DAYS OF AWE

Y0-BCT-289

Days of Awe

BEING A TREASURY OF TRADITIONS, LEGENDS

AND LEARNED COMMENTARIES CONCERNING

ROSH HA-SHANAH, YOM KIPPUR

AND THE DAYS BETWEEN

CULLED FROM THREE HUNDRED VOLUMES

ANCIENT AND NEW, BY SHMUEL YOSEF AGNON

INTRODUCTION BY JUDAH GOLDIN

SCHOCKEN BOOKS · NEW YORK

Copyright © 1948, 1965 by Schocken Books Inc.
Library of Congress Catalog Card No. 48-8316
Manufactured in the United States of America

10 9   80 81 82 83 84

Table of Contents

BOOK THREE: YOM KIPPUR

On the Fifth or Sixth or Seventh Rereading of Agnon's DAYS OF AWE—Maybe More

BY JUDAH GOLDIN

I

What is a classic? The question is probably as old as the first student of literature, but every student must ask it on his own over and over again, for in the answer he reveals not only something of the character of the specific literary work, but of the relation between his presence and a very large world, a treasury of experience and vocabulary, that he has appropriated. And so, to ask what is a classic, is to engage in literary criticism and self criticism, self examination and understanding, at the same time.

A work becomes a classic the minute I discover that my many moods, my perceptions, my spontaneous terms of reference, my recurring images are startlingly anticipated and given precise formulation by (and in) that work. It sharpens my eyesight, it cleans my mind of the fuzziness produced by my own lack of talent and laziness, it teaches me the words that I need for soliloquy and conversation. It is of course not strange nor solely a polite convention that so often when we speak of classics we refer to early, old compositions. For the masters of ancient pieces too saw clearly and spoke distinctly and with precision. The first to see and the first to record accurately continue to affect us ever after—this is the immortality of truth. And since no one exhausts reality, the classic is not only the ancient. Whoever correctly discovers and uses the right words reveals the world and my life to me, and ever after governs me. He teaches me also to recognize and speak the truth.

II

Since we are handling a serious work, it would be offensive to
indulge in whimsy. We have to state, therefore, that Agnon's
Yamim Noraim appeared twenty-seven years ago (the English
abridgement and translation appeared in 1948). It is no less a
fact, however, that for anyone to whom Rosh ha-Shanah and
Yom Kippur have meaning, and who has not cultivated a
deafness toward modern Hebrew literature, the volume, from
the moment of its appearance, seemed as though it had always
been here, as though it had always been the companion of the
Machzor (the holiday prayerbook), as though it was the volume
which one held in his hands at this season and looked into,
read snatches from, studied during moments of the long services when the mind is tempted to take its own, rather than
the congregational, course. The book never looked new, and
has remained fresh. Or even more accurately: it was never a
book (*Buch*), it was from the outset a *sefer*. The Hebrew word,
to be sure, does mean "book" but in the folk language it came
to be reserved for those literary works which are not to amuse
only, or for light reading, but possess a downright seriousness
and sacredness. A sefer you study, sometimes beginning at the
beginning and going straight through; sometimes you open it
at random, read a section and reflect over that section or part of
it; sometimes you consult it for specific bits of information: for
example, where do the Jews of Jerusalem go for *Tashlikh* (what
the translators call The Casting—of sins)? Do the Jews of
Kurdistan do at Tashlikh what Ashkenazi Jews do? Sometimes you read a passage in a sefer and begin to recall how the
parallel passage in another sefer puts it.

A sefer of course can also amuse you, as when it says, "It is
right to eat fish" on Yom Kippur eve, or that "The French
Jews are accustomed to eat red apples on Rosh ha-Shanah," or
when it reports: "It is not the custom of the inhabitants of

Jerusalem to wear kittels on Yom Kippur, the way people out-side of Palestine do. For if they were to wear kittels in order to resemble the ministering angels, why, most of the inhabitants of Jerusalem wear white cloaks over their clothing every day, and the resemblance would not be apparent."

But more than amusement, a sefer prefers to give delight, as in the story of the tailor who on the eve of the Atonement settles his accounts with God: Here, Master of the universe, is the list I kept scrupulously of all my offenses against You in the course of the past year, and here, Master of the universe, is the list I've been keeping of all the afflictions and distresses and losses You've put us through this year. If a proper bookkeeping be made, I'm afraid I've been more sinned against than sinning. But this is Yom Kippur eve, when we are all obliged to forgive one another. So I forgive You all, and You too will forgive us all the sins we have sinned against You. "To Life!"

Is delight a feature of Hasidic tales only? Not really. Here is a midrash on the Hosea verse (14:2) "Return, O Israel, unto the Lord thy God": "A king's son was at a distance of a hundred days' journey from his father. Said his friends to him, 'Return to your father.' He said to them, 'I cannot.' His father sent to him and said, 'Go as far as you are able, and I shall come the rest of the way to you.' Thus, the Holy One, blessed be He, said to Israel (Mal. 3:7): 'Return unto Me, and I will return unto you.' "

And, properly appreciated, a similar quality in a talmudic text: " 'And ye shall afflict your souls in the ninth day . . .' (Lev. 23:32). But do we fast on the ninth? Do we not fast on the tenth? But the purpose of this verse is to tell us that he who eats and drinks on the ninth and fasts on the tenth, is considered by the Writ as fasting on both the ninth and the tenth days."

Delight, amusement, the satisfying of curiosity also are produced by a sefer, for a sefer is a permanent thing, and seriousness is not so stupid as to reject lightness of touch.

III

Yamim Noraim, Agnon named his volume, calling a spade a spade. "Days of Awe" is probably as handy a rendition for a title in modern English as we are likely to get. But here again is an instance of how heartbreaking is the translator's task. For Yamim Noraim is not only the modern, popular expression for the days of Rosh ha-Shanah and Yom Kippur; it is the accurate term for the season which puts the fear of God into us. For this is the Judgment period, and when a man begins to think of his blunders and vulgarities and appalling occasions of bad conduct during the past twelvemonth term, it's enough to fill him with terror. The willy nilly sins against God and the sins against man and the sins against every animate and inanimate creature into which we are catapulted (let alone those we carefully plan) simply because no human being is infallible, have a way of parading before our memories and in our dreams with such sinister clarity that it is a supernatural triumph we are not in unrelieved despair. But "It is out of kindness" (kindness? *hesed! hesed ha-el,* God's trustworthy, sure love!) "toward his creatures that the Lord remembers them and reviews their deeds year after year on Rosh ha-Shanah, that their sins may not grow too numerous, and there may be room for forgiveness, and, being few, he may forgive them. For, if he were not to remember them for a long time, their sins would multiply to such an extent as to doom the world, God forbid. So this revered day assures the world of survival. For this reason it is fit that we celebrate the Rosh ha-Shanah as a festive day; but since it is a Day of Judgment for all living things, it is also fit that we observe Rosh ha-Shanah with greater fear and awe than all the other festive days."

When so much is at stake, even in rejoicing one trembles, and even the funny is not ridiculous. "Said Rabbi Israel Baal Shem Tov: When a man is drowning in a river, and splashes about trying to pull himself out of the waters that are overwhelming him, those who see him will certainly not make fun of his splashing. So, when a man makes all kinds of gestures as he prays, there is no reason to make fun of him, for he is saving himself from the raging waters—those husks and barbarous thoughts—that come upon him to distract him from his prayer."

IV

If more than two millennia and a half of reflection, questioning and answering and guessing, had not supplemented the bone-thin biblical text, who could have expected so much from the Yamim Noraim? Here is their substance in the Scriptural words: "And in the seventh month, on the first day of the month, ye shall have a holy convocation: ye shall do no manner of servile work; it is a day of blowing the horn unto you. And ye shall prepare a burnt-offering for a sweet savour unto the Lord: one young bullock, one ram, seven he-lambs of the first year without blemish; and their meal-offering, fine flour mingled with oil, three tenth parts for the bullock, two tenth parts for the ram, and one tenth part for every lamb of the seven lambs; and one he-goat for a sin-offering, to make atonement for you; beside the burnt-offering of the new moon, and the meal-offering thereof, and the continual burnt-offering and the meal-offering thereof, and their drink-offerings, according unto their ordinance, for a sweet savour, an offering made by fire unto the Lord" (Num. 29:1–6).

Thus on the subject of Rosh ha-Shanah. On Yom Kippur, the same chapter continues: "And on the tenth day of this seventh month ye shall have a holy convocation; and ye shall afflict your souls; ye shall do no manner of work; but ye shall present a burnt-offering unto the Lord for a sweet savour: one young bullock, one ram, seven he-lambs of the first year; they shall be unto you without blemish; and their meal-offering, fine flour mingled with oil, three tenth parts for the bullock, two tenth parts for the one ram, a several tenth part for every lamb of the seven lambs; one he-goat for a sin-offering; beside the sin-

offering of atonement, and the continual burnt-offering, and
the meal-offering thereof, and their drink-offerings" (*ibid.*
7–10).

This too may be added, from Leviticus (16:32–34): "And
the priest, who shall be anointed and who shall be consecrated
to be priest in his father's stead, shall make the atonement, and
shall put on the linen garments, even the holy garments. And
he shall make atonement for the most holy place, and he shall
make atonement for the tent of meeting and for the altar; and
he shall make atonement for the priests and for all the people
of the assembly. And this shall be an everlasting statute unto
you, to make atonement for the children of Israel because of all
their sins once in the year."

Like the high priest on the Day of Atonement, one might say,
"There is more written here than I have read to you." But truth
to say, not terribly much more. And if we bear in mind the
historical reality, that for almost two thousand years out of the
two millennia and a half there has been no Temple and none
of the appurtenances for cult and sumptuous ritual, even these
few words come dangerously close to retreating into the entirely archaic. They escaped that fate because one student generation after another perceived that in addition to their literal
content these words carried innuendoes. Legalists, moralists,
mystics, homilists, exegetes, folklorists, poets, chroniclers, sophis-
ticates and simple-minded, masters and disciples, at home
(wherever home might be) and abroad, in riches and in poverty, in synagogues and schools, in private and in public, in
grief or in ecstasy or in patient and impatient expectation of
the ultimate redemption—all Israel extracted from these words
a multitude of teachings for a whole *curriculum vitae.* Thus
the Yamim Noraim became the season of concentrated Teshuvah
with detailed instructions for the return journey to God, for
charity towards our fellowmen, indeed even to the beasts. ("It
is necessary to give one's beast whatever it needs to eat on Yom
Kippur." "Once it happened that Rabbi Israel Salanter [19th

cent.] was going to the House of Prayer for Kol Nidre. On the way he saw an animal belonging to a Gentile, which was lost. He saw that the animal was in distress, and troubled himself to lead it home over stones and rocks, through fields and gardens. Meanwhile, all the congregation was waiting for him. When he did not come, they went out to look for him. They found him trying to lead the animal into its master's stall.")

And since charity delivers from death, on the climactic tenth day, *The* Day (as even the talmudic treatise is called) on Yom Kippur, one acted the part of the angels, proving to oneself that one could rise above the mundane, that in God's righteous love one would be acquitted in this Trial, and therefore one dressed in white—and the ark was given a white curtain, and the reading desk was laid with a white coverlet, and when the feast before the Fast was finished, a white tablecloth was spread on the table, and where just a few minutes before there had been dishes with food now holy books were laid.

Not merely one's own world, but the whole world, the cosmos was affected. Rosh ha-Shanah became the anniversary of Creation, the anniversary of Abraham's and Isaac's preparedness to yield to God's extremest demand; Yom Kippur, the anniversary of the receiving of the Tables of the Law that were not to be broken again. The alarms sounded on the shofar on Rosh ha-Shanah became statutory obligation, invocation of the stored up merits of the Fathers, summons to shake off habitual lethargy, and anticipatory echo of that great blast whose signal declares Redemption; even as it is said (Isa. 27:13), "And it shall come to pass in that day, that a great shofar shall be blown; and they shall come that were lost in the land of Assyria, and they that were dispersed in the land of Egypt; and they shall worship the Lord in the holy mountain at Jerusalem."

God alone is king—or, in view of an ancient manner of speaking as well as political realities still with us, He is King

over all kings and kings of kings. Rosh ha-Shanah is the time
to affirm this, and not in whispers only. In seemingly infinite
ways the long recitations of this day and of Yom Kippur and
of the days between repeat and underscore this. Prayers and
shofar-service reinforce one another as they proclaim this theme.
At least since about the first quarter of the second century
kingships (*Malkhiyot*), Remembrances (*Zikhronot*), and
Ram's-Horns (*Shofarot*) have been the three pillars of the worship structure, even as in public fasts earlier Remembrances
and Ram's-Horns constituted the principal parts of the special
service. "Kingships, Remembrances, and Ram's-horns," a 15th
century philosopher explains, ". . . arouse the hearts of men
to a belief in the . . . three principles and their ramifications. . . . For Kingships corresponds to the principle of the
existence of God, to which the formula of the prayer testifies:
'And so we wait for Thee, O Lord our God, we wait soon to
see the splendor of Thy might, when Thou wilt raze the idols
from the earth . . . when the world will be perfected under
the sovereignty of the Almighty . . . inhabitants of the world
will perceive and know, that to Thee every knee is bowed, and
every tongue avows Thee. . . . They will all take upon themselves the yoke of Thy kingship . . .'

"The section of Remembrances teaches the doctrines of divine providence and reward and punishment, to which the
formula of this prayer testifies: 'Thou callest to mind how the
world was made and rememberest all those formed of old;
before Thee all hid things are laid bare. . . .'

"The section of the Ram's-horns is an allusion to the third
principle, which is the Revelation of the Torah from heaven.
Therefore it begins: 'Thou wast revealed to Thy people in the
cloud of Thy glory on Thy holy mountain, to speak with
them. From the heavens Thou madest Thy voice heard. . . .'"

The view of this philosopher is not too far removed from the
ideas inherent in the liturgy as a whole. More immediately to
the point is the idiom of the *Malkhiyot, Zikhronot,* and *Sho-*

farot benedictions. Malkhiyot: "Our God and God of our fathers: Reign over the whole wide world in Thy glory . . . and let everything made know that Thou didst make it. . . ." Zikhronot: "Our God and God of our fathers: In a remembrance for good recall us before Thee . . . and remember in our behalf, O Lord our God, the covenant and the love and the oath which Thou didst assert to our Father Abraham at Mount Moriah . . . and there is no forgetfulness before Thy glorious throne. . . ." Shofarot: "Our God and God of our fathers: Sound the great shofar for our freedom . . . and gather our dispersed far and wide from the ends of the earth, and bring us to Zion, Thy city, with rejoicing. . . ."

On Rosh ha-Shanah the obligation to hear the sounding of the shofar is a statutory obligation. But such "trumpetings" stir up so much fear and excitement and hope, it was well-nigh predictable that in the early mornings of a whole month before the arrival of the New Year such sounds would come to be practised in rehearsal for the solemn performances, and that Yom Kippur would not be permitted to withdraw without the accompaniment of one more long sustained blast. "It is the custom in all Israel," wrote Rav Hai Gaon of the tenth-eleventh century, "to blow the ram's horn at the close of Yom Kippur; we have found no reason to believe that it is an obligation, but it seems to be a memorial of the Jubilee, as it is said: 'Then shalt thou make proclamation with the blast of the shofar on the tenth day of the seventh month; in the day of atonement shall ye make proclamation with the shofar throughout all your land' (Lev. 25:9). Since the reckoning of the Jubilee year is not certain, the custom was established of blowing the ram's horn every year as a memorial of the Jubilee. This is the sense of the saying: 'In the Jubilee year . . . on Yom Kippur, the Court blew the ram's horn. Slaves were sent home and fields returned to their original owners' (Rosh ha-Shanah 8b). This is the memorial of the Jubilee which they kept during the time when the Temple still stood."

Is there any wonder that in times when it cost one's life to observe a religious commandment, men crawled into cisterns, into cellars, into vats if necessary, to hear the required shofar sounds—and even then were concerned, had they heard the sound itself, or only its echo?

v

All this (and even that is "no more than a paintbrush takes from the tube") out of about two fistfuls of biblical verses? Is artifice exempt from all restraint? "Why was the Confession composed in the plural, so that we say, We have sinned, rather than, I have sinned? Because all Israel is one body and every one of Israel is a limb of that body; that is why we are all responsible for one another when we sin. So, if one's fellow should sin, it is as though one has sinned oneself; therefore, despite the fact that one has not committed that iniquity, one must confess to it. For when one's fellow has sinned, it is as though one has sinned oneself." Thus, apparently, that remarkable mystic of the sixteenth century, Rabbi Isaac Luria.

Or again, this time from Rabbi Menahem Mendel of Rymanov: "Why is the wearing of shoes prohibited on Yom Kippur? Because all the worlds are elevated on Yom Kippur when Israel does complete Teshuvah; the earth upon which we live is elevated too, and is called holy ground. Therefore, it is forbidden to step upon the earth wearing shoes, as it is written (Exod. 3:5): 'Put off thy shoes from off thy feet, for the place whereon thou standest is holy ground.' "

Again and again one moves far away from the literal, the lexicographical limitations of the word; yet only out of context is the movement an act of violence. For the text of the Bible and later the text of the Talmud and the Midrashim too were not simply historical documents, but the spectacles through which one saw immediate life in sharper focus. Without these texts one literally could not see life. And like all who wear eyeglasses, these generations of students and saints and plain folk were hardly conscious of the fact that they were wearing anything at all. This is the way one sees clearly. Of course many of these men were scholars; but the notion that scholars see only texts is one of the silliest bits of misinformation to be taken in by. *Il regarde ce que je regarde, mais je vois ce qu'il ne voit pas.* It's not texts scholars see—we're talking of scholars, not journeymen—but life, life looked at through the texts that are eyewitness reports on life. The texts are the lenses to see life with. Actually, it's only when we take off our glasses that we squint, that we become aware of the fact that something is not quite right, the view is hazy and the object blurred. And who, in the variety of life's experiences, has twenty-twenty vision?

So life, everything in life, comes into sight through these texts; and soon it is impossible to distinguish between text and life. The words of the verse or of the legal formula or of the sage's saying throw into sharp relief the authenticity of life's subtleties. "A tale is told of one who sat in study before the zaddik Rabbi Mordecai of Nadvorna, of blessed memory [19th cent.], and before Rosh ha-Shanah came to obtain permission to be dismissed. That zaddik said to him, 'Why are you hurrying?'

"Said he to him, 'I am a Reader, and I must look into the festival prayer book, and put my prayers in order.'

"Said the zaddik to him, 'The prayer book is the same as it was last year. But it would be better for you to look into your deeds, and put yourself in order.' "

Or this: "It is fit and proper during these Days of Awe to study the admonitory books of the early and later moralists, which awaken a man's heart to Teshuvah. One ought not make them all of his study, for they lose their effect on the soul when one has concentrated too much on them. For as it is with cures of bodily ailments, so it is with soul ailments. One ought rather to study admonitory books a little every day, until he feels himself that the words have come into his innermost parts and turned him to his Father who is in heaven."

"Children of Israel, know that the soul will not be at ease in this world though it come into all the kingdoms of the earth, knowing that there is a world where it will be at ease and rest. So it is written (Jer. 6:16): 'Thus saith the Lord: Stand ye in the ways and see, and ask for the old paths, where is the good way, and walk therein, and ye shall find rest for your souls.' "

" 'The Lord, the Lord' (Exod. 34:6). 'I am he who is the Lord before a man sins, and I am he who shall be the Lord after a man sins' (Rosh ha-Shanah 17a). Rabbi Samuel Eliezer Edels [16th–17th cent.] raised a question: 'What need is there for compassion before a man sins?' But it is cited in the *Duties of the Heart* [11th cent.] that one of the righteous said to his disciples: If you had no sin, I should be afraid of that in you which is greater than sin, pride. For pride, which is more serious than sin, is to be found in the man who thinks he has not sinned.—From which we learn that even before he sins a man certainly needs compassion to atone for a proud heart."

"A tale is told of a certain hasid who went to see his rabbi. Before entering the house he thought to himself, It might be worth while to receive the 'forty stripes,' so that the zaddik will find no defect in me. He was still thinking of this when the door opened, and he entered. Greeting him, his rabbi said, 'What is the reason why the sages, of blessed memory, took one from the forty stripes, making them thirty-nine, when it is written in the Torah, "Forty stripes he may give him" (Deut. 25:3)? Yet the sages commanded that only thirty-nine stripes be given. The reason is that when a man commits a transgression and is flogged, perhaps if he received a full forty stripes according to the letter of the Torah he might think that he had wiped away his iniquity. Therefore, the sages, of blessed memory, went and took one from the forty (Makkot 22a), in order that the sinner might know that he had not yet received all his punishment, and had still to better his ways.' "

Artificial exegesis? Then so is the product of the sculptor who perceived what was in the stone the others rejected.

VI

From more than one thousand books, during many years of *studying* (I would not have hesitated to use the word "reading" if it hadn't fallen into such passive meanings and inactivities in recent times), Agnon has assembled homilies, comments, laws, reflections, letters, recollections, conversations, critical observations, word-of-mouth reports—whatever refracted something of the authentic light of the Yamim Noraim. He marked margins with his fingernail—how sure is his touch! It took him, he says, two and a half years of sixteen hours a day to compose this book—by which he surely means, 2½ years of 16 hours per day simply to organize what over years and years he had been observing, thinking about, and treasuring up for who knows what purpose. A work like *Yamim Noraim* cannot be produced by twice two and a half years of reading, even sixteen hours a day. Anthologies, golden treasuries, reliques, smorgasbord samplings of the so-called finest specimens of this or that literature, possibly—if the compiler has the necessary industry and the bright formula. I'm reminded suddenly of *The Riches of Chaucer* Charles Cowden Clarke hoarded up in the nineteenth century, with the instructive by-line, "from which his impurities have been expunged . . . his rhythms accentuated." One need not go off to English literature for illustrations; there are several closer to home that have become the rage. And how pretty are the pictures they summon up; how sweet the sentiments; how homogenized the piety they exhibit.

Ta shema: come now, listen to what *Yamim Noraim* is: an assembly of all the voices of Israel, the demanding and the soft-spoken, the very early and the ones off the beaten track along with the later and those on the main route of this extraordinary tradition, that loves the world and therefore rebukes it. An anthology is the product of calculated rummaging, and in 2½ years, working 16 hours a day, a man can collect a lot, enough for one book, and even more. In that interval it is also not impossible to arrange the collection in a more or less reasonable order. The net result is something like literature on its good behavior, like a shop window with the very attractive samples on display. *Yamim Noraim,* on the other hand, is not preoccupied with literature. It is the result of faithful listening in on voices for a long long time, until the characteristic tone is learned well. It is an attempt to capture the way a whole continuing folk has responded to the collision with life and death. This naturally involves *everything,* not only the sacred good sense of Rabbi Hayyim of Brisk who, when asked why he was so lenient in matters of food for the the sick on the Day of Atonement, replied, "Not that I am lenient when it comes to Yom Kippur, but that I am strict when it comes to saving a life"; it involves no less the astonishing confidence and insight of that rabbi who was inclined to be strict in regard to the great Fast, because *his* teacher had observed that "Since the Yom Kippur fast is enjoined by the Torah, then fasting on that day must have its basis in the very nature of our being; and, therefore, this fasting nourishes the body the way food does on the other days!"

Since *Yamim Noraim* undertakes to register the response of all Israel, it not only quotes the reminiscence of a farmer in America suddenly overwhelmed by the Kol Nidre melody as birds with their singing assist the cantor in his song, but also reports the carefully drawn up orders of the service which every worshipper will follow, for example:

The Reader takes his stand before the Ark and lowers his prayer shawl over his face. Two men are stationed, one at the right and one at the left of the Reader, as it is said. . . . Each of them takes a Torah Scroll in his hand, one standing on one side of the Reader, and the other on the other side, and says with him three times, "With the knowledge of the Omnipresent" (=God's consent). . . . Then the Reader chants Kol Nidre in the chant handed down by our fathers from past generations. . . . After reciting Kol Nidre three times, the

congregation cries out with the Reader, "And forgiven shall
be. . . ." Then the Reader recites once, "Pardon, I pray Thee.
. . ." Then the congregation recites three times in a loud
voice, "And the Lord said: I have pardoned. . . ." Then the
Reader recites after them. . . . Then the Reader recites the
benediction with the phrase "who has kept us alive". . . . The
congregation finishes before the Reader so as to be able to respond, Amen. . . . If Yom Kippur falls on a Sabbath, the
Ninety-second Psalm is recited.

And so on, and on. To get the full flavor of Agnon's delight in
the decorousness of ordered detail, one must really refer to the
Hebrew volume; see, for example, this order of the Yom Kippur
Eve service in *Yamim Noraim,* pages 298 and 299. That several
such long passages in the Hebrew original cannot be reproduced
effectively in the English version is quite a commentary on the
impoverishment of our vocabulary and on how far from the
shore we have been swept.

VII

But to be perfectly honest, we are all shipwrecked, and ulti-
mately it has little to do with Hebrew or English, or Esperanto
for that matter. Start thinking of the mess we so frequently make
of our lives, and words fail: no words seem to express exactly
the deep regrets we want to feel and all the heartache we must
learn to put up with. Suddenly we envy the originality of that
brilliant countryman who, lost in the woods on Yom Kippur,
without a prayer book to his name, recites the alphabet and
directs it skyward: It's beyond me, God; You combine these
letters into the right words and sentences, for You know what
I want to say.

The sinner who craves forgiveness confesses; which is reasonable, if only one knew how adequately to confess. And so
there are the ingenious lists arranged in alphabetical order.
Since for people with the fear of God in them even a list from
A to Z seems abridged, the sentences are doubled for each let-

ter: two for A and two for B and two for C; and when the
alphabet gives out, there are still categories to refer to, such as,
"For the sins for which we owe a burnt-offering . . . for which
we owe a sin-offering . . . for which we deserve the punishment
of. . . ." The mood is so overpowering that one becomes, so to
speak, addicted to confessing, and recites the Confessional at
each of the Day's services, though by the hour of the Closing of
the Gates of Prayer an abbreviated, modified form is all one
has the strength for—if you count the recitation in private at
the afternoon service *before* Yom Kippur begins, there are five
recitations. This still does not account for the recitations along
with the Reader. The very fact that these catalogues of transgressions are drawn up as formulae and in the editorial we,
reveals the delicacy and impeccable manners of the liturgists.

"The order of the confessions in our prayer books and festival prayer books is alphabetical; everyone recites them. The
man who knows he has committed one particular sin ought to
cry as he mentions that sin and confess to it with particular
emotion. And if he has committed a sin that is not mentioned
in the confession, he says that sin in a whisper to himself and
confesses to it from the depths of his heart and cries over it.
But he ought not to raise his voice, for one does not confess for
a personal sin loudly, as it is said, 'Blessed is he whose transgression is forgiven, whose sin is covered' (Ps. 32:1). But if
his sin is well known, he may confess it loudly, if he wishes."

As everyone knows, of course, and as Rabbi Eleazar ben
Azariah expounded: "It is written, 'From all your sins *before
the Lord* shall you be clean' (Lev. 16:30). Yom Kippur makes
atonement for transgressions committed in man's relations with
the Omnipresent. But Yom Kippur does not make atonement
for transgressions in men's relationships with one another, until
the transgressor has appeased his fellow." In other words, confession brings relief when there is genuine reform. Yom Kippur
has little tolerance for humbug.

Even at the risk of appearing greedy (for he *has* given us so much), I must express surprise at Agnon's omitting the following (or have I overlooked it, despite my rereadings? If so, I beg his pardon):

"Once, as Rabban Johanan ben Zakkai was coming forth from Jerusalem, Rabbi Joshua followed after him and beheld the Temple in ruins. 'Woe unto us!' Rabbi Joshua cried, 'that this, the place where the iniquities of Israel were atoned for, is laid waste.'

" 'My son,' Rabban Johanan said to him, 'be not grieved; we have another atonement as effective as this. And what is it? It is acts of loving-kindness, as it is said, "For I desire mercy and not sacrifice" (Hosea 6:6).' " [Abot de-Rabbi Natan, IV]

I think I know why Agnon omitted this passage, for it has been abused by all the sentimentalists. But we need not pay them any mind, for they abuse many fine things, and this anecdote does report a revolutionary discovery—that, unlike what all historic religions display, unlike even the natural impulse of every pious creature to bring something to, do something for, his God—as any lover is frustrated if he is reduced to words only—it *is* possible to worship God and to show one's love for and to Him, without giving Him a material gift. In at least this respect He is unique. If we cannot win His good opinion by means of holocausts, we can win it by acts of loving-kindness to our fellowman.

An idea like this takes a long time to sink in, and in reality it never entirely displaces the primary impulse. If only there were the Temple: what a busyness could go on, what a tangible reassurance it would be to see the High Priest change from one set of garments to another, the Pelusium linen and the Indian linen, to know that he must bathe and rinse, prepare the beasts, sprinkle the blood, go in and out of the Holy of Holies on this one occasion of the year, pronounce the Confessionals and sound the ineffable Name. Oh, to prostrate oneself, to await the report of the dispatched scapegoat! How glorious was that high priest Simeon,

>   "When he looked forth from the Tent
>   And when he came out from the sanctuary!"

Turn to pages 253–255 and examine what Ben Sira wrote about him twenty-one hundred years ago.

Deprived of such exhibitions for close to two thousand years, the House of Israel seized hungrily on descriptions by poets and liturgists to nourish their imagination in their famine, to satisfy their longing for the color and romance which worship and ceremony ordinarily provide. If after the first century there ever was a time the Temple was sorely missed, it was on the Day of Atonement. Where now will the sins of Israel be atoned? So long as they could, many made their way to the Wailing Wall. But it only underscored their sense of desolation. On Yom Kippur one recited the whole service of the high priest, wept that because of our sins gone is this magnificence; but at least the course of recitation gave the imagination an opportunity to dwell briefly in the House of the Lord.

And from recollection to recollection: the House lies in ruins —those Lebanon cedars, the Ten great sages, murdered by the empire—they too are a sacrifice, they too are a vicarious atonement. "The liturgical poem beginning, 'These I do remember,' which is recited after the description of the Temple service, is in memory of the ten who were martyred by Rome, who were killed for the sake of the unification of the Name of God. For when the Temple still stood and the altar stood in its habitation, sacrifices were offered upon the altar every day. But now what is offered are the souls of the righteous."

". . . At this time we can say: Abraham built one altar, and that woman built seven. . . . But our brothers are beaten and driven like cattle to the slaughter, to death and annihilation, blows and humiliation—nevertheless they have not forgotten Your Name. This being the case, what is so miraculous about the Binding of Isaac?"

VIII

Agnon has perfect pitch. One is grateful to the publisher who explains in his closing note, "Passages for which no sources are given are by the author; they serve as an introduction or transition, and are most of the time summarizations of source material." The fact is, you can hardly tell when the source lets up and Agnon takes over. Even when he is not citing sources, his voice is indistinguishable from theirs, or theirs from his. And only by consulting the primary sources fastidiously can you begin to discern the miracle of his sound effects.

"That marvel Rabbi Solomon Judah Rapoport [19th cent.] wrote: The liturgical poems of the Sephardim are mediators between the soul of man and its Creator, and the liturgical poems of the Ashkenazim mediators between Israel and its God. [Bikkure ha-Ittim VIII]

"However, in essence there is no difference in the prayers between one place and another, except for a few changes that do not affect the style of their blessings. But all Israel, in all their habitations, unite their hearts as one to pray to one God in one prayer, in the tradition that has been handed down to us by Rav Amram Gaon [9th cent.] according to the usages of the two academies of Sura and Pumbedita, who received it from the Saboraim, who received it from the Amoraim, who received it from the Tannaim, who received it from the members of the Great Assembly, who were the ones who instituted the prayers for Israel."

Where does Solomon Judah Rapoport stop and S. Y. Agnon begin? And how would one distinguish between the cadence of Agnon and the cadence of Amram; in fact, between Agnon's and that of a much older source that furnishes the background incantation?

" 'The hallowed stones are poured out at the head of every street' (Lam. 4:1). When the Temple was destroyed, the Holy One, blessed be He, scattered its stones over all the world, and every place where a stone fell, a House of Prayer was built. [Aggadat Eliyahu, quoting a midrash]

"It is for this reason that a House of Prayer is called a little sanctuary, because it has a little of the Temple, a stone of the Temple, which is sunk into every House of prayer. [*Ibid.*]

"It's therefore not nice behavior on the part of those who, when they feel crowded in the synagogue, leave it and go outdoors."

I wish the last paragraph had not been omitted. There is nothing stuffy about the remark; it's an old, old complaint, but entirely Agnon's too, both sentiment and language.

The Aramaic passages he translates into Hebrew read as though they never were in anything but the Holy Tongue. He will begin with one source, pass on—even in the same paragraph—to another, and bring two generations into a dialogue as immediate as though they had been speaking on the same day, with Agnon keeping the conversation going, because he is at home in their tone of voice, inflections, idiom, and concerns. Literary craftsmanship is certainly behind this: conscious, alert, discriminating selection of the right words and the appropriate sentence construction, images and mannerisms. We are not talking after all of a rustic bard; let us not forget that Agnon is an artist. How is it then that the work never loses its poise, never sinks into the contrived, into affectation?

Here style is an *effect*, a result, a necessary consequence of something vaster than literary exercise. Effect of what? It is the natural outpouring of what in Hebrew is called *Ahavat Yisrael*, and which may certainly be translated into English as *Loving Israel*, with "loving" as a transitive participle, and yet perhaps in some recessed echoes of the word suggesting also the adjective which describes that historical entity known as Israel, that long sequence of descendants of Abraham who understood and understand that the seed of Abraham must be at the same time disciples of Abraham. Passage after passage in *Yamim Noraim* carries a kind of vibrato of this theme. Exclamations of Levi Yitzchak of Berditchev are well known.

But many many citations are astir with it. How in fact could those responsible for the text of the English version have dared to omit the saying attributed to the martyred Rabbi Solomon of Karlin, "Der grester yezer horeh is az mi far-gest az mi is ein ben melekh," "The worst of the impulses to evil is to forget one's royal descent"? (And that Agnon should have left it untranslated from the Yiddish is canny instinct!) The genealogy of that remark can be traced back to the second century Akiba; it can be traced almost a millennium farther back than that, to the heartbroken lover of Israel who announced the promise, still read on the Sabbath between New Year and Atonement Day, "I will love them *nedavah* . . . I will be as the dew unto Israel; he shall bloom as the lily, and cast forth his roots as Lebanon. His branches shall spread, and his beauty shall be as the olive tree, and his fragrance as Lebanon. They that dwell under his shadow shall again make corn to grow, and shall blossom as the vine; the scent thereof shall be as the wine of Lebanon" (Hosea 14:5–8). That love can be traced right down to yesterday and found in the love poetry of the late Rabbi Kook, as well as in the very selections to which Shmuel Yosef Agnon (long may he flourish) is irresistibly drawn again and again.

"Rabbi Akiba said: Oh your good fortune, Israel! Before whom are you made clean, and who is it that cleanses you? (None but) your Father who is in heaven, as it is said (Ezek. 36:25), 'Then *I* will sprinkle clean water upon you, and ye shall be clean.'"

"How exalted is the rung of Teshuvah! The night before he did Teshuvah this very man was separated from the Lord God of Israel, as it is said, 'But your iniquities have separated between you and your God' (Isa. 59:2); he cried out and was not answered, as it is said, 'Yea, when ye make many prayers, I will not hear (Isa. 1:15); he performed the commandments, and they were thrown back in his face, as it is said, 'Who hath required this at your hand, to trample my courts?' (Isa. 1:12); 'Oh that there were even one among you that would

shut the doors' (Mal. 1:10); and today, after doing Teshuvah,
that same man clings to the Divine Presence, as it is said, 'But
ye that did cleave unto the Lord your God are alive everyone
of you this day' (Deut. 4:4); he cries out and is immediately
answered, as it is written, 'And it shall come to pass, that before they call, I will answer' (Isa. 65:24); he performs the commandments and they are accepted with pleasure and joy, as it
is said, 'For God hath already accepted thy works' (Eccl. 9:7).
Yes, even more—they are much desired, as it is said (Mal. 3:4):
'Then shall the offering of Judah and Jerusalem be pleasant
unto the Lord, as in the days of old, and as in ancient years.' "

". . . Let the admonishers who come to admonish Israel be
careful to speak softly. . . .

"There is a tale about an admonisher who came to Tiktin
and spoke words of admonition. The Gaon Rabbi Meir of
Tiktin burst into tears and said to the admonisher, 'Why have
you shamed me publicly, and broken the rule against shaming
one's fellow man in public?'

"Said he to him, 'God forbid, rabbi! I was not speaking of
you.'

"Cried the rabbi, 'But *they* are all righteous! And who of
them could have sinned if not I?' "

"A certain rich man once stayed behind in the House of
Prayer on the night of Yom Kippur after the prayer, to read
through the Book of Psalms. Said the Gaon Rabbi Joseph Dov
of Brisk [19th cent.] to him: 'A soldier who deserts the army
and leaves the country is guilty of the death penalty. But if he
should not leave the country, but merely desert one regiment
to join another belonging to the same king—for example, if
he was assigned to the infantry and deserted to the cavalry,
or the other way around—what is the verdict then? Perhaps
because he is still serving his king, he isn't considered a deserter? Or perhaps, because he is not serving in the regiment
where he was assigned, he is called a deserter anyhow?'

"The rich man stood there, wondering what the rabbi was trying to say.

"Then the rabbi continued and said, 'But I have clear proof that, nevertheless, that soldier is called a deserter. For everyone must serve his king in his own regiment. In the same way, each and every man in Israel must serve the King over all the world with the service that has been laid upon him. The rich man must do charity on the eve of Yom Kippur and give back their pledges to the poor who cannot redeem them; and the poor man who cannot do charity has to do Teshuvah and pray a great deal. Therefore it is the way of the poor to stay in the House of Prayer on the night of Yom Kippur to recite Psalms, and the way of the rich who have given a great deal of charity to go home and sleep.

" 'Now you, my friend, have deserted your own regiment, and have come to serve your Creator with the service of the poor, thinking to do your duty in that way. You too are called a deserter, for every man must serve his Creator in the camp where he is assigned.' "

These are thoroughly typical.

What is *Ahavat Yisrael?* It is that clean tenderness towards the people summoned once and then repeatedly to exemplify God's strict and compassionate will, regardless of obstacles within and without. *Ahavat Yisrael* has, to be sure, the sizeable element of loving a distinct people (one loves a person; beware of those who love the injunction to love!), not just an accidental human mass, but an assembly listening, sometimes attentively, sometimes with half a mind, to the Voice whispering, calling, prodding, threatening, promising, comforting, always urging to lift life on earth to decency, to dignity, to purity, to that graciousness of thought and speech and act which makes visible everywhere and in every face the image of God.

Lebanon, Lebanon, Lebanon, the prophet called; roots as Lebanon, fragrance as Lebanon, the scent . . . as the wine of

Lebanon. For, Agnon reassures us dozens of times quoting the verse of Zion's greatest lover, "Though your sins be as scarlet, *ka-sheleg yalbinu,* they shall be white as snow." What else is called Lebanon? The Temple, the *bet ha-mikdash,* the Sacred House. And, as Agnon (only Agnon?) concludes: "And our sages, of blessed memory, said (Mishnah Taanit IV. 8): 'In the days of the gladness of his heart' (Cant. 3:11)—that is the building of the Temple. May it be rebuilt speedily in our days. Amen."

Davenport College
Yale University
August 1964

NOTE

I like the English translation of *Yamim Noraim* and have used it throughout except where I felt a different rendition did more justice to the original. Several corrections, however, may be recommended:

Page 15, lines 4–5: Even though Agnon too understands the clause as the translators render it, it should be translated, "The intermediaries descend to Gehinnom and are there singed and then rise again" etc.

Page 90, lines 5–6: The first two clauses in the quotation from Jeremiah should not be read as interrogatives, despite the literal sense. They are taken, midrashically, as positive declarations, thus: "This son of Mine, Ephraim, is precious to Me; indeed he is My darling child."

Page 242, lines 9 and 10: The regularly printed editions certainly read this way; but it may be that they do not preserve the correct reading. See in this connection, J. N. Epstein, *Introduction to Tannaitic Literature* (Hebrew), Jerusalem, 1957, page 514.

J. G.

Preface

For the benefit of those who wish to be informed in the matters of Rosh ha-Shanah and Yom Kippur and the Days Between, I have assembled some sayings from the Torah and
from the Prophets and from the Writings, from the Talmud
Babylonian and Palestinian, from the halakhic Midrash and
the aggadic Midrash, and from the Zohar and from other
books written by our Early Rabbis and Latter Rabbis, of
blessed memory; and I have arranged all these sayings in
three books, according to the order of each of the periods,
each period and its matter.

To make this book palatable to all, I have abridged lengthy
passages and at times altered the style of the Rabbis; for those
holy authors, their generation being fit and all men eager to
hear words of Torah, had not the time to improve their
style. Yet, although I have not kept to their style, I have
kept their meaning very well indeed. The laws which I cite
in this work, such as the laws of Rosh ha-Shanah and the
laws of Yom Kippur, I cite not to set up as an authority, but
to lend dignity to the work.

Those customs which are common to all the festivals and
not the matter of Rosh ha-Shanah and Yom Kippur solely, I
have not given at this point. Nor have I given prayers and
liturgical poems and penitential prayers here, for every person has prayer books with liturgical poems and penitential
prayers at hand, a thing which is not true of other matters relating to Rosh ha-Shanah and Yom Kippur, which are scattered about in various places.

I have taken some things from the books by the Latter

Rabbis, despite the fact that the Early Rabbis anticipated them. The reason why I made use of the Latter Rabbis is because they assembled scattered writings and included the works of the Early Rabbis in theirs.

After giving praise and thanks to the merciful God who has set my lot among those who study his Torah and has found me worthy to compose this work, I wish to thank all those scholars and rabbis who aided me with their good counsel, especially Rabbi Samuel Bialoblotzki, who toiled devotedly at my side, reading the work from beginning to end, elucidating points of the Law, examining textual variants, and adding many sections to the work. With his great expertness in all departments of the Torah he was of great aid in the preparation of the work. Last and dearest of all, chief of those involved in this effort, is Mr. Salman Schocken, who roused me to do this work.

Jerusalem   SHMUEL YOSEF AGNON

BOOK ONE

Rosh ha-Shanah

1. The Motive of Rosh ha-Shanah

And the Lord spoke unto Moses, saying: Speak unto the children of Israel, saying:

In the seventh month, in the first day of the month, shall be a solemn rest unto you, a memorial proclaimed with the blast of horns, a holy convocation. Ye shall do no manner of servile work; and ye shall bring an offering made by fire unto the Lord. [Lev. 23:23–25]

And in the seventh month, on the first day of the month, ye shall have a holy convocation: ye shall do no manner of servile work; it is a day of blowing the horn unto you. And ye shall prepare a burnt-offering for a sweet savour unto the Lord: one young bullock, one ram, seven he-lambs of the first year without blemish; and their meal-offering, fine flour mingled with oil, three tenth parts for the bullock, two tenth parts for the ram, and one tenth part for every lamb of the seven lambs; and one he-goat for a sin-offering, to make atonement for you; beside the burnt-offering of the new moon, and the meal-offering thereof, and the continual burnt-offering and the meal-offering thereof, and their drink-offerings, according unto their ordinance, for a sweet savour, an offering made by fire unto the Lord. [Num. 29:1–6]

And when the seventh month was come, and the children of Israel were in the cities, the people gathered themselves together as one man to Jerusalem. Then stood up Jeshua the son of Jozadek, and his brethren the priests, and Zerubbabel the son of Shealtiel, and his brethren, and builded the altar of the God of Israel, to offer burnt-offerings thereon, as it is written in the Law of Moses the man of God. And they set the altar upon its bases, for fear was upon them because of the

people of the countries, and they offered burnt-offerings
thereon unto the Lord, even burnt-offerings morning and
evening. [Ezra 3:1–3]

And when the seventh month was come, and the children
of Israel were in their cities, all the people gathered themselves together as one man into the broad place that was before the water gate; and they spoke unto Ezra the scribe to
bring the book of the Law of Moses, which the Lord had
commanded to Israel. And Ezra the priest brought the Law
before the congregation, both men and women, and all that
could hear with understanding, upon the first day of the seventh month. And he read therein before the broad place that
was before the water gate from early morning until midday,
in the presence of the men and the women, and of those that
could understand; and the ears of all the people were atten-
tive unto the book of the Law. And Ezra the scribe stood
upon a pulpit of wood, which they had made for the purpose; and beside him stood Mattithiah, and Shema, and Ana-
iah, and Uriah, and Hilkiah, and Maaseiah, on his right
hand; and on his left hand, Pedaiah, and Mishael, and Mal-
chijah, and Hashum, and Hashbaddanah, Zechariah, and
Meshullam. And Ezra opened the book in the sight of all the
people—for he was above the people—and when he opened
it, all the people stood up. And Ezra blessed the Lord, the
great God. And all the people answered: 'Amen, Amen,'
with the lifting up of their hands; and they bowed their
heads, and fell down before the Lord with their faces to the
ground. Also Jeshua, and Bani, and Sherebiah, Jamin, Ak-
kub, Shabbethai, Hodiah, Maaseiah, Kelita, Azariah, Joza-
bad, Hanan, Pelaiah, even the Levites, caused the people to
understand the Law; and the people stood in their place.
And they read in the book, in the Law of God, distinctly;

and they gave the sense, and caused them to understand the reading.

And Nehemiah, who was the Tirshatha, and Ezra the priest the scribe, and the Levites that taught the people, said unto all the people: 'This day is holy unto the Lord your God; mourn not, nor weep.' For all the people wept, when they heard the words of the Law. Then he said unto them: 'Go your way, eat the fat, and drink the sweet, and send portions unto him for whom nothing is prepared; for this day is holy unto our Lord; neither be ye grieved; for the joy of the Lord is your strength.' So the Levites stilled all the people, saying: 'Hold your peace, for the day is holy; neither be ye grieved.' [Neh. 8:1–11]

THE DAY OF JUDGMENT

"Blow the horn at the new moon, at the full moon for our feast-day" (Ps. 81:4). Rabbi Phineas and Rabbi Hilkiah said in the name of Rabbi Simon: All the ministering angels assemble before the Holy One, blessed be he, and say, "Master of the universe, when is the New Year's Day?" And he says to them, "Is it me you are asking? Let us both of us ask the Court below!" Because of the verse (ibid.): "For it is a statute for Israel, an ordinance of the God of Jacob." [Midrash Tehillim]

It has been taught: Rabbi Eliezer says, In the month of Tishri the world was created, in Tishri the patriarchs were born, in Tishri the patriarchs died. On Rosh ha-Shanah Sarah, Rachel and Hannah were remembered on high and conceived, on Rosh ha-Shanah Joseph left prison, on Rosh ha-Shanah the bondage of our ancestors ceased in Egypt. In the month of Nisan they were redeemed, and in Tishri they will be redeemed in time to come. [Rosh ha-Shanah 10b–11a]

The world is judged at four seasons: at Passover, in regard to grain; on the Feast of Weeks, in regard to the fruit of the tree; on Rosh ha-Shanah, all the inhabitants of this world file before Him. As it is said, "He that fashioneth the hearts of them all, that considereth all their doings" (Ps. 33:15). On the Feast of Booths, the world is judged in regard to rain. [Mishnah Rosh ha-Shanah I.2]

All things are judged on Rosh ha-Shanah, and their fate is sealed on Yom Kippur, are the words of Rabbi Meir. Rabbi Judah, in the name of Rabbi Akiba, says: All things are judged on Rosh ha-Shanah, but the fate of each and every one of them is sealed in its proper season; at Passover, the fate of the grain, at the Feast of Weeks, that of the fruit of the tree, and at the Feast of Booths, that of rain. [Tosefta Rosh ha-Shanah I.13]

MEMORIAL BOOKS FOR THE DEEDS OF MEN

Said Rabbi Kruspedai, in the name of Rabbi Yohanan: Three books are opened on Rosh ha-Shanah: one for the wholly righteous, one for the wholly wicked, and one for the intermediates. The wholly righteous are at once inscribed and sealed in the book of life; the wholly wicked are at once inscribed and sealed in the book of death; and the intermediates are held suspended from Rosh ha-Shanah until Yom Kippur. If they are found worthy, they are inscribed for life; if found unworthy, they are inscribed for death. [Rosh ha-Shanah 16b, version of En Yaakov]

It has been taught: The School of Shammai say: There will be three classes on the final Day of Judgment, one of the wholly righteous, one of the wholly wicked, and one of the intermediates. The wholly righteous are at once inscribed and sealed for life in the world to come; the wholly wicked are at once inscribed and sealed for Gehinnom [perdition], as it is said, "And many of them that sleep in the dust of the earth shall awake, some to everlasting life, and some to reproaches and everlasting abhorrence" (Dan. 12:2). The intermediates descend to Gehinnom, but when they scream in their suffering they rise again, as it is said, "And I will bring the third part through the fire, and will refine them as silver is refined, and will try them as gold is tried; they shall call on My name, and I will answer them" (Zech. 13:9). And it was of them that Hannah said (I Sam. 2:6): "The Lord killeth, and maketh alive; He bringeth down to the grave, and bringeth up."

The School of Hillel say: He that abounds in grace inclines toward grace. And it was of them that David said, "I love that the Lord should hear my voice and my supplications" (Ps. 116:1), and it is to them that the entire passage refers, including the verse (Ps. 116:6): "I was brought low, and He saved me." [Rosh ha-Shanah 16b–17a]

It is out of kindness toward his creatures that the Lord remembers them and reviews their deeds year after year on Rosh ha-Shanah, that their sins may not grow too numerous, and there may be room for forgiveness, and, being few, he may forgive them. For, if he were not to remember them for a long time, their sins would multiply to such an extent as to doom the world, God forbid. So this revered day assures the world of survival. For this reason it is fit that we celebrate the Rosh ha-Shanah as a festive day; but since it is a Day of Judgment for all living things, it is also fit that we observe Rosh ha-Shanah with greater fear and awe than all the other festive days. [Sefer ha-Hinukh, Mitzvah 311]

THE QUALITY OF MERCY

There is another reason why the Holy One, blessed be he, set the Day of Judgment in the month of Tishri, and not in another month. It is for Israel's good that the Day of Judgment was set in the month immediately preceded by the harvest season when the poor are given the gleanings, the forgotten sheaves, and the corners of the fields—so that, when the Holy One, blessed be he, comes to sit in judgment on the world, he may judge Israel not with the quality of divine justice, but with the quality of divine mercy. For great is the efficacy of charity that turns the quality of strictness into the quality of mercy. [Hayye Avraham, quoting Parashat Derakhim]

THE ZODIACAL SYMBOL FOR TISHRI

The zodiacal symbol for Tishri is a balance—which is an intimation that all the deeds of mankind are weighed in the balance in order "to give every man according to his ways, according to the fruit of his doings" (Jer. 17:10). [Kad ha-Kemah]

II. Elul: A Month of Preparation

TESHUVAH TAKES PRECEDENCE

It is by reason of his great love for his people Israel, that the Holy One, blessed be he, favored us and commanded us to turn to him whenever we sin. Although Teshuvah ["turning," repentance] is good at all times, the month of Elul is choicest for Teshuvah, which is more acceptable during the month of Elul than the rest of the year, that month having been a month of God's good will ever since we were chosen his people. For after Israel had committed the sin of the golden calf, and the tablets of the Ten Commandments had been broken, Moses ascended Mount Sinai for a second time to bring back the Torah to his people, and tarried there until

Yom Kippur, which is the end of the period of atonement.
[Hayye Adam]

THE RAM'S-HORN

Rabbi Joshua ben Korhah says: Forty days Moses spent on
Mount Sinai, reading the Written Law by day, and review-
ing the Oral Law by night. After forty days he took the
tablets and descended into the camp. And on the seventeenth
day of Tammuz he broke the tablets and slew the sinners of
Israel. He spent forty days in the camp, burning the golden
calf and grinding it to dust, slaying all who had kissed the
calf, and destroying idol worship from Israel. It was then,
too, that he set every tribe in its place. And on the New Moon
of Elul, the Holy One, blessed be he, said to Moses: "Come
up to me into the Mount" (Exod. 24:12). Then a ram's-horn
was blown throughout the camp, for, behold, Moses was ascending Mount Sinai, that Israel stray not again, and worship idols. On that day the Holy One, blessed be he, was exalted by that same ram's-horn, as it is said, "God is gone up
amidst shouting, the Lord amidst the sound of the horn"
(Ps. 47:6). Therefore the sages instituted the custom of blowing the ram's-horn on the first day of Elul. [Pirke Rabbi Eliezer XLVI]

Therefore it is customary to blow the ram's-horn at the end
of the Morning Prayer from the New Moon of Elul until the
eve of Rosh ha-Shanah. In some places it is blown at the
Afternoon Prayer as well, and there are still others where the
ram's-horn is also blown at the Evening Prayer. [Rema, Orah
Hayyim, No. 581]

. . . But I [Ephraim Zalman Margaliot, 18th–19th cent.]
never heard of such a custom in our district [Brody]. [Mateh
Efrayim]

RETURN, O BACKSLIDING CHILDREN

There are places where during all the month of Elul it is customary for the beadle to call out after the Afternoon Prayer, "Return, O backsliding children" (Jer. 3:14). [Birke Yosef]

The word Elul has the numerical value of the word *binah* ("understanding"). Through understanding comes Teshuvah, as it is written (Isa. 6:10): "And understanding with their heart, return, and be healed." [Siddur Rabbi Yaabetz]

I AM MY BELOVED'S AND MY BELOVED IS MINE

Every man must prepare himself thirty days beforehand with Teshuvah and prayer and charity for the day when he will appear in judgment before God, on Rosh ha-Shanah. Then let him give all his heart to the service of God. And those who interpret the Torah metaphorically say, "The initials of the words, **A**ni **L**e-dodi **V**e-dodi **L**i ('I am my beloved's, and my beloved is mine'—Cant. 6:3), when read consecutively read Elul. If Israel will long to turn in a complete Teshuvah to their Father who is in heaven, then his longing will go out to them, and he will accept them in Teshuvah." [Mateh Moshe]

Therefore let every man do Teshuvah during all the month, and let him scrutinize his actions with a view to mending them, and let him seclude himself one hour every day and examine the six hundred and thirteen commandments and count them over, one by one. Whether he has committed one transgression or many transgressions, let him confess himself of them, and put them down in a book for a remembrance, and consult a sage, to show him his way in Teshuvah. [Yosif Ometz]

It is also fit that a man study the books of the God-fearing diligently in order to awaken his heart to Teshuvah, and engage less in other studies during those days. To the same effect wrote Rabbi Hayyim Joseph David Azulai [Birke Yosef; 18th cent.]: "I have seen that some of the rabbis, who are always engaged in the study of the Law, set aside part of their regular curriculum during the month of Elul to recite penitential prayers and supplications."

FAST

There are some whose custom it is to fast from the beginning of the New Moon of Elul until the close of Yom Kippur, a period of forty days, corresponding to the forty days that Moses remained on the Mount.

But the later sages wrote that it is not fit for most men to fast often, except for those who are healthy and know that the fast will not injure them and will not distract them from their Torah study. We of this generation who are weaklings, particularly the students among us, and those who are pressed for food all year round as it is—it is better for us to eat a little and to study twice as much. For engaging in the study of the Torah is more important than fasting. [Hayye Adam; Nagid u-Metzaveh]

The essential purpose of Teshuvah is to regret the past and commit oneself not to return to that folly again in the future; for, even if a man fast frequently from Sabbath to Sabbath and perform every known form of chastisement, if he has not taken it upon himself not to return to his sin—behold, he is as one who takes a ritual bath while holding an unclean reptile in his hand. [Siddur Derekh ha-Hayyim]

At the beginning of Elul the weekly portion beginning, "Judges and officers shalt thou make thee in all thy gates" (Deut. 16:18), is read, for the starting point of Teshuvah and its essential purpose is that the man doing Teshuvah must station an officer and judge at all of his gates, meaning the senses, such as those of the eyes, ears, nose, mouth, which are the gates that the Creator, blessed be his name, opened in man for his use. [Bene Yisakhar]

A FAST FROM SPEECH

Many men make it a habit to engage in no secular conversation from the beginning of the New Moon of Elul until after Yom Kippur, for there is nothing in the world better for the purification of the soul than the curbing of idle talk. Besides, it is also a great aid to devotion in prayer when alien thoughts do not confuse the worshiper.

A tale is told of a devout man who died and appeared to his wife in a dream. She saw that his hair and his beard were all lit up like a great torch. Said she, "What have you done to be worthy of this?" Said he to her, "I was wont to speak as little as I could of matters other than Torah and the fear of God, for the Holy One, blessed be He, watches over the man who speaks as little as he can of secular matters." [Kav ha-Yashar XII]

THE RECITAL OF PSALMS

It is customary to say Psalms in public every weekday, after the prayer, from the beginning of the New Moon of Elul until Yom Kippur.

The same is the custom among the devout of the Land of Israel; they recite Psalms every day from the New Moon until Yom Kippur.

Let the person who wishes to merit Teshuvah make it a practice to recite Psalms. There are many barriers to doing

Teshuvah. One person may not be sufficiently awake and even he who arouses himself faces many barriers, for the gates of Teshuvah are shut in the face of many. There are others who do not know how to do it, and pass their days and die, God forbid, without having done Teshuvah. But, even if a man is not awake for Teshuvah, he will merit the awakening, by reciting of Psalms, and will open all the closed gates and come into the gate of Teshuvah that belongs to his particular soul, until he merits a complete Teshuvah. [Kitzur Likkute Moharan]

THE ALERT ANTICIPATE TESHUVAH

The alert begin Teshuvah on the Sabbath when the New Moon of Elul is blessed. Rabbi Jacob Saphir ha-Levi [19th cent.] relates in the book describing his travels through Yemen, that it is the custom in the community of Sanaa, on the Sabbath when the New Moon of Elul is blessed, for the rabbi and his court to make the rounds of all the Houses of Prayer, bearing in their hands a circular letter containing admonitions, warnings, and arousements for the Days of Awe. They read this letter aloud in public to arouse the people to Teshuvah.

And Rabbi Jacob writes, "I accompanied them on their rounds because that custom was precious in my eyes. At the time of the Additional Prayer we arrived in the House of Prayer of the kabbalist, Mori Yihye Kohen. There they entreated me to be the Reader for the Additional Prayer, because I was to leave that place after the Sabbath. When in repeating the Prayer of Benedictions I reached the line, 'May it be Thy will to lead us joyfully up to our country and plant us within our borders,' my heart broke, and I could not hold back the tears. Then I cried aloud until I could cry no more; and all the holy assembly, agitated and broken-hearted, poured forth a flood of tears. That Sabbath was a veritable Yom Kippur for us."

THE WAYS OF LIFE

Once our master Rabbi Hayyim of Zans [19th cent.] told a parable:

A man had been wandering about in a forest for several days, not knowing which was the right way out. Suddenly he saw a man approaching him. His heart was filled with joy. "Now I shall certainly find out which is the right way," he thought to himself. When they neared one another, he asked the man, "Brother, tell me which is the right way. I have been wandering about in this forest for several days."

Said the other to him, "Brother, I do not know the way out either. For I too have been wandering about here for many, many days. But *this* I can tell you: do not take the way I have been taking, for that will lead you astray. And now let us look for a new way out together."

Our master added: "So it is with us. One thing I can tell you: the way we have been following this far we ought follow no further, for that way leads one astray. But now let us look for a new way."

There was still another parable that our master used to relate:

There was once a poor countrywoman who had many children. They were always begging for food, but she had none to give them. One day she found an egg.

She called her children and said, "Children, children, we've nothing to worry about any more; I've found an egg. And, being a provident woman, I'll not eat the egg, but shall ask my neighbor for permission to set it under her setting hen, until a chick is hatched. For I am a provident woman! And we'll not eat the chick, but will set her on eggs, and the eggs will hatch into chickens. And the chickens in their turn will hatch many eggs, and we'll have many chickens and many eggs. But I'm a provident woman, I am! I'll not eat the chickens and not eat the eggs, but shall sell them and buy me a heifer. And I'll not eat the heifer, but shall raise it to a cow, and not eat the cow until it calves. And I'll not eat it then, either, and we'll have cows and calves. For I'm a provident woman! And I'll sell the cows and the calves and buy a field, and we'll have fields and cows and calves, and we won't need anything any more!"

The countrywoman was speaking in this fashion and playing with the egg, when it fell out of her hands and broke.

Said our master: "That is how we are. When the Holy Days arrive, every person resolves to do Teshuvah, thinking in his heart, 'I'll do this, and I'll do that.' But the days slip by in mere deliberation, and thought doesn't lead to action, and what is worse, the person who made the resolution may fall even lower. Therefore every person ought to exercise great caution so as not to fall even lower, God forbid."

There was still another parable from the Midrash that our master used to relate:

Once a king's son sinned against his father, the king. His father expelled him from his house. As long as he was near his home, people knew he was a king's son, and befriended him, and gave him food and drink. But as the days passed, and he got farther into his father's realm, no one knew him, and he had nothing to eat. He began to sell his clothing to buy food. When he had nothing left to sell, he hired out as a shepherd. After he had hired out as a shepherd he was no longer in need, because he needed nothing. He would sit on the hills, tending his flocks and singing like the other shepherds, and he forgot that he was a king's son and all the pleasures that he had been used to.

Now it is the custom of the shepherds to make themselves small roofs of straw to keep out the rain. The king's son wanted to make such a roof too, but he could not afford one, so he was deeply grieved.

Once the king happened to be passing through that province. Now it was a common practice in that kingdom for those who had petitions to the king to write out their petitions and throw them into the king's chariot. The king's son came with the other petitioners, and threw his note, in which he petitioned for a small straw roof such as shepherds have. The king recognized his son's handwriting, and was saddened to think how low his son had fallen that he had forgotten that he was a king's son, and felt only the lack of a straw roof.

Our master ended: "It is the same way with our people: They have already forgotten that they are each of them king's sons, and what they really lack. One cries that he is in want of a living, and another cries for children. But the truth, that we lack all the treasures we had of old—that is something they forget to pray for!" [Darkhe Hayyim]

A TIME FOR ATONEMENT

It is written in the sacred books:

"The thirty days before Rosh ha-Shanah, the great Judgment Day when man is permitted to turn in Teshuvah—to what are they comparable? To the thirty days of grace which a Court grants a debtor in which to pay his debts and be freed of his creditors."

But the man who is reverent of the word of God begins to turn in Teshuvah the day before the eve of the New Moon, which is the day called the Minor Day of Atonement. Even those who do not follow the practice of rising early on the

eves of other New Moons make a Minor Day of Atonement
on the eve of the New Moon of Elul, to prepare their hearts
for Teshuvah. [Mateh Efrayim]

THE MINOR DAY OF ATONEMENT

On the eve of the New Moon, there gather in the House of
Prayer no fewer than ten fasters, who recite penitential prayers [Selihot] and supplications and read all the Book of
Psalms, prolonging the reading until the Afternoon Prayer.
Then they take the Torah Scroll out of the Ark, and read the
scriptural portion beginning, "And Moses besought the Lord
his God" (Exod. 32:11), and the cantor chants the prayer,
"Answer us, O Lord." In Jerusalem the priests raise their
hands in benediction during the Afternoon Prayer. It is customary to visit the graves of the pious; in Jerusalem Rachel's
tomb is visited and prayers and supplications recited there,
particularly on the eve of the New Moon of Elul and during
all the month of Elul and the ten days of Teshuvah. If the
New Moon falls on a Sabbath, the Minor Day of Atonement
is advanced to the Thursday before.

ALL THE MONTH OF ELUL

All the month of Elul before eating and sleeping let every
man sit and look into his soul, and search his deeds, that he
may make confession. [Maharil]

A BROKEN HEART

Once before Rosh ha-Shanah, the pious Rabbi Elimelekh of
Lizhensk [18th cent.] was sitting and worrying: "How shall
I face the Omnipresent on the Judgment Day—have I not
committed many transgressions?" And he continued to
reckon them over one by one, as was his holy way.

And in the end he said, "Well then, my broken heart will

stand me in good stead on the Judgment Day." [Ohel Eli-melekh]

AMENDMENTS

Once on the New Moon of Elul, the zaddik Rabbi Levi Isaac of Berditchev [18th cent.] was standing at his window. A Gentile cobbler passed by and asked him, "And have you nothing to mend?"

At once the zaddik sat himself down on the ground and weeping bitterly cried, "Woe is me, and alas my soul, for the Day of Judgment is almost here, and I have still not mended myself!" [Zikhron la-Rishonim]

SEASON'S BLESSING

From the beginning of Elul on, whenever a man writes a personal letter, he should mention at the beginning that he is praying in his friend's behalf for a good year to come, something on the order of, "May you be inscribed and sealed for a good year," or "May He who suspends the earth over nil, inscribe you for life on this day of good will." [Maharil]

It is a practice common to all the Diaspora of Israel for people to send one another messages of blessing for the New Year.

VISITING GRAVES

It is customary during this period to visit the graves of one's ancestors and relatives. It is also customary to prostrate oneself on the graves of the pious and to be liberal with supplications and with charity to the poor in the graveyard.

III. The Sabbath before Rosh ha-Shanah

A SAGE EXPOUNDS

On the last Sabbath in Elul it is the custom for the rabbi to expound.

Whenever the sage expounds, the Holy One, blessed be he, pardons the iniquities of Israel; and when they respond, "Amen, blessed be his great Name," after the exposition, He at once tears up the adverse decree. For that reason it is the custom in all the Diaspora to have a sage expound in public on the Sabbath before Rosh ha-Shanah, in order to turn the people away from the iniquity that is in their hand.

It is necessary for the sage who expounds to have "his teachings well in hand"—meaning that the works of his hands ought to agree with his Torah study, and that he practice what he preaches.

Everyone who reproves the congregation must treat them with respect, reproving them only by suggestion, as was Moses' way, who reproved Israel in none but a calm fashion, as a man reproves his fellow, and in the third person, as Rashi interprets at Deuteronomy 1:1.

Though there is no more than one person present who listens to and accepts the words of the sage, let him not deny the congregation the benefit of his words, that he may save the soul of that one person, as it is said, "Behold, I set before you this day" (Deut. 11:26). Lo, God spoke in the singular, despite the fact that there was a multitude in the desert—intimating that if only a single person in Israel be saved, it is best not to deny the congregation words of admonition. [Sefer ha-Hayyim]

A SERMON BY RABBI JACOB BEN MOSES HA-LEVI

It is written, "And it shall come to pass, when all these things are come upon thee," and afterward, "that then the Lord thy God will turn thy captivity, and have compassion upon thee, and will return and gather thee" (Deut. 30:1, 3). Now the promise of these verses has never been fulfilled; yet let no man be skeptical; for indeed we have the promise from the mouth of the Holy One, blessed be he, himself, that he will bring and hasten redemption when people do Teshuvah and leave off their evil deeds.

Therefore let every man regret his sins, great or small, and do Teshuvah. And let no man be lazy and say, "I still have time," lest, God forbid, the hour slip by. Nor let any man say, "My sins are too many, and Teshuvah too arduous. How can I endure all that wearisome trouble?" Therefore it is written in the same scriptural portion, "For this commandment which I command thee this day, it is not hidden from thee, neither is it far off . . . but the word is very nigh unto thee, in thy mouth, and in thy heart, that thou mayest do it" (Deut. 30:11–14). That is to say, this commandment, which is Teshuvah, is nigh to thee in thy mouth and in thy heart that thou mayest do it. "In thy mouth"—that is, oral confession of transgressions. "And in thy heart"—is the contemplation of Teshuvah in one's heart, for the very contemplation of Teshuvah is of value.

Every man ought to be very, very much on guard against malicious talk, for it is a serious transgression, like one of the three cardinal transgressions, idolatry, incest, and bloodshed.

In the same way, every person ought to be on guard against anything that smacks at all of theft, though it seem in his eyes not theft itself; as is the way of the householders who assess taxes and lay their burden more heavily on their fellows than on themselves, not perceiving that that smacks of theft. It is good to remove oneself from that temptation, for it is indeed a serious transgression.

In the same way, every man should be on guard against flattery; he ought not to flatter his fellow, saying, "You are a fine man, in action, and in scholarship, and in looks," and the like. For that is a serious transgression indeed.

In the same way, every man should be on guard against jesting. He should not think to himself: "I'll jest in company, so people will think me charming, or play tricks in company to make people laugh." This is indeed a serious transgression. For whoever jests, the beginning of his punishment is suffering and the end extinction (Abodah Zarah 18b; Yerushalmi Berakhot II.8). But it is a good deed to make the bride and groom rejoice, by jesting in their company and causing them to rejoice, as well as to flatter the bride and praise her. It is a good deed to call her "a lovely bride, and a gracious," and other similar phrases.

Therefore, if a man has committed one of these transgressions, or any of the other transgressions, let him look closely into his actions, that he may put the transgressions far away from him, and never commit them again.

And if, God forbid, sufferings come upon a man, let him accept them in the spirit of love, and not rebel at them, saying, "Why am I poor and a pauper, and have more sufferings than other people?" Let him not speak in this way. But rather let him say, " 'The Lord is righteous; for I have rebelled against His word' (Lam. 1:18), and I have done that which is evil in his sight; therefore have I not prospered."

Let every man confess his sins; and when he says, "And Thou art righteous" after the Confession, let him say it with real devotion. For then the Holy One, blessed be he, says to the angels, "Come and see how dear Israel are, who justify God's judgment of them!" Let every man stand in the breach against his will to evil.

His case may be compared to that of a king who has many foes and is fearful of them. So he goes and inspects all of his fortresses and strengthens the breaches at every place where the enemy could possibly enter. The king makes his plans: "Perhaps they will climb stealthily over at this point; and let us build castles and a tower for our defense at that point."

So it is with the will to evil. He is the enemy that lies in

ambush and besieges man day and night, inciting him to
transgress, that he may be caught in his trap. For that is why
the will to evil was created, and he is compelled to do his part,
and is an expert at it. Therefore let every man be alert to
stand in the breach against the will to evil, and let every man
constantly be searching and delving deep in his mind, that he
may come to know every place where his will is inciting him
to transgression. Let every man say, "I will amend my ways,
and stand in the breach, and not heed the will to evil, and
build in my mind a defense against him, that he may not take
me in his trap." By accustoming himself to stand against the
will to evil, a man comes to despise transgressions more than
at first he desired them. It is also true that the will to evil
leaves a man when he sees that he is turning his back on him,
rather than hear him.

At the end of the sermon, the rabbi returned to the intent
of the scriptural portion of the week and interpreted the
words, "And a redeemer will come to Zion" (Isa. 59:20), as
meaning that we ought to pray to God to hasten the redemption, concerning which it is written in that portion (Deut.
29:28): "The secret things belong unto the Lord our God;
but the things that are revealed belong unto us." [Maharil]

iv. Selihot: Penitential Prayers

WHEN THE PENITENTIAL PRAYERS ARE RECITED

As the month of Elul is the month of Teshuvah, it is customary from the beginning of the month of Elul until Yom Kippur to rise very early to recite penitential prayers and supplications. During that period men rise at midnight to supplicate and plead for their lives before the Holy One, blessed be
he, who sits on his throne of judgment and judges who

among all his creatures is to live and who is to die. We have evidence of this in what King David said (Ps. 119:6): "At midnight I will rise to give thanks unto Thee because of Thy righteous ordinances."

Another reason for this practice is that at midnight a man's mind is composed, the body being inactive and the blood purified, so that he can concentrate with his mind and heart during the last watch and achieve more than he can during the day. . . . Therefore the Early Hasidim established the custom of rising during those nights to supplicate and pray before the Creator, blessed be he, until the light of day. . . . And the Holy One hears the prayers that a person prays at night and his supplications and answers them, because that is the hour of divine good will—when the Holy One, blessed be he, is reminded of the destruction of the Temple and the exile of Israel among the nations, and has compassion upon them, and is gracious to them. . . . It follows that he who pleads before the Holy One, blessed be he, during the last watch of the night—his supplication is heard and accepted by the Holy One, blessed be he, who sits on a throne of mercy to accept the prayers of Israel. [Sefer ha-Musar IV; Israel al-Nakawa, Menorat ha-Maor, Perek ha-Tefillah]

It is the Ashkenazic custom to begin waking early four days before Rosh ha-Shanah. If Rosh ha-Shanah should fall on a Monday or a Tuesday in that week, so that there are less than four days left in which to recite penitential prayers, they begin a week earlier; and, in order that it may be a definite day, it is their custom to begin waking for penitential prayers on the first day of the week. [Hayye Adam]

And why are four days set aside? Because we find a similar practice in relation to sacrificial animals, which must undergo examination for blemishes four days before they are sacrificed. In reference to all sacrifices it is written (e.g. Num.

29:8), "And ye shall *present* a burnt-offering," and in reference to Rosh ha-Shanah it is written, "And ye shall *prepare*
a burnt-offering" (Num. 29:2)—teaching us that on Rosh
ha-Shanah every man ought to *prepare* himself for self-
sacrifice. Therefore four days are set aside for us to examine
all our sins, and return to God. [Ateret Zekenim]

AT THE CLOSE OF THE DAY OF REST

We always rise early on the first day of the week for penitential prayers, because it is the day after the Sabbath, and
people make it a practice to study on the Sabbath when they
are free from work and can study Torah. For that reason it
is good to begin the penitential prayers on Sunday, when
the folk are happy at having fulfilled the commandment to
study the Torah, and also because of the pleasure they have
taken in the Sabbath. Our sages, of blessed memory, said that
the Divine Presence dwells neither in the midst of sadness,
nor in the midst of idleness, but in the midst of joy at having
fulfilled a commandment (Shabbat 30b). Therefore, it is good
to pray when one is in the midst of joy at having fulfilled a
commandment. [Leket Yosher].

It is customary for the beadle of the city to make the rounds
of the entire city and to knock three times on every door, crying, "Israel, O holy folk, awake, arouse yourselves, and rise
to the service of the Creator." Then all rise early for penitential prayers, this being true of the women and the children
old enough to understand as well as of the men.

THE READER

If there is a regular Reader, let him lead the prayer; if there is
not, a Reader is sought out, one who is excellent in learning
and in deed, who knows how to pray and knows how to appease his Creator with his actions, is agreeable to the congre-

gation and can defend his generation, has a wife and children, and is at least thirty years old, so that his mind is composed. For at that age maturity sets in, and a man's heart becomes humble and his spirit broken. These qualities are necessary because during the Days of Awe we are suspended in judgment and there is need for great devotion.

It is the practice for the leaders of the community and the leaders of the generation to stand before the Ark in the role of Readers because they are in awe of God, and aware of the sorrow of Israel, and defend their generation, and pray with particular devotion. If it is impossible to find anyone who has all these virtues and qualities, every Israelite is presumed fit to be a Reader, if only he is agreeable to the congregation.

Nor is any Reader appointed who has enemies in the congregation. Rabbi Meir ben Isaac Katzenellenbogen [15th-16th cent.] wrote in his Responsa [No. 64], "And if the congregation desire him for their Reader, he is obligated to remove the hatred from his heart, and to say explicitly that he will include his enemy in his prayer, the same as every other man." Now the same was the custom of the ancients; when a man could sense a feeling of ill will against him in the heart of the Reader, he would compel the Reader to say that he would include him in his prayer.

Is a man who has been stricken by the quality of divine justice, so that he has lost the use of his arms, fit to be a Reader? Surely, he is fit; he is even preferable. For the King who is King above all kings wishes to make use of broken vessels, and his is not the way of a lord of flesh and blood, as it is said, "A broken and a contrite heart, O God, Thou wilt not despise" (Ps. 51:19). For none but a priest is declared unfit because of a defect, and a Levite only because of a defect in his voice. [Yam shel Shelomo, Hullin, quoting Maharam mi-Rothenburg]

Now it is customary that he who is the Reader on the first night of the penitential prayers is the Reader during the Days of Awe as well, because he who takes a fee for his services during the holiday sees no blessing from that fee. Therefore, it is the practice for each of the Readers who worship on the Days of Awe to be the Reader on the first day of penitential prayers, or the eve of Rosh ha-Shanah, so that their fee becomes inclusive. [Nefesh Hayyah]

I have heard my master and teacher, Rabbi Solomon Shapira, of blessed memory, expound that the man who is the Reader on the Days of Awe and does not worship during the penitential prayers is comparable to one who wishes to come before a king and has the key to the inner chamber but not the key to the outer. Therefore it is common sense that the man who is the Reader on the Days of Awe must be the Reader during the penitential prayers. [Leket Yosher]

The devout and saintly men of Yemen refuse to be Readers, for the Reader takes the place of the High Priest, and the prayers of the community must pass through him. Therefore, if his thoughts should be distracted from his prayer even for a moment, or if he should slip over a single word, his prayer would not be heard on high, and the prayer of those who send him to be their emissary would not be accepted. It follows that he bears the iniquity of all the folk, and the Holy One, blessed be he, can call him to account at once. Hence, whosoever undertakes to be a Reader is honored by the people as though he were offering himself as a communal sacrifice. [Reshumot I]

It is fitting that the Reader know how to awaken the heart of the folk to devotion, with a joyful melody where joy and enthusiasm are needed, and with a tearful melody where weeping is needed for confession and Teshuvah. But let the Reader not show himself vain because of his melodies.

A certain king was once asked, "And how do you like the chanting of so-and-so?" (The latter's voice was pleasant, and he was a skilful chanter.)

The king said to those who asked him, "Now how shall his reading be pleasant to me, when he reads only for sake of pleasing me and finding favor in my eyes? But if his aim were to achieve the favor solely of the Creator by those same means, his chanting would be pleasing to me."

The same may be said of every one of the Readers and "cantillators" who aims by his prayer and his singing of liturgical poems to find favor in the eyes of men, but does not have God, be blessed, in mind—his prayer is not accepted by the Creator. [Hovot ha-Levavot, Shaar Yihud ha-Maaseh]

THE ORDER OF THE PENITENTIAL PRAYERS

Penitential prayers are recited calmly and with devotion, in the order to be found in our prayer books, according to the local custom. There are some whose custom it is to stand during these prayers.

It is the practice in Yemen to blow the ram's-horn during the recitation of the Thirteen Qualities of divine compassion, in addition to the usual blasts after the Morning Prayer.

YE WHO USHER IN COMPASSION

Among the other penitential prayers, the liturgical poem: "Ye who usher in compassion, usher in our pleas for compassion before the Master of compassion. . . . Ye who usher in tears, usher in our tears before a King appeased by tears

. . ." is recited, and there is in it no suggestion of an associa-
tion of the name of God with other powers. [Shibbole ha-
Leket, No. 282]

Rabbi Loew ben Bezalel of Prague [16th cent.] refused to
recite the poem because, he said: We must not pray to the
angels, for to Him alone is it fitting to pray, and it is not fitting to pray to any other being. [Likkute Mahariah; Hatam
Sofer, Orah Hayyim, No. 146]

I heard Rabbi Hayyim of Volozhin [18th–19th cent.]
speak in amazement at the popular custom of addressing the
prayer, "Bless me for peace," to the angels on Sabbath eve, as
well as the hymn "Angels of Compassion" during penitential prayers. And this is what he said:

"What place is there for such a plea? For the angels have
no free will of their own, since they are not free agents, but
act solely under necessity. For if a man is worthy, they must
bless him, even against their will, and if, God forbid, he is
not worthy, they must of necessity curse him." He added
that, from the day he had known his own mind, he had never
recited the liturgical poem, "Bless me for peace," on Sabbath
eve, and had never recited the liturgical poem "Angels of
Compassion" during the penitential prayers; but thus he
would recite: "Patriarchs of the world, beloved of the Most
High, pray, beseech ye, of God."

But he did not rebuke those who did recite the prayer, "Ye
who usher in compassion." [Shaare Rahamim]

PREPARATION FOR PRAYER

"Rabbi Eliezer said: Let a man ever first prepare his prayer,
and afterward worship" (Rosh ha-Shanah 33a). His dictum
is relevant to the blessings of Rosh ha-Shanah and Yom Kippur, for every man must prepare his prayer in advance so as
not to err. This is particularly true of the Reader, who in ad-

dition stands in awe of the congregation. Therefore let every man review and study the prayers and liturgical poems to be fluent in the hour of prayer on Rosh ha-Shanah. Let him teach his children and the members of his household the order of the service and the order of the blessings and the order of the various services, so that he will not need to halt his prayer on Rosh ha-Shanah to show them the correct order. [Mateh Moshe]

If a man does not know the meaning of the prayers, but worships God, be blessed, because He commanded that he should be worshiped—though he does not know even the meaning of the words, his prayer ascends and pierces the firmament, for the sacred words of the Torah and prayer contain a superior sanctity, and when they issue from the heart of a man who is praying for the sake of heaven, they bring about great amendments in the superior worlds. [Or Yesharim, quoting the Baal Shem Tov]

Whosoever of the congregation has been chosen to be the Reader or to blow the ram's-horn needs, three days before Rosh ha-Shanah, and before Yom Kippur as well, to seclude himself from every thing that leads to ritual uncleanliness, because he needs a special purity. For so it is written in the Zohar on Lev. 18:1:

Rabbi Eleazar said, I perceived that on the days of Rosh ha-Shanah and Yom Kippur my father would listen to no man's prayer unless he had examined him three days beforehand. Indeed, Rabbi Simeon ben Yohai wished on Rosh ha-Shanah and Yom Kippur to listen to no man's prayer in the House of Prayer, unless he had examined him three days before the holiday, to decide whether he was worthy of worshiping, both in respect to his deeds, and to his knowledge of the meaning of the prayers. [Shene Luhot ha-Berit, Rosh ha-Shanah]

A tale is told of one who sat in study before the zaddik Rabbi Mordecai of Nadvorna, of blessed memory [19th cent.], and before Rosh ha-Shanah came to obtain permission to be dismissed. That zaddik said to him, "Why are you hurrying?"

Said he to him, "I am a Reader, and I must look into the festival prayer book, and put my prayers in order."

Said the zaddik to him, "The prayer book is the same as it was last year. But it would be better for you to look into your deeds, and put yourself in order." [Likkute Mahariah]

v. The Eve of Rosh ha-Shanah: "Remember the Covenant"

PENITENTIAL PRAYERS

On the eve of Rosh ha-Shanah, one rises for penitential prayers two or three hours after midnight, and goes to the House of Prayer and chants more penitential prayers and supplications than on all the other nights; and that night is called the "Night of Remember the Covenant," for on that night we beg the Holy One, blessed be he, to bethink him of the covenant of the patriarchs and to shield us for their sake. This is a custom that Rabbenu Gershom, the "Light of the Exile" [10th–11th cent.] established in his hymn, "Remember the Covenant."

For, the Talmud tells (Shabbat 30a), when Israel sinned in the desert, Moses stood before the Holy One, blessed be he, and recited many prayers and supplications before him, but was not listened to. But when he recited, "Remember Abraham, Isaac, and Israel, Thy servants" (Exod. 32:13), he was listened to at once.

ADMONISHMENT FOR REMEMBER THE COVENANT

"Remember the Covenant with Abraham and the Binding of Isaac and return the captivity of the tents of Jacob, and save us for the sake of Thy name" (penitential prayers for the eve of Rosh ha-Shanah). Let us try to understand the intent of the poet who begins with the phrase, "Remember the Covenant" and concludes with "and help us for the sake of Thy name," as well as to understand why we call this watch by the name of "Remember the Covenant," after the liturgical poem of that name, since we recite many liturgical poems at that watch. There is also apparently occasion to inquire closely as to the reason for the ado over the binding of Isaac, which we are always praying that God will remember unto us.

It has been said of the woman and her seven sons who were killed for the sanctification of the Name of God that she said to them, "Go and say to Abraham your Father, 'You have built one altar, and I have built seven.' " (Gittin 57b). And I say, at this time we can say: Abraham built one altar, and that woman built seven, and we in this bitter exile have built thousands and tens of thousands, for so many of our brothers, the children of Israel, living among the peoples, have given their lives for the Torah and commandments, have been beaten and punished rather than eat unclean food, and have gone hungry and thirsty rather than take an unclean thing in their mouths and contaminate themselves or desecrate the Sabbath, or commit other transgressions. It is explained in the Talmud (Ketubot 33b), "If they had lashed Hananiah, Mishael and Azariah, they would have bowed down to the image." But our brothers are beaten and driven like cattle to the slaughter, to death and annihilation, blows and humiliation—nevertheless they have not forgotten your

Name. This being the case, what is so miraculous about the Binding of Isaac?

Yet we shall see that the sacred root of the thought of every Israelite that impels him to give his life for the Torah and the Service and for the sanctification of the Name of God—is all derived from Abraham our father who bequeathed it to his children after him, as it is written, "That he may command his children and his household after him, that they may keep the way of the Lord" (Gen. 18:19). That is the principle behind the covenant that God made with Abraham in the name of his seed that they might possess that strength, which lacking, they ought not to be called his "seed," for the principle behind the yearning of Abraham our father, for seed was "That he may command . . . that they may keep the way of the Lord. . . ."

Lo, the consummation and basis for the making of the covenant was the tenth trial of Abraham, that is, the trial of the Binding of Isaac, in which he took his son, his only child, intending to slaughter him, with great love to do the will of our Maker, be blessed. By means of the Binding, Abraham introduced into the heart of his children after him the courage to give their lives for the sanctification of the Name of God. And all his successors follow his example, and are named after him.

For that reason we always mention the Binding of Isaac, for in it are included all the services and martyrdoms of every generation. The woman said, "Go to Abraham," whose strength during the Binding of Isaac was also present in the sacrifice of her seven sons.

The principle behind Teshuvah is "a humble and a contrite heart," such as Abraham had, who said, "And I am but dust and ashes" (cf. Gen. 18:27). And, as it is explained in the Zohar [III. 240a]: "Rabbi Abba began: 'The sacrifices of

God are a broken spirit' (Ps. 51:19).—This passage has already been interpreted to mean that the Holy One, blessed be he, does not desire the sacrifice that a man brings to atone for his sin, but what he wants is 'a humble and a contrite heart.' For when a man is about to become unclean, he draws upon himself a spirit of uncleanliness and this spirit overpowers him and turns the man to its desire. When he is about to cleanse himself and masters the spirit of uncleanliness, he is helped to cleanliness. When the Temple was in existence, the man would offer a sacrifice of atonement, which would be in abeyance until he regretted his sins, and until he broke the spirit of haughtiness that was in him. This was the breaking of that spirit of uncleanliness. As soon as that spirit of uncleanliness was broken, and he made his sacrifice, his sacrifice was favorably accepted, as is fit. But if that spirit was not broken, his sacrifice was worthless, and was given to the dogs. For that sacrifice is not the portion of the Holy One, blessed be he, for it is said, 'The sacrifices of God are a broken spirit,' implying that that spirit of uncleanliness must be broken and not be the master. . . . That man who takes no pride in himself and takes no pleasure in the pleasures of the world—him the Lord 'will not despise' (*ibid.*), he is dear in His eyes."

For lo, there are many who come with great enthusiasm to the House of Prayer to recite penitential prayers and supplications before our Maker, be blessed, but they do honor to God only with their lips, and their hearts are elsewhere. For the multitude of their iniquities separates them from their Master, and causes that spirit of uncleanliness to master them. Hence the advice given, first to attain a humble and a contrite heart, by means of which that spirit of uncleanliness will be shattered of itself, and with it man's pride. It is necessary to beg mercy and to beseech God to be allowed to arrive at that quality, by mentioning before him the covenant that he made with Abraham our father. For Abraham was our father, and the strength of the father persists in the son. Now, Abraham's great strength consisted in the quality of humility, for he said, "And I am dust and ashes" (cf. Gen. 18: 27). All his desire and yearning was that he might command his children "that they may keep the way of the Lord," and this principle was behind the making of the covenant. That is why the recitation of "Remember the Covenant" is a good counsel to attain the way of God. What is essential is the quality of humility.

To what can this be compared? To a father who had an only son who did not listen to the voice of his parent and teacher, and was continually squandering his father's money. Before his death, he called his son and said to him, "Know, my son, that you will be left a great fortune. I know by your present actions that you will lose it all and it will pass into the hands of strangers. Therefore remember, my son, that I have a certain garden; do not sell it, for it is your father's inheritance, and when you are in dire straits, the garden will sprout your salvation and ease." After his father passed away, the son lost his wealth and riches and was left in poverty and need. Then he remembered that his father had told him that from that garden his salvation would sprout. He walked in the garden thinking, "How is it possible to find salvation here?" Then he looked, and, behold, under a certain tree there was a mark and a sign. He dug and found a precious treasure.

The reference is self-evident. For here we are speaking of that aiding patriarchal merit of which the Writ speaks (Lev. 26:44) "And yet for all that, when they are in the land of their enemies, I will not reject them, neither will I abhor them, to destroy them utterly, and to break My covenant with them." "Then will I remember My covenant with Jacob, and also My covenant with Isaac, and also My covenant with Abraham will I remember" (v. 42).

So, let every man remind himself that he is of the seed of Abraham, and that that seed is a precious treasure from which his salvation can sprout. And let that thought arouse him to attain the great strength of our father Abraham. For the strength of the father persists in the child. Then he will be aroused to return in a complete Teshuvah before our Maker, and to have a broken and a contrite heart. As it is written, "Who is a God like unto Thee, that pardoneth the iniquity, and passeth by the transgression of the remnant of his heritage?" (Mic. 7:18). The sages comment (Megillah 15b), "The reference is to one who considers himself as a remnant in the world." And that was the quality Abraham had, who said, "And I am dust and ashes." By means of the awakening of the realms below, the awakening of the realms above will come to pass: "And I shall remember for thee the covenant of Abraham. . . ."

So we pray: "Remember the Covenant of Abraham and the Binding of Isaac," to awaken in ourselves the holy enthusiasm of the realms below. "And restore the captivity of the tents of Jacob and save us for Thy Name's sake" is to awaken the holy enthusiasm of the realms above, that we may turn in a complete Teshuvah in truth, as it is written (Mal. 3:7): "Return unto Me, and I will return unto you." And the sages said (Cant. Rabbah V): "Make for Me an opening as wide as the eye of a needle, and I shall make an opening for you as wide as the door of a chamber." Also (Yoma 38b): "He who comes to cleanse himself is assisted by heaven." [Bet Yaakov]

HEAR OUR VOICE

Rabbi Meshullam Issachar ha-Levi Hurwitz of Stanislav [19th cent.], before beginning to recite the prayer, "Hear Our Voice," during the penitential prayers of "Remember the Covenant," opened the Ark with tears and supplications and related:

A certain king had an only son, tender and delicately reared from childhood. And his father loved him and raised him and reared him in the ways of righteousness, and led him to the bridal canopy; and all he wished was to see his son going in the straight way. "And he looked that it should bring forth grapes, and it brought forth wild grapes" (Isa. 5:2). The good qualities that his father planted in his son he exchanged for ugly, and he went after the stubbornness of his evil heart, deserted the wife of his youth and clung to a foreign wife. His father the king seeing his erring deeds, his heart turned to hate his son, and he banished him from his house and from his palace, and sent him to another land far from his country.

The son wandered for many years from village to village and from city to city. His clothes became torn and tattered. His face changed, until it was not to be recognized that he was the son of a king. When many days had passed and he had had his fill of wandering, he remembered his father the king, and his palace, and began to think about his condition, and why his father had banished him. His yearning to return to the house of his father became stronger day by day. He made up his mind to return to the house of his father, and to return in complete repentance.

And when he came before his father the king, he cried and begged his mercy, and fell at his feet, and asked to be forgiven for the sin that he had sinned. But his father did not recognize him, because his face had changed greatly. Then he began to scream bitterly, "Father, father, if you do not recognize my face, you must remember my voice, for my voice has not changed." Then his father recognized him, and had pity on him, and gathered him into his house.

Then the rabbi said:

"So is it with us. We are sons to the Lord, our God, the King above all kings. The Holy One, blessed be he, loved us and desired us, and exalted us above every folk, and led us to the bridal canopy, and gave us his sacred Torah that corrects a man, that he may go in the straight way of righteousness; but we have turned aside from the highway he leveled before us, we have departed from his goodly commandments, and have been banished far from our land, and our iniquities have turned away these things, so that our face has been changed and our comeliness has turned in us into corruption.

"And now with the coming of the Sacred Days we are regretful of our deeds, and are returning to our Father that is in heaven, and cry to him, 'Hear our voice! If you do not recognize our appearance, you must recognize our voice, for we are your children; spare and have compassion on us, and receive, with compassion and willingly, this our prayer.'" [Responsa, Bar Levai]

OPTIONAL AND OBLIGATORY BLOWING OF THE RAM'S-HORN

After the conclusion of the penitential prayers, the Morning Prayer is recited. The ram's-horn is not blown after the prayer as it is on the other days of Elul, in order to mark a halt between the optional and obligatory blowings, that is to say, between the blasts during Elul which are but a custom, and the blasts on Rosh ha-Shanah, which the Torah commanded. [Levush]

This is done in order to confuse Satan, to keep him ignorant of the coming of Rosh ha-Shanah when he brings
charges against men, and to have him believe that the Day of
Judgment has already passed. [Mateh Moshe]

THE ANNULMENT OF VOWS

After the prayer, it is customary to annul those vows that a
man made in his heart, either waking or dreaming, and then
forgot and did not keep, that he may enter the New Year
without owing any debts.

What is the procedure in the annulment of vows? Each
person chooses three men, and stands before them, and recites the entire section in the prayer book, and the annullers
reply three times, "May all vows be annulled you, may all
vows be pardoned you, may all vows be absolved you. . . ."
To what does this refer? To the vow a man makes to himself.
But for the vows a man makes to his fellows, annulment is
not effective. [Siddur Derekh ha-Hayyim]

And this is the custom in the Land of Israel: There gather
together on the eve of Rosh ha-Shanah a sacred assembly of
scholars and God-fearing persons, and if there is no time on
the eve of Rosh ha-Shanah, they gather between Rosh ha-
Shanah and Yom Kippur. If it is impossible to perform the
annulment before an assembly, there must be a Court, that
is, a quorum of three.

This is the custom among the inhabitants of Aden: On the
eve of Rosh ha-Shanah, after the Morning Prayer, it is customary to read all the Psalms of Teshuvah before the annulment, in order that the community might arouse themselves
and put their hearts to return to God.

This is the procedure of annulment: Ten of the wisest and

best men of the city are chosen. The head of the Court is the
first to come out of the House of Prayer into the courtyard,
and to confess silently, and all the community annul him his
vow. Afterward, the second in prestige comes out and they
annul him his vow, as they did the first; and so every one of
the ten. Afterward, the same ten come in as one and annul
the vows of the entire community.

After the annulment, the passages beginning "Who is a
God like unto Thee" (Mic. 7:18–20) are publicly recited.
Then they recite the Kaddish, and depart in peace. Such is
their tradition from earliest times. [Nahlat Yosef]

CHARITY

Rabbi Jacob ben Moses ha-Levi [14th–15th cent.] expounded:

Whosoever gives charity to the poor on the eve of Rosh
ha-Shanah, let him give it with a liberal eye, and the same
with all charity. Those who give their tithe to make candles
to light during the hour of prayer act unjustly, for the tithe
belongs to the poor. Let the donor give them their alms at
dawn, that they may be able to buy their holiday needs. If the
poor man is accustomed to a liberal feast, let no man say,
"Why should I aid this spendthrift?" For you are commanded to be liberal with him, and to aid him, as it is said
(Deut. 15:7–8): ". . . nor shut thy hand from thy needy
brother; but thou shalt surely open thy hand unto him . . .
sufficient for his need in that which he wanteth." [Maharil]

In Jerusalem the Holy City, it is customary for all to visit
the Wailing Wall and there to pray; and they there distribute
charity among the poor.

All that day before Rosh ha-Shanah let every man engage
in the study of the Torah and in good deeds and in doing
Teshuvah, particularly for those transgressions which a man
commits in his relationship with his fellow man. Let him not

wait for the eve of Yom Kippur, but rather let him prepare
himself earlier that day to seek forgiveness from his fellows.
[Kitzur Shulhan Arukh]

FESTIVAL PRAYER BOOKS

I am exceedingly wroth at the many people who expend
much money on expensive white clothing, and are not heed-
ful of buying themselves attractive festival prayer books for
Rosh ha-Shanah and Yom Kippur to fulfil the verse, "This is
my God and I will glorify Him" (Exod. 15:2), meaning,
adorn yourself before Him by the observance of his commandments [see Shabbat 133b]. For indeed an attractive
prayer book is greatly effective in devotion. It is even harder
when a man and his son have only one old prayer book. Why
do they spare their money, and refuse to buy separate prayer
books for themselves and their children! [Moed lekhol Hai,
No. 35]

THE LIGHTING OF CANDLES

Women light candles in honor of the day before the nightfall, that they may enter a New Year in the midst of light and
joy. They recite the benedictions over the holiday candle and
the benediction containing the phrase "who has kept us
alive," as they do on the other holidays. If it falls on the Sabbath, they insert the phrase "to light the Sabbath candle" into
the holiday benediction.

vi. The Evening and Its Service

TO THE HOUSE OF GOD

One goes to the House of Prayer while it is still daylight, full
of reverence and awe. Let no man depend on his intelligence,
saying, "All the year I have performed commandments and
good deeds, and I need not be afraid"; for Solomon, peace be

upon him, has already said (I Kings 8:46) : "For there is no man that sinneth not."

We enter the House of Prayer and pray the Afternoon Prayer and prolong it a little, since it is the last prayer of the year, to show Him, that we are not ungrateful for the days and years that he, out of his mercy, has given us.

After the Afternoon Prayer let every man meditate in his heart on all the deeds he has done. If there are some good deeds among them, let him take it upon himself to add to them; if his deeds were evil, let him regret them in his heart, and let him take it upon himself to repent of them, and let him prepare himself to receive the New Year in sanctity and purity. Let him look ahead and hope that the coming year will be good, for God conducts his world ever more beautifully [Sihot Moharan]. Let every man prepare himself to pray the Evening Prayer with powerful devotion.

Before the Evening Prayer it is customary in many communities to chant the liturgical poem "Little Sister" in which there is the plea, "May the old year expire, and with it its curses, and may the New Year begin and with it its blessings."

It is customary to spread a white veil on the Ark, white covers for the Torah Scrolls and white napkins on the tables, and to let them remain so until after Yom Kippur. For the whiteness refers to forgiveness, after the Writ (Isa. 1:18): "Though your sins be as scarlet, they shall be as white as snow." It also alludes to the quality of divine kindness, as the Writ says (Mic. 7:18) : "For He delighteth in kindness."

IN THE MULTITUDE OF PEOPLE IS THE KING'S GLORY

It is customary for the countryfolk to come to the city for Rosh ha-Shanah and Yom Kippur, to pray "in the multitude of people."

On Rosh ha-Shanah and Yom Kippur all Israel gather together from all their places and villages into one place, which
is not true of any other holiday. There is a reason for this custom, for it is well known that when a king is crowned, people
come from all the towns in his realm to the capital to see the
king being honored; and, "in the multitude of people is
the king's glory," his honor is when a crowd is present to
crown him and accept the yoke of his kingship. And so it is
written, "And there was a king in Jeshurun, when the heads
of the people were gathered, all the tribes of Israel together"
(Deut. 33:5)—meaning that at the time when Jeshurun
[Israel] crown a king over them, that is, on Rosh ha-Shanah
and Yom Kippur, when they recite the word "King" in their
prayer, the heads of the people must be gathered, and all the
tribes of Israel together. [Sefer ha-Matamim]

It is fit that the inhabitants of the city communities should
do honor to the countryfolk when the latter come to join their
quorum, as was the case with those who brought the first
fruits to Jerusalem: "The great men of Jerusalem used to go
out of the city to greet them and did them honor" (Mishnah
Bikkurim II.3). That is the thought set down in the hymn
of the eve of Yom Kippur beginning, "Thy children have
come under the shadow of Thy roof." Lo, we are pleading for
mercy after "coming under the shadow of the roof" of our
God, for it is the way of the householder to watch over his
guests, as we learn from the tale of Lot, who pleaded (Gen.
19:8) : "Forasmuch as they are come under the shadow of my
roof." [Sefer ha-Hayyim]

ESSENTIAL PURPOSE OF ISRAEL'S PRAYERS

The essential purpose of Rosh ha-Shanah prayers is that his
great Name be sanctified in the universe. Therefore let every
man weep and be sorrowful in his heart, especially on the

great and awesome Day of Judgment, because of the profanation of his great Name. Let this prayer from the depths of his
heart be more profound than the prayers he prays in his own
behalf; for now, in the Exile, there is reason continually to
weep and to be sorrowful over the profanation of his great
Name among the nations that do insult us and mock us, a
sacred folk, saying (Deut. 32:37–38) : "Where is your God?
Let him rise up and help you!" [Nehora ha-Shalem]

And Jacob [Israel] is persecuted by Esau [the nations of
the world] only when the essential purpose of his prayer is
the needs of this world. But in the hour when the children of
Israel will lift their eyes and their hearts to the sanctification
of God who is in heaven, there will be no nation and tongue
able to prevail over them. Such we see to be true of the hare
that is pursued by the hunter; when she breathes on the earth,
the dogs can follow and sniff her odor and catch her; but
when she breathes upward to the sky, her traces are lost and
the dogs will never be able to catch her. So it is with Israel.
[Sefer ha-Hayyim]

You must know that all our pleadings for life during these
Days of Awe refer to eternal and spiritual life in the world to
come. As to the man who arouses himself in Teshuvah—the
Holy One, blessed be he, knows whether it is for the man's
benefit that he live on in this world to gain perfection; if it is,
then the Holy One, blessed be he, inscribes him in the book of
life. But if he knows that it is better for the man to die, then
"precious in the sight of the Lord is the death of His saints"
(Ps. 116:15), and he removes that man from the world for
his own benefit, that he may enter on eternal life. [Nehora
ha-Shalem]

THE EVENING PRAYER

The Evening Prayer is recited according to the order found
in our festival prayer books. The special liturgical poems

usually inserted into the prayer on other festivals are not inserted into the Evening Prayer on Rosh ha-Shanah. Phrases
like "the holy God" are replaced during the Days of Awe by
the phrase "the holy King," because the kingship of God is
emphasized during these days.

Although the Prayer of Benedictions is recited silently all the
rest of the year, it is the custom on Rosh ha-Shanah and Yom
Kippur to recite it in a low voice. We are not fearful lest
people disturb one another, as they have prayer books in their
hands [Orah Hayyim, No. 581]. In any case, they should be
careful not to raise their voices too high; he who prays silently
is praiseworthy. [Shene Luhot ha-Berit]

There are some who make it a practice to pray silently on
Rosh ha-Shanah and on Yom Kippur. They do not stir from
their place during all the service, but stand slightly bent, their
eyes cast down and heart uplifted, and raise their voices no
more than is necessary for their own ears to hear what their
lips are saying, and they lay the fear of judgment on their
heart, and cling to their Creator in tranquillity.

There are some whose custom it is to pray very loudly
during the rest of the year as well, and to cry out in the midst
of their prayer, and to gesture strangely.

Said Rabbi Israel Baal Shem Tov [18th cent.]: When a
man is drowning in a river, and splashes about trying to pull
himself out of the waters that are overwhelming him, those
who see him will certainly not make fun of his splashing. So,
when a man prays with gestures, there is no reason to make
fun of him, for he is saving himself from the raging waters
that come upon him to distract him from his prayer. [Keter
Shem Tov]

Once on the night of Rosh ha-Shanah, when the zaddik
Rabbi Moses of Kobrin [19th cent.] stood before the Ark to
worship for the congregation, all his limbs began to tremble
and his teeth to chatter, and all his limbs and sinews were
moved as the trees of the forest are moved with a strong
wind. Then he seized the prayer stand, and the prayer stand
moved to and fro, and it was not in his power to stand upright, because of his violent trembling, until he bent back-
ward; it was as though he were taking the trembling into
himself. Then he stood his ground and began to worship.
[Or Yesharim]

Let those who pray through all the service in a bent position straighten themselves out before the conclusion of
each benediction and bend again at the word "blessed," and
straighten again at the Name of God. Similarly, at every
place where the Name of God is mentioned, let it be said in
an upright position, as our masters (Berakhot 12a) expounded the verse (Ps. 146:8): "The Lord raiseth up them
that are bowed down."

Rabbi Jacob ben Moses ha-Levi [14th–15th cent.] used to
pray with his head bowed even when he prayed alone, which
he did not do the rest of the year. He would also lower himself every time he mentioned Jerusalem. [Maharil]

WISHING ONE ANOTHER A HAPPY NEW YEAR

Before leaving the House of Prayer on the night of Rosh ha-
Shanah it is customary to bless one another with the benediction, "May you be inscribed and sealed for a good year."
Then it is customary to go home joyfully and to keep away
from all grief and sighing, so as not to give the Accuser an
opening, for the Accuser's only place is where there is grief
and sighing. One ought to trust in God, as it is written (Neh.

8:10): "For the joy of the Lord is your strength." [Seder ha-
Yom]

It is customary to enter one's home joyfully and to greet
one's wife and children with the blessing, "May you be inscribed and sealed in the book of life." If Rosh ha-Shanah
falls on the Sabbath, some people recite the song beginning,
"Peace be upon you," pleasantly and joyfully, but not singing
it as one does on other Sabbaths during the year. [Mateh
Efrayim]

KIDDUSH: SANCTIFICATION AND THE EVENING
MEAL

Then the table is set, and the Kiddush is recited over the
wine. If Rosh ha-Shanah falls on the Sabbath, the prayer beginning, "And the heaven and the earth were finished"
(Gen. 2:1–3), is recited at the beginning of the Kiddush, as is
the practice on every holiday that falls on a Sabbath, and the
phrases referring to the Sabbath are inserted; the benediction
containing the phrase "who has kept us alive" follows the
Kiddush.

The hands are washed, the upper of the two loaves is
broken, and the benediction ending "who brings forth bread
from the earth" is recited.

It is customary to dip the portion of the bread which is to
be eaten in honey and to recite the sentence, "Be it thy will
that a good and a sweet year be renewed for us." [Midrash
Pinhas]

It is customary to eat an apple sweetened in honey at this
meal, and to recite the sentence, "Be it thy will that a good
and a sweet year be renewed for us," over it. The benediction
ending "creator of the fruit of the tree" is recited at the begin-

ning, even though the apple may be eaten in the middle of
the feast.

The French Jews are accustomed to eat red apples on Rosh
ha-Shanah, and in Provence it is the custom to eat white
grapes and white figs and a sheep's head. Every novel, light,
and good food is a good omen for all Israel. [Mahzor Vitri,
No. 323]

CARING FOR THE POOR

One should be careful to feed the poor at one's table, and to
send gifts to the poor and to the paupers, as it is written,
"Send portions unto him for whom nothing is prepared"
(Neh. 8:10). Rabbi Israel Isserlein, of blessed memory [15th
cent.], said: Every man ought to pray that proper paupers
come his way, for if poor folk come not his way, taxes and
other such things will. [Leket Yosher]

NOURISHMENT

Rav Tahlifa taught: All one's nourishment is fixed in advance on Rosh ha-Shanah, except for expenditures for the
Sabbaths and expenditures for the holiday, etc. For he who
has spent less is given less, and he who has spent more is
given more. [Betzah 16a]

FOR THINE OWN SAKE, O LIVING GOD!

The pious Rabbi David Moses of Tchortkov [19th cent.] related: On the eve of Rosh ha-Shanah after the Kiddush the
pious rabbi of Berditchev used always to take the part of
Israel. He would say, "Master of the universe, the fortune of
Israel is all devoted to your service. For, lo, what does an
Israelite do when he is making a good living? He raises children to Torah-study, spends liberally on the pleasure of the

Sabbath, opens his hand to give charity and the like; so that
a Jew's main expense is in keeping the commandments. So
why should you not save Israel?"

Thus we may interpret the entreaty we recite on Rosh ha-
Shanah and during the ten days of Teshuvah: "Remember
us for life, O King who wishes life, and write us in the book
of life for thine own sake, O living God." The meaning is
that all we ask for in the way of life and a good inscription
we ask for the sake of God, that we may be able to serve God
and observe his statutes, and that we may live on for his sake.
[Tiferet Yisrael]

SILENCE

It is a good custom not to speak at all from the first night
until the close of Rosh ha-Shanah, neither in the secular
tongue nor in the sacred tongue, neither in the House of
Prayer nor in any other place, neither with Gentiles nor with
Jews. If one wishes to greet others, let him nod with his head.
And the Writ says (Ps. 65:2): "For Thee silence is praise."
[Kuntres Minhag Tov]

VII. The Morning and Its Service

THE MORNING PRAYER

One rises earlier for the Morning Prayer on Rosh ha-Shanah
than on other days. There are places where it is customary for
the beadle of the House of Prayer to call out while it is yet
night, an hour before sunrise, that all may be in the House of
Prayer at sunrise; there are other places where the beadle
does not call out, but all rise of their own accord. The children, too, are taught to rise early for the prayer.

It is customary to take a ritual bath before the prayer for

the sake of purity, despite the fact that a ritual bath was taken
on the eve of Rosh ha-Shanah. This is particularly necessary
for the Readers and the priests and those who blow the ram's-
horn.

There are places where it is customary for the entire congregation to wear kittels [white robes] on Rosh ha-Shanah,
and there are places where only the Readers and the priests
and those who blow the ram's-horn and those who announce
the notes to be blown wear kittels over their clothes.

And the Reader takes his stand before the Ark and begins
with the song, "Lord of the Universe," singing easily and
pleasantly a melody of supplication and appeasement that is
accepted in all the Diaspora of Israel.

Cantors who recite pleas to the angels and, even worse, ad-
jurations, ought to be rebuked and restrained. Our rabbis,
of blessed memory, said: "Scream not to Michael and not to
Gabriel; call to Me and I shall answer you. 'The Lord is nigh
unto all them that call upon Him, to all that call upon him in
truth' " (Ps. 145:18). How much more is this true of cantors
who pray for the congregation, for they are sustained by the
aiding merit of the many worshipers and need no inter-
cessors. Let them but be worthy and let them conduct themselves in the ways of God that are good and pure [Siddur
Rabbi Yaabetz]. But the cantor is permitted to use the language of supplication in his pleading, such as, "May the will
come from thee," so long as he does not mention the names of
angels. [Mateh Efrayim]

THE KING

When the line, "And awesome in Thine awesome works," is
reached, a special Reader appears before the Ark and sings
"The King" with a fine melody. Beginning low he gradually

raises his voice to be heard by all the congregation with awe
and dread [Maharil]. Thus he raises his voice at every
"King" in the prayer. [Minhagim le-Rabbi Yuspa Sham-
mash]

In many communities it is customary for the Reader to
sing "The King" while standing in his place, and then to
walk to the Ark with bowed head, and to conclude "who
sitteth on a high and lofty throne."

Then the Reader and the congregation continue the Morning Prayer, reciting "Hear, O Israel" and the accompanying
benedictions, and afterward the Silent Prayer of Benedictions.

A TALE

It is told of the pious Rabbi Aaron of Karlin [18th cent.]
that once he was the Reader during the Morning Prayer of
Rosh ha-Shanah. When he began to sing "The King" he
cried and wept so bitterly that he was not able to continue.
He was afterward asked what had happened. He replied
that he had been reminded of the saying of the sages, of
blessed memory (Gittin 56a): "When Rabban Yohanan ben
Zakkai appeared before Vespasian he said, 'Peace unto you,
O king, peace unto you, O king.' Said Vespasian to him, 'If
I am a king, why have you not come to me until now?'"
Therefore, he said, when I began to sing "The King," my
heart grew sad within me, for He is a king, and I have not
come before him until now to turn in Teshuvah. [Seder ha-
Dorot he-Hadash]

THE DWELLERS ABOVE

It has come down to me through knowing men that the pious
Rabbi Levi Isaac of Berditchev [18th cent.] used, before the
repetition by the Reader of the Prayer of Benedictions on
Rosh ha-Shanah, to sing in a loud voice:

The dwellers above and the dwellers below
shake and quake in fear of your Name.
The dwellers in chasms, the dwellers in graves,
shiver and quiver in fear of your judgment.
But the just, in the Garden of Eden,
burst into song and sing your Name.
That is why I, Levi Isaac of Berditchev, am come before you,
with my prayer and with my plea.
What do you want of Israel?
"Speak!" To whom do you speak?
To the children of Israel.
"Talk!" To whom do you talk?
To the children of Israel.
"Command!" Whom do you command?
The children of Israel.
"Thus ye shall bless!" Whom do you command to bless?
The children of Israel.
Therefore I ask you, what do you want of Israel?
Do you not have many nations,
Chaldeans, Persians, Ishmaelites, Midianites.
What do you want of Israel?
What then? It must be that Israel is dear to you,
Who are called children of the Omnipresent.

Then he started the Prayer of Benedictions. The melody
too has come down to me. [Eser Orot]

THE REPETITION OF THE MORNING PRAYER OF BENEDICTIONS

The Ark is opened in order to awaken compassion upon us
in heaven, and that the gates of heaven may be opened to our
prayer while we are supplicating. For this reason it is customary to recite each time the Ark is opened, "Our Father,
our King, open the gates of heaven to our prayer." It is not

compulsory to stand when the Ark is opened, but one stands
out of reverence. [Ture Zahav, Yoreh Deah, No. 242,13]

The Prayer of Benedictions is repeated, with the addition
of many inserted hymns and liturgical poems, recited in the
order in which they are found in the festival prayer books,
and with the Ark being opened during the recital of some of
them.

LITURGICAL POEMS

The liturgical poems that people are accustomed to chant
were composed during the period of religious persecution,
when Israel was unable to read the words of the Torah, because their enemies decreed that they were not to engage in
the study of the Torah. Therefore the wise men in their midst
ordained that there was to be something in every prayer to
remind and warn the common people of the laws concerning
each of the festivals and the holidays and the Sabbath, and
details about the commandments. These were to take the
form of praise-givings, thanksgivings, rhymes and poems.
[Sefer ha-Ittim]

Most of the liturgical poems that the Jews of Germany, Poland and Italy are accustomed to recite were composed by
Rabbi Eleazar ha-Kalir, may he rest in Eden. While still an
infant lying in his cradle, this same Rabbi Eleazar was privi-
leged to see visions of God, and opened his mouth in praise of
the Omnipresent. There came a swarm of bees, and his
mouth was filled with honey. There are some who say he was
a mishnaic master, and there are some who say he lived
during the days of the Geonim; the opinion of those who say
that he lived around the time when the Ishmaelites conquered Palestine and it passed from the domination of the
kingdom of Edom, seems more correct to me.

There are some who are fulsome in praise of Rabbi Eleazar
ha-Kalir, and they have composed homilies on his liturgical

poems, something that had only been done with the Holy
Writ. But there are others who attack his poems, as did
Rabbi Abraham ibn Ezra [12th cent.], in his interpretation
of Ecclesiastes 5, because most of the liturgical poems by
Rabbi Eleazar ha-Kalir are riddles and parables interspersed
with the language of the Talmud, and full of homilies and
legends.

WHY HALLEL IS NOT RECITED

Hallel ["Psalms of Praise"] is not recited on Rosh ha-Shanah.
What is the reason? Said Rabbi Abbahu: The ministering
angels said to the Holy One, blessed be he, "Master of the
universe, why is it Israel does not sing hymns of praise on
Rosh ha-Shanah and Yom Kippur?" Said He to them, "Can
the king be seated on his throne of judgment with the books
of life and death open before him, and Israel sing hymns of
praise?" [Rosh ha-Shanah 32b]

OUR FATHER, OUR KING

After the repetition of the Prayer of Benedictions, the Ark is
opened and "Our Father, Our King" is said. Rabbi Akiba instituted this prayer, as it is stated: "Once Rabbi Eliezer ordered thirteen fast days, but no rains fell. . . . Rabbi Akiba
followed him before the Ark and said, 'Our Father, our
King, we have no king but Thee.' He was immediately answered" (Taanit 25b). If Rosh ha-Shanah falls on a Sabbath,
"Our Father, Our King" is not said, for Rabbi Akiba first
said it at a public fast, and no public fast can be ordered to
fall on a Sabbath. [Orhot Hayyim]

"Our Father, our King, inscribe us in a book." The five
repetitions of "Inscribe us in a book" correspond to the five
books of Moses. The first, "Inscribe us in the book of happy
life," corresponds to the Book of Genesis, in which the creation of all things, meaning life, is spoken of. The second, "In-

scribe us in the book of redemption and salvation," corresponds to the Book of Exodus, which speaks of the redemption from Egypt. "Inscribe us in the book of maintenance and sustenance" corresponds to the Book of Leviticus, which speaks of the holy sacrifices and thank-offerings, for the essence of sustenance must be in holiness. "Inscribe us in the book of aiding merit" corresponds to the Book of Numbers, which speaks of the Twelve Tribes that camped near their standards, every tribe being a Chariot to its root, that is to say, to the patriarchs, because of whose aiding merit we are alive. "Inscribe us in the book of forgiveness and pardon" corresponds to the Book of Deuteronomy, in which Moses our master upbraids Israel for all they did that was wrong, and which contains the scriptural portion of Teshuvah, by means of which we merit forgiveness and pardon. [Tiferet Uziel]

THE READING FROM THE TORAH

The Scrolls are taken out of the Ark for the reading of the Torah, and the usual prayers are recited. The chapter beginning, "And the Lord remembered Sarah" (Gen. 21), is read from the first Scroll, because Sarah was "remembered" on high on Rosh ha-Shanah. For the one called for the closing portion, the Reader reads the scriptural portion about the offering of the day (Num. 29:1–6) from the second Scroll; the prophetic portion about the events surrounding the birth of Samuel (I Sam. 1:1–2:10) is read, because Hannah was "remembered" on Rosh ha-Shanah.

There is a special melody for the reading of the Torah on Rosh ha-Shanah and Yom Kippur to remind people of the awesome character of the day, that they might lend their ears to the reading and thus make amends for their faults in reading from the Torah during the rest of the year. [Maharil]

CIRCUMCISION ON ROSH HA-SHANAH

My father and teacher, Rabbi Judah ben Rabbi Kalonymos, said in the name of the sages, Rabbi Judah the Saint [ca. 1200] and Rabbi Samuel the Saint, speaking in the name of Rabbi Kalonymos the Elder ben Rabbi Isaac ben Rabbi Eleazar the Great, that a long time ago an infant was to be circumcised in Mainz on Rosh ha-Shanah. Some of the holiest men in the country were consulted—Rabbenu Gershom ben Judah, the "Light of the Exile" [10th–11th cent.], Rabbi Simeon the Great ben Isaac, Rabbi Judah ha-Kohen, who compiled a book of laws, Rabbi Judah the Great, first of those who were martyred, and other scholars of the holy academy. They all instructed that the circumcision be performed after the reading of the Torah and Prophets, just before the blowing of the ram's-horn, in order that the Holy One, blessed be he, might remember unto us his covenant with Abraham and the Binding of Isaac. [Or Zarua, Hilkhot Rosh ha-Shanah]

It is now customary to perform the circumcision after leaving the House of Prayer. In former times, when circumcisions were performed in the House of Prayer, they were done between the reading of the Torah and the blowing of the ram's-horn. But in our days it is customary to circumcise at home *after* the service and not during it—because it is a great deal of bother to leave the House of Prayer and assemble the people at home and then return. [Kaf ha-Hayyim, Jerusalem]

BETWEEN THE MORNING PRAYER AND THE ADDITIONAL PRAYER

It is the custom in Israel to pause, if even for only a short while, between the Morning and Additional Prayers on Rosh ha-Shanah and Yom Kippur, in order to make a break be-

tween the two services. It is the custom in Germany to change
the veil of the Ark at that time.

VIII. The Blast of the Ram's-Horn

LIFT UP THY VOICE LIKE A HORN

Rabbi Joshua ben Korhah said: The ram's-horn was created
for the particular good of Israel. By the ram's-horn the Torah
was given to Israel, as it is said (Exod. 19:19): "And when
the voice of the horn waxed louder and louder." Because of
the ram's-horn the wall of Jericho fell, as it is said (Josh.
6:20): "And it came to pass, when the people heard the
sound of the horn, that the people shouted with a great shout,
and the wall fell down flat." And it is the ram's-horn that the
Holy One, blessed be he, is destined to blow when the son of
David, our righteous one, will reveal himself, as it is said
(Zech. 9:14): "And the Lord God will blow the horn." It is
also the ram's-horn that the Holy One, blessed be he, is destined to blow when he leads the exiles of Israel into their
land, as it is said (Isa. 27:13): "And it shall come to pass in
that day, that a great horn shall be blown; and they shall
come that were lost in the land of Assyria, and they that were
dispersed in the land of Egypt; and they shall worship the
Lord in the holy mountain at Jerusalem." For that reason, it
is also said (Isa. 58:1): "Cry aloud, spare not, lift up thy
voice like a horn." [Tanna debe Eliyahu Zutta XXII]

WITH TRUMPETS AND SOUND OF THE HORN

"With trumpets and sound of the horn shout ye before the
King, the Lord" (Ps. 98:6). This is like the story of a king
who went hunting in the forest. He got deep into the forest,
and could not find the king's highway that would lead him

back to his palace. Seeing some countrymen, he asked them the way, but they could not answer him, for they did not know it either. Finally, he found a wise man, and asked him the way. Realizing who the king was, the wise man trembled and showed him to the highway, for he knew the way. So he led the king back to his kingdom. Now the wise man found great favor in the eyes of the king, who lifted him up above all the lords of the realm, and clothed him in costly garments, and ordered his old clothes to be laid in the king's treasure house. Sometime afterward the wise man sinned against the king, who grew wroth and commanded the lords who stood highest in his kingdom to judge the man as a transgressor against the king's commandment. Then the wise man was in sad straits, for he knew that they would decide against him. So he fell on his face before the king and pleaded for his life and asked to be allowed before the verdict to put on the same clothes he had been wearing when he had led the king out of the forest. The king accepted his request. And it came to pass when the wise man had put on those clothes, that the king recalled the great kindness that the wise man had done him by returning him to his palace and to his royal throne. The king's compassion was kindled, and the wise man found grace and kindness in his eyes, and the king allowed his sin to pass unpunished, and returned him to his position.

So it is with us, O people of Israel! When the Torah was about to be given, the Holy One, blessed be he, went from nation to nation, asking them to accept the Torah, but they would not. We accepted it with such joy and delight that we said, "We will do," before "We will hear" (cf. Exod. 24:7). We took the yoke of the kingdom of heaven upon ourselves, and made Him king over us, and accepted his commandments and his sacred Torah. But now, we have transgressed and rebelled against him, and on Rosh ha-Shanah we are fear-

ful of the Day of Judgment, when he sits in judgment on all
the hidden things, and pronounces the verdict of every man
according to his deeds. Therefore we sound the ram's-horn
and put on the same dress we were wearing at the time of the
giving of the Torah, when we accepted the Torah and
crowned him king with the ram's-horn, as it is written: "And
when the sound of the horn waxed louder and louder" (Exod.
19:19)—in order that he may remember that aiding merit of
ours, forgive us our iniquities and wilful transgressions, vin-
dicate us in judgment, and inscribe us at once for a long and
happy life. Amen. So be his will! [Kedushat Levi]

THE RAM'S-HORN

"Blow the horn at the new moon, at the full moon for our
feast-day. For it is a statute for Israel, an ordinance of the God
of Jacob" (Ps. 81: 4–5).

Said Rabbi Abbahu: Why do we sound the horn of a ram?
Because the Holy One, blessed be he, said: Blow me a ram's-
horn that I may remember unto you the Binding of Isaac the
son of Abraham, and I shall account it unto you for a binding
of yourselves before me. [Rosh ha-Shanah 16a]

"And Abraham lifted up his eyes, and looked, and behold
behind him a ram caught in the thicket by his horns" (Gen.
22:13)—teaching us that the Holy One, blessed be he, showed
our father Abraham the ram tearing himself free from one
thicket and becoming entangled in another. Said the Holy
One, blessed be he, to Abraham: Thus are your children destined to be caught in iniquities and entangled in misfortunes,
but in the end they will be redeemed by the horns of a ram.
Therefore it is said (Zech. 9:14): "And the Lord God will
blow the horn." [*Ibid.*]

Rav Huna ben Rabbi Isaac said: This teaches us that the
Holy One, blessed be he, showed Abraham the ram tearing

itself free from one thicket and becoming entangled in another. Said the Holy One, blessed be he, to Abraham: Thus are your children destined to be caught by the nations and entangled in misfortunes, and to be dragged from kingdom to kingdom, from Babylon to Media, from Media to Greece, and from Greece to Rome, but in the end they will be redeemed by the horns of a ram. Therefore it is said (Zech. 9:14): "And the Lord shall be seen over them, and His arrow shall go forth as the lightning; and the Lord God will blow the horn." [*Ibid.*]

Rabbi Hanina ben Dosa says: No part of that ram went to waste. The ashes of that ram became the base of the inner altar. The sinews of the ram were torn, corresponding to the ten strings of the harp which David played. The skin of the ram became the girdle of Elijah's loins. As for the two horns of the ram—the voice of the left horn was heard on Mount Sinai. And the right horn is larger than the left and is destined to be blown in time to come at the assembling of the dispersed, as it is said (Isa. 27:13): "And it shall come to pass in that day, that a great horn shall be blown." [Pirke Rabbi Eliezer XXXI]

Rabbi Levi said: All the good things, blessings and consolations which the Holy One, blessed be he, is destined to give to Israel will be given only from Zion. Salvation—as it is said (Ps. 14:7): "Oh that the salvation of Israel were come out of Zion!" Blessings—as it is said (Ps. 134:3): "The Lord bless thee out of Zion." The ram's-horn, as it is said (Joel 2:15): "Blow the horn in Zion." [Lev. Rabbah XXIV; Yalkut on Isa. 2]

THE LAW OF THE RAM'S-HORN

It is an affirmative commandment from the Torah to hear the blowing of the ram's-horn on Rosh ha-Shanah, as it is said:

"It is a day of blowing the horn unto you" (Num. 29:1).
Despite the fact that the Torah does not explicitly state that
the blowing on Rosh ha-Shanah is to be on a ram's-horn, it
does say of the jubilee year: "Then shalt thou make proclamation with the blast of the horn on the tenth day of the
seventh month; in the day of the atonement shall ye make
proclamation with the horn throughout all your land" (Lev.
25:9). So, on the basis of tradition we may infer that, just as
the blowing at the beginning of the jubilee year is on a ram's-
horn, so the blowing on Rosh ha-Shanah is on a ram's-horn.

In the Temple one ram's-horn and two accompanying
trumpets were blown on Rosh ha-Shanah, the ram's-horn
producing long, and the trumpets short blasts, the essential
commandment of the day being the ram's-horn blasts. Why
are trumpets blown at the same time? Because it is said:
"With trumpets and sound of horn shout ye before the King,
the Lord" (Ps. 98:6). But in other places only the ram's-horn
is blown on Rosh ha-Shanah. [Maimonides, Hilkhot Shofar I.]

WHICH HORN MAY BE USED

All horns may be used, except those of cows and oxen, because their horn is called *keren* and not *shofar*. And also the
horn of the cow and the ox is not acceptable because the
Accuser must not be made to serve as a defender, that it may
not be said: Yesterday they made the golden calf, and today
they come to appease their Maker with the horn made from
it.

The ram's-horn should be bent, that the children of Israel
may bend their hearts toward their Father who is in heaven.
It is also best to blow the horn of a ram so that he may remember unto us the Binding of Isaac.

If the mouthpiece of the ram's-horn has been overlaid

with gold as a decoration, it is unfit, for the gold separates the mouthpiece of the ram's-horn from the mouth of the blower.

It is permitted to pour water or wine or vinegar into the ram's-horn on the holiday in order to make a clear sound. This is not considered to be repairing vessels on a holiday, which is forbidden. [Shulhan Arukh shel ha-Rav]

WOMEN AND THE BLOWING OF THE RAM'S-HORN

Every man is obliged to hear the sound of the ram's-horn, but women and children are free of the obligation. But although women are exempt, they may assume the precept, if they wish. Although the Scribes have prohibited the blowing of the ram's-horn on a holiday when it is not during the course of observing a commandment, nevertheless the prohibition has been waived for women, in order to satisfy them. [*Ibid.*]

REASONS FOR THE RAM'S-HORN

Next comes the opening of the sacred month, when it is customary to sound the ram's-horn in the Temple at the same time that the sacrifices are brought there, and its name of "feast of the ram's-horn" is derived from this. It has a twofold significance, partly to the nation in particular, partly to all mankind in general. In the former sense it is a reminder of a mighty and marvellous event which came to pass when the oracles of the laws were given from above. For then the sound of the trumpet pealed from heaven and reached, we may suppose, the ends of the universe so that the event might strike terror even into those who were far from the spot and dwelling well nigh at the extremities of the earth, who would come to the natural conclusion that such mighty signs portended mighty consequences. And indeed what could men receive mightier or more profitable than the general laws which came from the mouth of God, not like the particular laws, through an interpreter?

This is a significance peculiar to the nation. What follows is common to all mankind. The horn is the instrument used in war, both to sound the advance against the enemy when the moment comes for engaging battle and also for recalling the troops when they have to separate and return to their respective camps. And there is another war not of human agency when nature is at strife in herself, when her parts make onslaught one on another and her law-abiding sense of equality is vanquished by the greed for inequality. Both these wars work destruction on the face of the earth. The enemy cut down the fruit trees, ravage the country, set fire to the foodstuffs and the ripening ears of corn in the open fields, while the forces of nature use drought, rainstorms, violent moisture-laden winds, scorching sun-rays, intense cold accompanied by snow, with the regular harmonious alternations of the yearly seasons turned into disharmony, a state of things in my opinion due to the impiety which does not gain a gradual hold but comes rushing with the force of a torrent among those whom these things befall. And therefore the law instituted this feast figured by that instru- ment of war the horn, which gives it its name, to be as a thank-offering to God the peace-maker and peace-keeper, who destroys faction both in cities and in the various parts of the universe and creates plenty and fertility and abundance of other good things and leaves the havoc of fruits without a single spark to be rekindled. [Philo of Alexandria, The Special Laws II]

TEN REASONS FOR THE RAM'S-HORN

Wrote our master Saadia Gaon [9th cent.]: There are ten

reasons why the Creator, be blessed, commanded us to blow the ram's-horn on Rosh ha-Shanah. The first is, because Rosh ha-Shanah marks the beginning of Creation, on which the Holy One, be blessed, created the world and reigned over it. Kings do the same, who have trumpets and horns blown to let it be known and heard everywhere when the anniversary of the beginning of their reign falls. So we, on Rosh ha-Shanah, accept the kingship of the Creator, be blessed. Thus said David: "With trumpets and sound of the horn shout ye before the King, the Lord" (Ps. 98:6).

The second reason is that, since Rosh ha-Shanah is the first of the ten days of Teshuvah, the ram's-horn is blown to announce their beginning, as though to warn: Let all who desire to turn in Teshuvah, turn now; and if you do not, you will have no reason to cry injustice. Kings do the same: first they warn the populace in their decree, and whoever violates the decrees after the warning complains unheeded.

The third reason is to remind us of our stand at the foot of Mount Sinai, as it is said (Exod. 19:19): "The voice of the horn waxed louder and louder," in order that we may take upon ourselves that which our forefathers took upon themselves when they said (Exod. 24:7): "We will do and obey."

The fourth reason is to remind us of the words of the prophets, which were compared to a ram's-horn, as it is said (Ezek. 33:4-5): "Then whosoever heareth the sound of the horn, and taketh not warning, if the sword come, and take him away, his blood shall be upon his own head . . . whereas if he had taken warning, he would have delivered his soul."

The fifth reason is to remind us of the destruction of the Temple and the battle alarms of the foe, as it is said (Jer. 4:19): "Because thou hast heard, O my soul, the sound of the horn, the alarm of war." When we hear the sound of the ram's-horn, we beseech God to rebuild the Temple.

The sixth reason is to remind us of the Binding of Isaac, who offered himself to heaven. So ought we to be ready at all times to offer our lives for the sanctification of his Name. And may our remembrance rise before Him for our benefit.

The seventh reason is that, when we hear the blowing of the ram's-horn, we fear and tremble and bend our will to the will of the Creator—for such is the effect of the ram's-horn, which causes shaking and trembling, as it is written (Amos 3:6): "Shall the horn be blown in a city, and the people not tremble?"

The eighth reason is to remind us of the great Day of Judgment, that we may all fear it, as it is said (Zeph. 1:14–16): "The great day of the Lord is near, it is near and hasteth greatly . . . a day of the horn and alarm."

The ninth reason is to remind us of the gathering of the dispersed of Israel, that we may passionately long for it, as it is said (Isa. 27:13): "And it shall come to pass in that day, that a great horn shall be blown; and they shall come that were lost in the land of Assyria."

The tenth reason is to remind us of the revival of the dead, that we may believe in it, as it is said (Isa. 18:3): "All ye inhabitants of the world, and ye dwellers in the earth, when an ensign is lifted up on the mountains, see ye; and when the horn is blown, hear ye." [Avudraham]

AWAKE, O YOU SLEEPERS

Despite the fact that the blowing of the ram's-horn on Rosh ha-Shanah is an explicit decree in the Scripture, it is also an allusion, as if to say: Awake, O you sleepers, awake from your sleep! O you slumberers, awake from your slumber! Search your deeds and turn in Teshuvah. Remember your Creator, O you who forget the truth in the vanities of time and go astray all the year after vanity and folly that neither profit nor save. Look to your souls, and better your ways and actions. Let every one of you abandon his evil way and his wicked thought, which is not good. [Maimonides, Hilkhot Teshuvah III. 4]

FROM THE PLACE OF MAN TO THE PLACE OF GOD

As in the material world sound travels great distances from place to place, so that two places that are remote from one another are bound and connected only by sound, so in the spiritual realm it is possible by sound to transcend space and rise above it.

That is the reason why all of Israel engage in producing sound on Rosh ha-Shanah, that is, in sounding the ram's-horn and voicing their prayer. For Rosh ha-Shanah is the first of the ten days of Teshuvah, and the principle behind Teshuvah is that we are returning from all the evil places where we have gone astray because of our iniquities, and are returning back to the true Place of the World, the Divine, where the root of all earthly places is. It is only possible to attain thither by means of sacred sounds which rise in prayer and supplication to God; each of us praying from the place where he has gone astray. And God hears our voice with compassion, enabling us to return from our present place and rise to that which transcends place and space, to the Place of the World, the Divine, where all is restored to perfection. [Likkute Etzot Hadash III]

SECRET LANGUAGE

The reason for the blowing of the ram's-horn was revealed to me in a dream: It is as though two friends, or a father and son, who do not wish that what the one writes to the other should be known to others, were to have a secret language, known to no one but themselves. So it is on Rosh ha-

Shanah, the Day of Judgment; it was not the will of the Omnipresent that the Accuser should know of our pleas. Therefore He made up a language for us, that is the ram's-horn, which is only understood by Him. [Tiferet Uziel]

THE MEANING OF ALL MEANINGS

Once the Baal Shem Tov [18th cent.] commanded Rabbi Zev Kitzes to learn the secret meanings behind the blasts of the ram's-horn, because Rabbi Zev was to be his caller on Rosh ha-Shanah. So Rabbi Zev learned the secret meanings and wrote them down on a slip of paper to look at during the service, and laid the slip of paper in his bosom. When the time came for the blowing of the ram's-horn, he began to search everywhere for the slip of paper, but it was gone; and he did not know on what meanings to concentrate. He was greatly saddened. Broken-hearted, he wept bitter tears, and called the blasts of the ram's-horn, without concentrating on the secret meanings behind them.

Afterward, the Baal Shem Tov said to him: "Lo, in the habitation of the king are to be found many rooms and apartments, and there are different keys for every lock; but the master key of all is the ax, with which it is possible to open all the locks on all the gates. So it is with the ram's-horn: the secret meanings are the keys; every gate has another meaning, but the master key is the broken heart. When a man truthfully breaks his heart before God, he can enter into all the gates of the apartments of the King above all kings, the Holy One, blessed be he." [Or Yesharim]

CAUTIONS FOR THE RAM'S-HORN BLOWER

A great and renowned king sent his sons out hunting, and they lost their way. They began to shout, thinking their father might hear them. But there was no reply. So they said among themselves: "Perhaps we have forgotten our father's tongue, and that is why he does not answer our words; so let us raise our voices without words." And they decided to choose one of them to go forth to shout for them, and they cautioned him, "Remember, we are all depending on you."

This is the reference: The Holy One, blessed be he, sent us to raise sparks of sanctity [emanations from the Godhead], but we have lost our father. Perhaps we receive no reply because we have forgotten our father's speech. So we choose one person and say to him: "Now, we are sending you forth, O ram's-horn blower, to awaken his compassion for us with your wordless voice. Be cautious, for we are all depending on you."

Nevertheless, let the ram's-horn blower think himself of no importance, for he merely resembles an instrument made of hide, in which there are vents through which the instrument makes music. Ought the instrument to boast because the music issues from it?

Such is the case with man: Thought and speech and all the faculties rest in him as in an instrument. Ought he to boast? Why, he himself is nothing at all! [Likkute Yekarim]

"Lift up thy voice like a horn, and declare unto My people their transgression, and to the house of Jacob their sins" (Isa. 58:1). I heard my teacher and master, the devout Rabbi Dov Baer, expound on the verse: "And it came to pass, when the player played, that the spirit of the Lord came upon him" (II Kings 3:15). He said: Here you have a man who plays well. As he plays, many distracting thoughts come to him, and he glories in his voice. That is not true of the instrument, which is dumb and certainly is not distracted while playing. That is the meaning of the phrase, "And it came to pass, when the player played"; that is, if "the player," the man, is like the "played," that is, like the instrument played upon, and is not distracted just as the instrument is not distracted, then—"the spirit of the Lord came upon him." That, too, is the meaning of the verse, "Lift up thy voice like a horn": that is to say, like the horn, which is not distracted by alien thoughts, so you, too, "lift up thy voice," without being distracted by alien thoughts. Then—"and declare unto My people their transgression, and to the house of Jacob their sins." For that which comes from the heart enters the heart. [Tiferet Uziel; Orah la-Hayyim]

CAUTIONS FOR THE LISTENER

The righteous Rabbi Moses of Kobrin [19th cent.] was a caller for the ram's-horn blasts. Once he said in a loud voice: Master of the universe, have compassion on the souls of Israel: open their hearts to do Teshuvah before you.

At another time he said: My brothers, my dear ones, do not rely on me. But let every one do Teshuvah for himself. [Or Yesharim]

BEFORE THE BLOWING OF THE RAM'S-HORN

Since the blowing of the ram's-horn awakens his compassion, and raises the memory of Israel to our Father who is in heaven, many are accustomed to make great preparations for it. After the reading of the Torah, the ram's-horn blower, the caller, and the reader of the Additional Prayer go out for a ritual immersion for the sake of extreme purity. While the latter are away, the rest of the congregation are busy: one looking into the meaning and the significance of the ram's-horn blasts; another, studying the Mishnah; still another, reciting Psalms. They try to unite their hearts to love and fear His Name, and to awaken their hearts to a complete Teshuvah. After their ritual immersion, the three men put on kittels and ascend the platform, the place where the Torah is read.

If a scholarly and virtuous man is present, let him address strong words to the people. He ought not to indulge in pleasant parables, though they are sweet to the palate, because they are out of place at that time. Rather let him try to captivate the hearts of his listeners and say things to compel them to return in Teshuvah, in the manner of the talmudic text (Mishnah Taanit II.1): "Brethren, it is not written of the men of Nineveh that God saw their sackcloth and their fasting, but: 'And God saw their works, that they turned from their evil way'" (Jonah 3:10). Let his verse be timely, either about the ram's-horn or the Day of Judgment, and let him expound it simply or alluding to a moralistic purpose. [Mateh Efrayim]

On both days of Rosh ha-Shanah the zaddik Rabbi Zevi Hirsh of Liska [18th cent.] would preach long and awe-inspiring sermons. The moment he went up to the pulpit and stood in front of the Ark, terror and fear would seize the people. For when he took hold of the veil and put it up to his face and prayed a short prayer, his hands would tremble and his limbs knock together because of the greatness of the fear and terror that seized him. It was his holy way to begin: "Brethren, children of Israel!" At once the hearts of the listeners would melt, and the eyes of the old men standing on the benches would be flooded with tears. While preaching he would lift his hands which were spread open to the sky above the heads of the community, and would roar like a lion—a feat really beyond the strength of so weak a man. At every pause he would scream bitterly: "Woe is me! Who knows what the New Year will bring!" When he preached to them, he would say: "Believe me, I am including myself and my children, too!" He would always take the Binding

of Isaac as his text, to plead in behalf of Israel and to awaken
the aiding merit of our holy forefathers and the Binding of
Isaac, that the love between Israel and their Father in heaven
might cover all their transgressions. [Darkhe ha-Tov veha-
Yashar]

THE ORDER OF THE BLASTS

The ram's-horn blower and he who calls the blasts go up on
the platform, the former facing the east, and the latter
standing at his side. Now, why is the ram's-horn blown from
the platform? Out of respect for the congregation. Another
reason is because it is the place where the Torah is read, as
a reminder that the Torah was given to Israel to the accompaniment of the ram's-horn. The ram's-horn blower does
not go down from the platform even to accompany the Torah
Scroll to the Ark, but stands there until the end of the entire
Additional Prayer, and there blows the additional blasts as
well.

There are places where the ram's-horn is blown from the
platform during both days of Rosh ha-Shanah, and there are
other places where it is blown from the platform on the first
day and he who blows the ram's-horn does so from his place
on the second day. [Orhot Hayyim]

It is customary to place all the ram's-horns to be found in
the House of Prayer near the ram's-horn blower, so that if
there is an accident and he cannot blow on his own ram's-
horn, he can take another horn from the supply.

There are some congregations whose custom it is to recite
Psalm 47, beginning, "O clap your hands, all ye peoples;
shout unto God with the voice of triumph," seven times
before the blasts of the ram's-horn.

The seven times that Psalm 47 is recited correspond to the

seven firmaments which the Holy One, blessed be he, created. Then the fifth verse of Psalm 118: "Out of my straits I called upon the Lord; He answered me with great enlargement" is recited; and then six additional verses: Lamentations 3:56; Psalm 119:160, 122, 162, 66, 108. The initials of these six verses form the Hebrew acrostic *Kera Satan* ["Cut off Satan"]. Last of all, the verse: "God is gone up amidst shouting, the Lord amidst the sound of the horn" (Ps. 47:6), is recited.

The ram's-horn blower holds the mouth of the ram's-horn curved side up, as it is said, "God is gone up amidst shouting," and grasps the ram's-horn in his right hand and rests his four fingers on it as though to hide the judgment; then he covers it and loudly and melodiously recites the benedictions containing the phrases, "to hear the voice of the ram's-horn" and "who has kept us alive." He does not blow upon the ram's-horn until the caller has prompted him, and blows standing, from the right side of his mouth.

Then the caller calls, Tekiah, and he blows the sound of Tekiah, and the caller calls, Shevarim Teruah, and he blows the sound of Shevarim Teruah, and the caller calls, Tekiah, and he blows the sound of Tekiah. They do this three times. Then the caller says to the ram's-horn blower, "Sit down," that is to say, "Catch your breath"; and the ram's-horn blower removes the ram's-horn from his lips and lays it in its cover and rests a while. Then the caller again calls, Tekiah, Shevarim, Tekiah, three times for the ram's-horn blower and after each call he blows the phrases. Then the caller says to him again, "Sit," and the ram's-horn blower removes the ram's-horn from his lips and lays it in its cover and rests a while. Then the caller again calls, Tekiah, Teruah, Tekiah, for him three times, and after every call the ram's-horn blower blows the phrases. For the last blast the caller

says, Tekiah Gedolah, and the ram's-horn blower makes it
last longer than all the other Tekiah phrases.

Rabbi Jacob ben Moses ha-Levi [14th–15th cent.] wrote:
The reason why the last Tekiah is longer is because of the
Writ, "When the ram's-horn soundeth long, they shall come
up to the mount" (Exod. 19:13), which, our sages of blessed
memory expounded (Taanit 21b), is a sign of the removal
of the Divine Presence. Here, too, the long blast is a sign of
the removal and end of the blasts.

When the holiday of Rosh ha-Shanah fell on the Sabbath,
the ram's-horn would be blown in the Temple, but not in
the country. After the Temple was destroyed, Rabban
Yohanan ben Zakkai ordained that on the Sabbath the ram's-
horn was to be blown in every place where there was a Court.
Rabbi Eliezer said: Rabban Yohanan ordained this only for
Yabneh. The others said to him: It is the same whether it
be Yabneh or any other place that has a Court. Jerusalem
was further superior to Yabneh, in that in every city from
which Jerusalem could be seen and heard, which was near
Jerusalem and accessible to it, the ram's-horn was blown on
the Sabbath; while in Yabneh it was blown only in the
Court. [Mishnah Rosh ha-Shanah IV.1–2]

Rabbenu Nisim ben Reuben Gerondi [14th cent.] wrote
that the ram's-horn was blown on Rosh ha-Shanah when it
fell on a Sabbath, in the Court of Rabbi Isaac Alfasi [11th
cent.]. And Rabbi Mendel of Kotzk [19th cent.] gave as a
reason for it the passage in Berakhot 8a: From the day of
the destruction of the Temple, the Holy One, blessed be he,
has nothing but four cubits of law [Halakhah] in the world.
The four cubits of law take the place of the Temple; and in
the Temple the ram's-horn was blown on Rosh ha-Shanah

when it fell on a Sabbath; and the four cubits of law in that generation were concentrated in the Court of Rabbi Isaac Alfasi. [Siah Sarfe Kodesh II.]

IX. The Additional Prayer: Kingships, Remembrances, Ram's-Horns

THE ADDITIONAL PRAYER

After the blowing of the ram's-horn, the cantor says in a loud voice, "Happy is the people that know the joyful shout; they walk, O Lord, in the light of Thy countenance" (Ps. 89:16). And there are some who add verses seventeen and eighteen from the same Psalm. On the Sabbath when the horn is not blown, verse sixteen is not said. Then the cantor chants, "Happy are they that dwell in Thy house" (Ps. 145), and takes the Torah Scroll in his hand and returns it to the Ark.

Then he takes his stand before the Reader's desk and does not begin at once, but delays a little to awaken himself to devotion, and chants the Reader's plea and the half-Kaddish in its set melody, with awe and trembling. Then the Additional Prayer is prayed while standing in a bent position.

The Additional Prayer consists of nine blessings on Rosh ha-Shanah; included among them being Kingships, in order that we may take upon ourselves the yoke of the kingdom of heaven, Remembrances, that our remembrance may rise before Him, and Ram's-horns. [Shulhan Arukh shel ha-Rav, Orah Hayyim, No. 591,1]

In Yemen they follow the tradition of Rabbi Moses ben Maimon [12th cent.]. The congregation does not recite the Silent Prayer of Benedictions, but the Reader recites it for everyone, for those who know it as well as for those who do not, because the prayer and its benedictions are long, and most of the worshipers cannot concentrate on them. But they all stand up and concentrate and listen to the benedictions, and when the Reader kneels, all the people kneel and respond, Amen, after every benediction. [Nahlat Yosef]

THE REPETITION OF THE ADDITIONAL PRAYER OF BENEDICTIONS

Then the Prayer of Benedictions is repeated, with the addition of many inserted hymns and liturgical poems, recited in the order in which they are found in the festival prayer books, and with the Ark being opened during the recital of some of them.

One of the inserted liturgical poems is that beginning, "Let us express the day's powerful sanctity." Afterward come the prayers known as Kingships, Remembrances, and Ram's-horns, introduced by the prayer beginning, "It is for us to praise the Lord of all." At the phrase "we bend the knee and prostrate ourselves," the congregation bend their knees and prostrate themselves. Then the Reader does the same. In some places only the Reader bends his knees and prostrates himself. It is the custom to help the Reader rise, lest he change his position during the Prayer of Benedictions.

At the end of the Kingships, as well as at the end of the Remembrances and at the end of the Ram's-horns, the ram's-horn is blown in the customary order. The blasts are altogether omitted on the Sabbath.

Afterward the priests go up to the Ark, "to bless the people of Israel with love." Then the Reader continues, reciting the prayers as they are to be found in the festival prayer book, and ending with the phrase, "Blessed art Thou, O Lord, maker of peace."

Rabbi Solomon Judah Rappoport [19th cent.] wrote: The liturgical poems of the Sephardim are mediators between the soul of man and its Creator, and the liturgical poems of the Ashkenazim mediators between Israel and its God. [Bikkure ha-Ittim VIII.]

However, in essence there is no difference in the prayers between one place and another, except for a few changes that do not affect the style of the blessings. But all Israel, in all their habitations, unite their heart as one to pray to one God in one prayer, in the tradition that has been handed down to us by Rav Amram Gaon [9th cent.] according to the usages of the two academies of Sura and Pumbedita, who received it from the Saboraim, who received it from the Amoraim, who received it from the Tannaim, who received it from the members of the Great Assembly, who were the ones who instituted the prayers for Israel.

THE TALE OF RABBI AMNON

I found a manuscript by Rabbi Ephraim ben Jacob of Bonn [12th cent.], describing how Rabbi Amnon of Mainz came to compose the liturgical poem beginning, "And we shall express the powerful sanctity," after a misfortune that had happened to him. The manuscript follows:

This is the story of what happened to Rabbi Amnon of Mainz, who was one of the great men of his generation, and rich, and of good family, and handsome, and well-formed. The lords and the archbishop began to demand that he convert to their religion, and he refused to listen to them. And it came to pass, after they had spoken to him day after day and he would not listen to them, though the archbishop himself was urging him, that one day he said to them, "I wish to take counsel and to think about this matter for another three days." He said this to put them off.

And it came to pass, that the moment he had left the presence of the archbishop he took it to heart that he had allowed a word of doubt to leave his lips, as though he needed to take counsel and thought to deny the living God.

So he went home, and would neither eat nor drink, and fell sick. And all his near ones and loved ones came to console him, but he refused to be consoled. For he said, "I shall go down to the grave mourning, because of what I have said." And he wept, and was sad at heart.

And it came to pass on the third day, while he was in pain and anxiety, that the archbishop sent after him. And he said, "I shall not go." And his foe continued to send many and ever more distinguished lords. But Rabbi Amnon still refused to go to the archbishop.

Then the archbishop said, "Bring Amnon against his will immediately." So they hurried and brought him. And he said to him, "What is this, Amnon? Why have you not come to reply to me and to do my desire at the end of the time you set for yourself in which to take counsel?"

And Amnon answered and said, "I shall pronounce my own sentence. Let the tongue that spoke and lied to you be cut out." For Rabbi Amnon wished to sanctify God, because he had thus spoken.

Then the archbishop answered and said, "No, the tongue I shall not cut out, for it spoke well. But the feet that did not come to me at the time you set I shall lop off, and the rest of the body I shall punish." Then the oppressor commanded, and they lopped off the fingers of Rabbi Amnon's hands and his feet. At every finger they asked him, "Will you be converted, Amnon?" And he said, "No."

And it came to pass when they had finished lopping off his fingers, that the wicked man ordered Rabbi Amnon to be laid on a shield, with all his fingers at his side. And he sent him home. He was rightly called Rabbi Amnon ["the faithful one"], for he had faith in the living God and lovingly suffered severe afflictions, simply because of one word he had spoken.

After these events, the Days of Awe approached, and Rosh ha-Shanah arrived. Rabbi Amnon asked his relatives to bear him to the House of Prayer just as he was, and to lay him down near the Reader. They did so. And it came to pass, when the Reader came to recite the Kedushah [Sanctification], that Rabbi Amnon said to him, "Hold, and I shall sanctify the great Name of God." And he cried in a loud voice, "And thus may the Sanctification ascend to you," that is to say, I have sanctified your Name for the sake of your Kingship and your Unity. And afterward he said, "And we shall express the powerful sanctity of this day." And he said, "It is true that you are the Judge and Arbiter," in order to justify the verdict, that those same fingers of his hands and his feet might rise before God, as well as the memory of the entire incident. And he said, "And the seal of every man's hand is on it . . . and You remember the soul of every living thing," for his fate was so decreed on Rosh ha-Shanah. When he had ended, his own end came, and he vanished from the earth before the eyes of all, for God had taken him. Of him it is said (Ps. 31:20): "O how abundant is Thy goodness, which Thou hast laid up for them that fear Thee."

Three days after Rabbi Amnon had been called to the Academy on High, he appeared to Rabbi Kalonymos ben Rabbi Meshullam [ca. 1100] in a dream of night, and taught him the liturgical poem beginning, "And we shall express the powerful sanctity of the day." And he ordered him to send it to all the Diaspora, to be his testimony and remembrance. Rabbi Kalonymos did so. [Or Zarua, Hilkhot Rosh ha-Shanah]

MAN'S HEIGHT

"Man, his foundation is dust, and his end is dust" [Rabbi Amnon's prayer]. At first glance, it is a low view of man, to say that his foundation is dust and his end is dust. But in truth these words are said in praise of man, who was hewn from a sacred source, from Abraham, our father, peace be upon him, who said (Gen. 18:27): "I am but dust and ashes." And the Midrash Tehillim says, "And his end is dust"—those are the days of the Messiah, of which David said (Ps. 44:26): "For our soul is bowed down to the dust." [Toledot Adam]

WHEN THE MINSTREL PLAYED

Rabbi Bezalel of Odessa was a famous cantor, and there was no singer like him in Israel. When he was a boy, he studied Talmud and the Codes and wished to become a ritual slaughterer. He came to the Seer of Lublin [18th–19th cent.] at Lantzut to have him inspect his knives. Said the zaddik to him, "I see that you are destined to become the best cantor in the country. Your throat is keener and smoother than your knives, and your lungs will be healthy all your life, and without defect."

Rabbi Bezalel took these words to heart, and left his knives to stand before the Ark as a Reader. From that time on, he passed from city to city praying before the Omnipresent, until he came to Rabbi Moses of Szopron, who appointed him the Reader in his House of Study, for like all the zaddikim the zaddik of Szopron was very fond of song, which has the power to bring people into the possession of the spirit of sanctity, as it is said of Elisha: "And it came to pass, when the minstrel played, that the spirit of the Lord came upon him" (II Kings 3:15). The zaddik was particularly fond of Rabbi Bezalel, the cantor, who by his voice could open the hearts of Israel before their Father who is in heaven.

Once Rabbi Bezalel fell into a transgression, the Compassionate One protect us. The zaddik heard about it and removed him from his cantorship. On Rosh ha-Shanah Rabbi Bezalel stood in a corner of the rabbi's House of Study, and prayed silently. When the Reader reached the stanza beginning, "Who opens a gate to those who knock in repentance" in the liturgical poem beginning, "And all believe," Rabbi Bezalel pulled his prayer shawl down over his face, and groaned so loud that all hearts shuddered.

The rabbi lifted his eyes to heaven, and said, "Call Bezalel, and let him again stand before the Ark. Bezalel has turned in Teshuvah." [Pinhas Minkovski, Reshumot IV]

KINGSHIPS, REMEMBRANCES, RAM'S-HORNS

The men of the Great Assembly composed three sections to be recited during the Additional Prayer on Rosh ha-Shanah, namely, Kingships, Remembrances, and Ram's-horns, to arouse the hearts of men to a belief in the corresponding three principles and their ramifications, that they might be declared meritorious when they are judged before God.

For Kingships corresponds to the principle of the existence of God, to which the formula of the prayer testifies: "And so we wait for you, O Lord, our God, we wait soon to see the splendor of thy might, when thou wilt raze the idols from the earth . . . when the world will be perfected under the kingdom of the Almighty . . . dwellers in the world will see and know, that every knee is bowed to thee, and every tongue avows thee. . . . They will all take upon themselves the yoke of thy kingdom. . . ."

The section of Remembrances teaches the doctrines of divine providence and reward and punishment: "You bethink you how the world was made, remember all those formed of old . . . before You all hid things are bare. . . ."

The section of the Ram's-horns is an allusion to the third principle, which is the revelation of the Torah from heaven. Therefore it begins: "You were revealed in the cloud of your glory to your holy people, to speak with them. From the heavens you let your voice be heard. . . ." So, because the gift of the Torah came through the medium of a very loud sound, the ram's-horn, the like of which never was heard before, it is called Ram's-horns, for similar thunders and lightnings had been heard and seen before, but the sound of the ram's-horn blowing, though there *was* no ram's-horn, never was and never will be heard again until the time of redemption, the hour when the true Torah will be made known to the whole world. That is the hour, according to some sages, of which it is said (Zech. 9:14): "And the Lord God will blow the horn."

I have read that the Ram's-horns are an allusion to the Binding of Isaac. This is not so. For if the section of Ram's-horns is an allusion to the Binding of Isaac, it would have been fit to mention the Binding of Isaac in the Ram's-horns and not in Remembrances, where it is mentioned.

It was to allude to these three principles which are the way to salvation, that Isaiah included them all in one verse, saying: "For the Lord is our Judge, the Lord is our Lawgiver, the Lord is our King; He will save us" (Isa. 33:22). "The Lord is our Judge," is an allusion to the principle of providence. . . . "The Lord is our Lawgiver," is an allusion to the revelation of Torah from heaven, which is the second principle. . . . Isaiah said: "Hearken unto Me, ye that know righteousness, the people in whose heart is My law; fear ye not the taunt of men" (Isa. 51:7); that is to say, even if we are not found meritorious in the time of judgment by virtue of God's judicial aspect, because it is impossible for one judge to violate the law left him by another, lo, by virtue of his aspect as revealer of the Torah and lawgiver, it is fit that we be found meritorious in the time of judgment.

Isaiah said, "The Lord is our King," in allusion to the third principle, which is the existence of the Divinity, who is King over all the universe, and is particularly called "the King of Israel and their Redeemer" (Isa. 44:6). That is to say, even if God would not wish to set aside a law because of his lawgiving aspect, it would be fit that he save us by virtue of his regal aspect, for the king has the right to set aside a law, and to do what he wishes in order to save his people.

Therefore Isaiah concluded, "He will save us"; that is to say, that as we have an advantage over the entire world in believing in these three principles on which human well-being depends, it is fit that he save us before all other peoples [Ikkarim I.4]

REMEMBRANCES

When the pious Rabbi Levi Isaac of Berditchev [18th cent.], and some say his pious son Rabbi Israel of Pikov, of blessed memory, would come to these verses at the end of the Remembrances: And by the hands of your servants, the prophets, it is written, saying, "I will remember My covenant with thee in the days of thy youth, and I will establish unto thee an everlasting convenant" (Ezek. 16:60), and it is said, "Is Ephraim my precious son . . ." (Jer. 31:20), he would chant with a pleasant melody sweeter than honey and a special movement:

My father, of blessed memory, told me:

Once a woman came to me, crying bitterly. I asked her: Why are you crying?

She replied: My head hurts me very badly.

I said to her: But if you cry, your head will hurt even more.

Said she to me: How shall I not cry? Here the Days of Awe

are coming, and I have an only son, and I am afraid that he will not be found meritorious in the time of judgment.

I said to her: It is a father's way to have compassion on his son, especially if he is an only son and precious, as it is said (Jer. 31:20): "Is Ephraim my precious son? Is he my darling child? For as often as I speak against him, I cherish his memory still. Therefore my heart yearns for him; I must have pity upon him, saith the Lord."

The melody that the zaddik used to sing as well as his special movement is still widespread among the hasidim. [Eser Orot]

NO FORGETTING

"For You remember all the forgotten things, and there is no forgetting before your throne of honor." At first the poet says, "remember all the forgotten things"; from which one would gather that there *is* forgetting before God; and afterward he says, "and there is no forgetting before your throne of glory"; from which one would gather that there is *no* forgetting before Him. How is this possible?

These words refer to commandments and transgressions. If a man has committed a transgression and forgotten it, and has not done Teshuvah, the Holy One, blessed be he, remembers it. If a man has observed a commandment, and does not mention it, the Holy One, blessed be he, remembers it. If a man has committed a transgression, and applies the Writ, "My sin is ever before me" (Ps. 51:5) to himself, the Holy One, blessed be he, lets it pass from his presence and forgets it. If a man has observed a commandment and praises himself for it, the Holy One, blessed be he, forgets it.

That is the meaning of the saying that God remembers all the forgotten things, that is to say, he remembers what men forget. "And there is no forgetting before your throne of

glory"; God forgets what men remember. [See Shemen ha-
Tov, No. 158; see also Keneset Yisrael]

LET A GREAT HORN BE BLOWN: A TALE

The holy comrades who were students of the Baal Shem
Tov [18th cent.] had a special house outside the city, and
there after every holy teaching that they heard from the
mouth of their rabbi, they would gather together and discuss
his words. My grandfather, of blessed memory, told me that
he knew where their place was, but did not dare to go there,
because he was a mere infant and of tender years. Once after
the Grace after Meals on Rosh ha-Shanah, the Baal Shem
Tov, of blessed memory, expounded the meaning of the verse,
"Let a great horn be blown for our liberation." When the
Baal Shem Tov had finished, he at once left and went into
his room, shutting the door behind him.

Immediately the comrades went to their house outside the
city, and my grandfather was left alone in the house of the
Baal Shem Tov. My grandfather began to imagine to himself that the Messiah was coming that day. From moment to
moment the illusion grew stronger within him that the Messiah was at hand, and would come into the city at any instant.
So strong was the illusion his heart was pounding. But there
was no one in the house for him to open his heart to. He felt
his senses failing him, so real was his illusion that the Messiah was coming to the city. He could think of no other way
to dispel his mood than to go to the holy comrades. So he
got up and ran in confusion through the streets of the city.
Everyone who saw him running wondered and asked him,
"Why are you running?" But he did not answer a word.

When he came to the holy comrades, he saw them all sitting around the table, and not a person was speaking. For it

seemed clear to them, too, that the Messiah was at hand. [Kevutzat Yaakov]

CONCLUSION OF THE ADDITIONAL PRAYER

There are places where it is customary to blow another thirty blasts at the conclusion of the Additional Prayer, because some of the congregation may not have heard all the blasts, as they should have. There are still other places where it is the custom to blow a hundred blasts during the entire Additional Prayer.

After the last blast has been blown, the Additional Prayer is concluded in the customary order.

x. The Afternoon: The Casting

AFTER THE ADDITIONAL PRAYER

It is customary for the worshipers to greet one another and to bless their children, as on other holidays. One does not say, "May you be inscribed for a good year," as one does during the Evening Prayer, because the righteous are judged after the first three hours of the day, and if one were to bless one's fellow after that time with the phrase, "May you be inscribed for a good year," it might be supposed that the man being addressed was considered an intermediate soul, one held in abeyance until Yom Kippur; that blessing would be disrespectful. Then the worshipers take leave of one another and go home.

It is not the custom to visit one's fellow in his house on Rosh ha-Shanah as on the other holidays, nor even to visit the rabbi of the city on Rosh ha-Shanah. But one visits one's father and mother to receive their blessing, especially if he knows that they wish it. [Mateh Efrayim]

KIDDUSH: SANCTIFICATION

"Blow the horn at the new moon. . . ." (Ps. 81:4) is said, and the Kiddush over the wine is recited. And if Rosh ha-Shanah falls on a Sabbath, the Sabbath verses are said first, as on other Sabbaths during the year.

THE FEAST OF THE DAY

Then we eat and drink and rejoice, because we are confident of having received a divine pardon. But we ought not to eat our fill, so as not to become light-headed. We ought particularly not to drink too much, that the awe of God might continue before us.

THE AFTERNOON PRAYER

When the time for the Afternoon Prayer has come, one ought to give his heart to prayer with great devotion, as our sages, of blessed memory, said: "Let a man ever be careful of the Afternoon Prayer for, lo, Elijah, the prophet, was answered only in the Afternoon Prayer" (Berakhot 6b); and besides, Isaac instituted this prayer, and on this Rosh ha-Shanah we recall his Binding, that his merit may turn the quality of divine justice into the quality of divine compassion.

The Afternoon Prayer follows the order to be found in our prayer books. If Rosh ha-Shanah falls on a Sabbath, the Torah Scroll is taken out of the Ark and three men are called to the reading of a section from the portion beginning, "Hearken" (Deut. 32). Some congregations are accustomed to read the liturgical poem "Heart's Companion" before the Afternoon Prayer, in order to arouse themselves to the love of God.

THE CASTING: TASHLIKH

After the feast of the day and in most of our communities after the Afternoon Prayer and before the setting of the sun, the ritual of the Casting is performed, after the scriptural verse (Mic. 7:19): "And Thou wilt cast all their sins into the depths of the sea."

The ritual of the Casting is performed on the first day of Rosh ha-Shanah. If one has no time during the first day, one performs it during the second. And when the first day falls on a Sabbath, there are places where it is customary to perform the Casting on the second day of Rosh ha-Shanah. [Mateh Efrayim]

In Jerusalem every one performs the Casting ritual even on the Sabbath. And such is the custom in Egypt, too. [Nehar Pekod]

What is the order of the Casting ritual? We go outside the city to a sea or a river, wherever there are fish. And if there is no such sea or river in that area, we go to a spring or fountain. (In Jerusalem the prayer of the Casting is said near cisterns which still hold water; the inhabitants of Safed go up to the roofs of their houses, where they can see Lake Kinneret, and there say the prayer of the Casting; in Aden it is customary to say it near the ritual bathhouse in the courtyard of the main House of Prayer.)

These verses are said: the verses from Micah beginning, "Who is a God like unto thee" (7:18–20), and the verses from Psalms beginning, "Out of my straits I called upon the Lord" (118:5–9), and the Thirty-first Psalm, and the verse from Isaiah (11:9): "They shall not hurt nor destroy in all My holy mountain; for the earth shall be full of the knowledge of the Lord, as the waters cover the sea."

Then the prayer composed by Rabbi Hayyim Joseph David Azulai [18th cent.] to awaken compassion for Israel, and to beseech the Holy One, blessed be he, to help us to be occupied in the service of God and in the service of the Torah, and to be remembered and inscribed in the book of life. And we mention before Him how many hundreds of years we have been calling on his great Name and believing in him and in his sacred Torah, and how we have been killed and burned to death and drowned for the sake of the sanctification of his Name. And we beseech him to return his Presence to Zion and to return Israel to their habitation. Then shall the earth be full of the knowledge of God, to revere and to love his great Name. And Psalm 130, beginning, "A Song of Ascents; Out of the depths have I called Thee, O Lord," is said.

And one shakes out the hems of his clothing three times, as an allusion to the fact that we are putting our heart to the casting out of our sins, in order to become clean of all sin. There is support for this custom in the Scripture (Neh. 5:13): "Also I shook out my lap, and said: 'So God shake out. . . .'" [Mahzor Ohole Yaakov]

WATERS UNTO THE SOUL

And why is it customary to go to seas and rivers on Rosh ha-Shanah? Because it is taught in the Midrash that when Abraham, our father, peace be upon him, went to bind Isaac his son, Satan went before him and turned into a great river before them, so that the waters reached up to Abraham's neck. At that moment Abraham raised his eyes to heaven and said: "Master of the universe, you have chosen me, and been revealed to me, and said to me, 'Through you shall my Name be known in my world,' and now, 'The waters have come in even unto my soul' (Ps. 69:2); if I, or Isaac, my son, should drown, through whom would your Name be declared one?"

Said the Holy One, blessed be he: "By your life, my Name

shall be declared one in my world through you." At once the
Holy One, blessed be he, rebuked the river, and Abraham
was saved. [According to Maharil]

AS THE FISH OF THE SEA

And it is customary to go to a river where there are fish,
because we are compared to fish suddenly caught in a net.
So are we caught in the severe net of divine judgment, and
gazing at the river contemplate Teshuvah. [Levush]

Another reason is given in Eliyahu Zutta: we visit rivers
with fish that the evil eye may not govern us, as it cannot
govern fish, and that we may be fruitful and multiply like
fish. And those who interpret metaphorically say: Just as fish
have no eyebrows and their eyes are always open, so let the
eye of Him who is on high always be open for our benefit.

INTO THE DEPTHS OF THE SEA

And a custom of Israel is Torah. Why do Jews go to a body
of water and say, "And Thou wilt cast all their sins into the
depths of the sea"? Because when one considers the phrase
"into the depths of the sea," the event of the Creation of the
world is made clear. For "the depths of the sea" refers to the
abyss, the deepest part of the sea. According to the nature of
the elements, the waters should cover the earth and the earth
be the center and the lowest part of all the world. But the
earth cannot have been given to the sons of man and those
who dwell upon it unless that was God's intention. He who
renewed the world according to his will did so for the purpose of the settlement of the earth.

Therefore we go to a body of water to see where it was
that he "placed the sand for the bound of the sea" (Jer. 5:22).
And it is said: "Thus far shalt thou come, but no further"

(Job 38:11). And we go there to behold the strength of the Maker of Creation. We go on Rosh ha-Shanah, which is the Day of Judgment, so that every man may take to heart the event of Creation and remember that God is King over the earth. And that is why the phrase "And Thou wilt cast all their sins into the depths of the sea" is said; for in truth he who considers the event referred to in the phrase "into the depths of the sea" perceives how the world was renewed and comprehends the existence of God and repents of all his sins; his iniquities are pardoned, and his sins are cast into the depths of the sea. [Torat ha-Olah]

A SYMBOL

A symbol is a means of arousing the brute soul; hence, is the custom to wear a white gown, called *sargenes* [or, kittel], as a symbol of the death gown, in order to make the sinner tremble, that he may remember the day of death; similarly, the custom of going to a body of water on Rosh ha-Shanah is a symbolic allusion, for the waters which now seem to be at this place were not here before and will not remain afterward. So, if the sinner says to himself, I will not repeat my sin, the sin like the waters will move on. [Sefer ha-Hayyim]

THE DIVINE PRESENCE NEAR WATER

"And the Lord spoke unto Moses and Aaron in the land of Egypt" (Exod. 12:1). This verse teaches us that all the lands were fit for the word of God until Palestine was sanctified, but from the time that Palestine was sanctified the prophets heard the word of God only near water, as it is said (Ezek. 1:3): "The word of the Lord came expressly unto Ezekiel the priest, the son of Buzi, in the land of the Chaldeans by the river Chebar." And it is said (Dan. 8:2): "And I was by the stream Ulai." And to Jonah, too, God spoke only on the water. Rabbi Judah says, "From the very beginning, God spoke to the prophets only on the water, as it is said (Ezek. 1:3): 'The word of the Lord came unto Ezekiel . . . by the river Chebar.'" [Mekhilta de Rabbi Shimon bar Yohai, Bo]

NEAR A SPRING

Our rabbis, of blessed memory, said (Horayot 12a): "Kings are anointed only near a spring, that their kingship may run long and smooth, as it is said (I Kings 1:33): 'And the king said unto them, Take with you the servants of your lord . . . and bring him down to Gihon.'"

And our rabbis, of blessed memory, said: "God says, Say Kingships to me, and thus crown me your king." And though this does not apply to him, be blessed, it does apply to us. We hope that our acceptance of the yoke of the kingdom of heaven and the pure spirit we have received on Rosh ha-Shanah will be continued forever.

A CURIOUS CUSTOM

I saw a very curious custom in practice among the Jews of Kurdistan. On Rosh ha-Shanah they all go to a river that flows at the foot of a hill, and say the prayer of the Casting. Afterward they all jump into the water and swim around like the fish of the sea, instead of only shaking the hems of their clothing on the bank of the river, as our brothers the children of Israel do in Europe. And when I inquired of them the reason for this curious custom, they answered that by this act they are purified of all their sins, for the waters of the river wash away all the sins they have committed during all the past year. [Masae Yisrael]

HOW TO PERFORM THE CASTING

It is best to avoid the people who are as light-minded as women, and say, *Ich vil geyn mayn aveyres shiteln* [I will shake off my transgressions], and, taking hold of the folds of their clothing, shake them, thinking to themselves that by so doing a man can shake off the transgressions that he committed all the year before. And he ought not to think so, for it really is a desecration of the great Name of God before the nations that know of the custom. For when they see Jews going to the river, they say laughingly, The Jews are going *shiteln ire zind in vasser* [to shake their sins into the water].

But if a person wants to observe the custom, let him say, *Ich vil geyn tashlikh makhen* [I will perform the Casting]. For the principal purpose of the custom is to pray to God, to cast our iniquities into the depths of the sea, because in saying these verses we are contemplating Teshuvah: for his eye is constantly fixed on Israel. And the custom of shaking the hems of our clothing is symbolic, too; we do it to shake off the shells of the evil spirits that cling to us because of the filth of our iniquities. For the same reason, it is the custom after the blessing of the New Moon to shake off the shells of the evil spirits that were aroused by the ac-cusation of the moon, as is known to those who know the secret wisdom of the Kabbalah. [Emek Berakhah]

On returning to the House of Prayer after the Casting, if the time for the Evening Prayer has not yet arrived, one ought not to be light-headed and sit around idle. One ought to remove oneself from the company of one's friends, even if it seems that they are talking about Rosh ha-Shanah. It is impossible for them not to be drawn from one subject to another, until they come to laughter and light-headedness

and slander. But let every one engage in his own affairs,
studying or reciting Psalms. [Mateh Efrayim]

XI. The Second Day of Rosh ha-Shanah

ORIGIN AND UNITY

Even in Palestine Rosh ha-Shanah is observed for two days,
unlike other holidays, only one day of which is observed in
Palestine. And this is not because of the uncertainty about
the date of Rosh ha-Shanah, but because we learned in the
Palestinian Talmud (Erubin III, end): "The observance of
Rosh ha-Shanah for two days was ordained by the Early
Prophets."

These two days are one sacred whole, and are considered
as one long day.

THE EVENING PRAYER

The Evening Prayer on the Second Day of Rosh ha-Shanah
follows the order to be found in the festival prayer books.
After the Evening Prayer people bless one another as they
do on other holidays. They do not say, "May you be inscribed
for a good year," for one's fellow is considered completely
righteous and to have already been inscribed for a good year
during the first day of Rosh ha-Shanah.

THE LIGHTING OF CANDLES

The women light candles in honor of the holiday, and
recite the benedictions ending, "who has commanded us to
light the holiday candles" and "who has kept us alive and
preserved us and allowed us to reach this present season." If
they have new dresses, they put them on before lighting the

candles, so that the benediction with the phrase "who has kept us alive" will refer to their dresses as well. If a woman does not have a new dress to put on, she can take a fresh fruit, so long as she lights the candles near the time of the Kiddush, so that the fruit may be eaten near the time of the benediction. [Mateh Efrayim]

KIDDUSH: SANCTIFICATION

And we return home, and recite the Kiddush over the wine, and recite the benediction with the phrase "who has kept us alive." And, because the days of Rosh ha-Shanah are considered to form one day, and the benediction has already been recited on the first day, a fresh fruit is set on the table during the Kiddush, so that the benediction refers both to the day and to the fresh fruit. Even if a man does not have a fresh fruit, he may still recite the benediction with the phrase "who has kept us alive."

In Poland and other northern countries, it is customary to recite the benediction over grapes and melons, which ripen in the north at that time. But in Palestine where the season of grapes and melons is already over, the benediction with the phrase "who has kept us alive" is recited over pomegranates or olives. And here in the holy city of Jerusalem (may it be rebuilt and re-established!), it is the custom in the Houses of Prayer of the Sephardim to pass out olives to the congregation on the evening of the second day of Rosh ha-Shanah.

A TALE

Rabbi Leib, the "Admonisher" of Polnoy, and Rabbi Leib ha-Kohen of Berditchev, and Rabbi Zusya of Hanipol, and Rabbi Mordecai of Neskhizh, may all their memories be blessed, were visiting at the home of the "Grandfather" of

Spola [18th–19th cent.] on Rosh ha-Shanah, and talked of the
coming of the Messiah and the redemption of Israel all during the meal.

Said Rabbi Zusya to Rabbi Leib the Admonisher: "Leib,
you are to blame more than all of us for the delay in the redemption. For you are the Admonisher of Israel. Why aren't
you admonishing them, until they do Teshuvah?"

The Grandfather of Spola got to his feet, and pointed one
hand straight up to heaven, and said, "Master of the universe,
I swear to you that Israel will not return to doing good
through being admonished and suffering. Then why do you
punish them to no purpose? For you see what the end will
be from the beginning. If so, I beseech you, be a good father
to Israel. Just as a father is compassionate with his son, even
if he isn't deserving, in the same way have mercy on your
sons." And saying this, he burst into tears, and all the others
cried with him. [Tiferet Arye Leib mi-Spola]

THE ORDER OF THE SECOND DAY OF
ROSH HA-SHANAH

The order of the second day of the holiday is like the first
and there is no difference in the prayers and the blowing of
the ram's-horn. The only difference is in the liturgical poems
and the readings from the Torah.

Most of the liturgical poems for the second day of Rosh ha-
Shanah were composed by Rabbi Simeon the Great of Mainz
[11th cent.]. They are based on the Kingships, Remembrances, and Ram's-horns. The first letters of the stanzas are
in alphabetical and reverse alphabetical order, and also spell
out the name of the author.

THE READING OF THE TORAH

After the Morning Prayer, two Torah Scrolls are taken out

of the Ark, and the scriptural portion of the Binding is read
(Gen. 22). And the reason for the reading of that particular
portion on that day, according to Rashi in his commentary
on the tractate Megillah, is that God may recall the Binding
of Isaac for our benefit. And in the second Scroll the same
portion as was read on the first day is read for the person
who is to read the portion from the prophets. Then the portion from Jeremiah beginning, "Thus saith the Lord: 'The
people that were left of the sword have found grace in the
wilderness'" (Jer. 31:2–20), is read, because it is about Israel
being remembered for their benefit, as it is there written, "I
do earnestly remember him still; therefore My heart yearneth
for him. I will surely have compassion upon him, saith the
Lord."

BEFORE THE BLASTS

If a wise man is present, he preaches a strong sermon on the
subject of the day, in order to awaken the people to Teshuvah.

This is the sermon that Rabbi Shmelke of Nikolsburg
[18th cent.] preached on the text: "Wherefore cometh not
the son of Jesse to the meal, neither yesterday, nor today?"
(I Sam. 20:27). "Wherefore cometh not the son of Jesse"—
that is the king, the Messiah. "Neither yesterday"—on the
first day of Rosh ha-Shanah. "Nor today"—on the second day.
Because both yesterday and today we have been praying for
bread only, for material things, and not for the Divine Presence, which is in exile. [Shemen ha-Tov]

It is customary in some countries to recite the benediction
with the phrase "who has kept us alive" before the blowing
of the ram's-horn on the second day of Rosh ha-Shanah as
well, even if the first day falls on a weekday when the ram's-
horn is blown, and the benediction already recited. And it is

customary for the ram's-horn blower to wear a new garment for the blowing of the ram's-horn on the second day of Rosh ha-Shanah, just as a fresh fruit is laid on the table at the Kiddush on the second evening. Even if he does not have a new garment, he still recites the benediction. There are other places where the benediction is not recited on the second day of Rosh ha-Shanah unless the first day fell on a Sabbath, and the horn was not blown.

THE ADDITIONAL PRAYER ON THE SECOND DAY OF ROSH HA-SHANAH

The order to be found in our festival prayer books is followed in reciting the Additional Prayer. Fewer hymns and liturgical poems are recited on the second day of Rosh ha-Shanah than on the first. After the prayer, the worshipers return home, where they recite the Kiddush over wine and eat the noon meal.

IN THE STRAITS

(A Memoir from the Days of the Russo-Japanese War)

Before Rosh ha-Shanah, a committee of Jewish soldiers passed through all the hospitals, and announced that there would be public prayer for Jewish soldiers on Rosh ha-Shanah. The committee did not labor in vain; every Jewish soldier gathered up what was left of his strength and came to the prayers.

It was an awful sight. Many of those who came were incapacitated, gloomy, and lean as corpses; many of us were armless, lame, leaned on crutches, were blind, and bore wounds of every description. Even those of us who were whole had faces that were forbidding and melancholy, with disheveled hair and overgrown beards. When it grew dark, we hung double curtains over the windows, so that the light would not be visible and invite Japanese fire.

The Evening Prayer began. One great sigh filled the house, and we all burst into tears. A crippled soldier leaning on his crutches served as the Reader, and his soft voice touched us to the soul. After the Evening Prayer, we blessed one another with wishes for a good year, but our hearts were sad. Who knew what would happen the next day? Many of us stayed behind to sleep over in the House of Prayer and recite Psalms.

The next morning a few Jewish doctors joined us in the synagogue, and we honored them with ascents to the Torah. During the blowing of the ram's-horn, something happened that frightened us badly. The soldier standing on guard outside the synagogue was a little deaf, and when the ram's-horn was blown, he thought that it was the battle alarm. He hurried into the House of Prayer, and told the congregation that we were being called into the field. The House of Prayer became a scene of confusion and tumult. Should we interrupt the blowing of the ram's-horn? Our hearts pounded and our faces became even more gloomy. It seemed to every one of us as though he could hear the blare of battle and the noise of the drums from afar. It was only after we had rushed outside that it became clear that the deaf guard had mistaken the ram's-horn for a bugle.

During the prayer beginning "We shall express the powerful sanctity" no words at all were heard in the House of Prayer; only tear-choked voices filled the atmosphere of the little house. The cantor's voice became stronger and stronger and struck sparks in the air: ". . . who will live and who will die, who in his time, and who before his time." Those were terrible and awful moments. [Bamatzor uva-Shevi, Reshumot II]   THE AFTERNOON PRAYER

The order of the Afternoon Prayer on the second day of Rosh ha-Shanah follows that of the first day, and is to be found in our festival prayer books.

HAVDALAH: BENEDICTION OF SEPARATION

Then the Havdalah is recited, just as it is at the close of
the Sabbath, except that no benedictions are recited over the
candle and the spices, and the prayer beginning "Lo, God of
my salvation" and the song "Elijah, the Prophet" are not
chanted.

WITH THE PASSING OF ROSH HA-SHANAH

Rabbi Nahman of Bratzlav [18th–19th cent.] used to say: To
me the main holiday is Rosh ha-Shanah. And as soon as Rosh
ha-Shanah is over, I listen to hear if there is a knocking at
doors, and Jews are arousing themselves to penitential prayers
for next year. For in no time at all the whole year passes by
in the twinkling of an eye. [Sihot ha-Ran, No. 214]

ENDED IS THE FIRST BOOK WHICH IS THE BOOK
OF ROSH HA-SHANAH

BOOK TWO

The Days Between Rosh ha-Shanah
and Yom Kippur

1. Seek Ye the Lord

"Seek ye the Lord while He may be found" (Isa. 55:6). Said Rabbah bar Abuha: "He may be found" during the ten days between Rosh ha-Shanah and Yom Kippur. [Rosh ha-Shanah 18a]

"Seek ye the Lord while He may be found"—during the ten days of Teshuvah, when He is resting among you. [Tanhuma, Haazinu]

"Thou makest me to know the path of life" (Ps. 16:11). Said Israel to God, "Make us to know the path of life." Said the Holy One, blessed be he, to them, "Lo, here are ten days for you to do Teshuvah between Rosh ha-Shanah and Yom Kippur." [Menorat ha-Maor, Ner 3]

"They walk, O Lord, in the light of Thy countenance" (Ps. 89:16)—during the ten days between Rosh ha-Shanah and Yom Kippur. [Midrash Tehillim]

TEN SACRIFICES

A reason why there are ten additional sacrifices on Rosh ha-Shanah is that they correspond to the ten sayings with which God created the world. For on Rosh ha-Shanah the whole world stands in judgment before the Holy One, blessed be he, and deserves to be found guilty of extermination, because the creatures are filthy with transgressions. But the Holy One, blessed be he, acquits his world. That is why we say that it is as though the world is re-created on Rosh ha-Shanah. [Pesikta Rabbati, ba-Hodesh ha-Shevii]

THE SPECIAL VIRTUE OF THE TEN DAYS

Despite the fact that Teshuvah and prayerful outcries are al-

ways good, they are best during the ten days between Rosh
ha-Shanah and Yom Kippur, and are immediately accepted,
as it is said: "Seek ye the Lord while He may be found" (Isa.
55:6). Of whom is this said? Of the individual. But the community is answered whenever they do Teshuvah and cry out
wholeheartedly in prayer, as it is said (Deut. 4:7): "For what
great nation is there, that hath God so nigh unto them, as the
Lord our God is whensoever we call upon Him?" [Maimo-
nides, Hilkhot Teshuvah II.6]

The ten days between Rosh ha-Shanah and Yom Kippur
were set aside for prayer and supplication, because all earthly
life is judged on Rosh ha-Shanah, and he who returns to God
is forgiven on Yom Kippur, as it is written, "And it came to
pass about ten days after, that the Lord smote Nabal, so that
he died" (I Sam. 25:38). And it has been expounded: The
ten days are the ten days of Teshuvah during which the judgment of Nabal was withheld by heaven, with the hope that
he might do Teshuvah (Rosh ha-Shanah 18a). And in the
Mishnah we find (Taanit II.1): "Brothers, it was not said of
the men of Nineveh that 'God saw their sackcloth and fasting,' but rather that 'God saw their works, that they turned
from their evil way' (Jonah 3:10). From this we learn how
great is Teshuvah, since it can tear up the evil decree, as it
is said (Isa. 6:10): 'Return and be healed,' and it is said (Jer.
3:14): 'Return, O backsliding children.'" [Mahzor Vitri,
No. 337]

TIPPING THE SCALE

Our rabbis taught: Ever let a man see himself as though he
were half-guilty and half-innocent. Happy is he if he does
one good deed, for he tips the balance in his favor. Woe is
him if he commits one transgression, for he tips the balance
against himself, as it is said, "But one sinner destroyeth much

good" (Eccles. 9:18). Because of a single sin committed, he loses much that is good.

Rabbi Eleazar ben Rabbi Simeon says: Because the world is judged by its majority, and the individual judged by the majority of his deeds, happy is the man who does a single good deed, for he tips the balance in his favor and that of the world. Woe is him, if he commits one transgression, for he tips the balance against himself and the world. For it is said, "But one sinner destroyeth much good" (Eccles. 9:18). Because of a single sin, he and all the world would have lost much that is good.

Rabbi Simeon ben Yohai says: Even if a man is completely righteous all his days, if he rebels at the last he loses the benefit of his early deeds. As it is said, "The righteousness of the righteous shall not deliver him in the day of his transgression . . ." (Ezek. 33:12). But even if a man was completely wicked all his days, if he does Teshuvah at the last, his wickedness is never again remembered against him, as it is said, ". . . and as for the wickedness of the wicked, he shall not stumble thereby in the day that he turneth from his wickedness" (*ibid.*). Then should such a man's deeds be considered half transgressions and half virtues?

Resh Lakish answered: Only when he regrets his early deeds does he lose their benefit. [Kiddushin 40b]

TWENTY-FOUR THINGS THAT HINDER TESHUVAH

1. Twenty-four things hinder Teshuvah. Of these four are great sins, and the man who commits any one of them, the Holy One, blessed be he, does not give an opportunity to do Teshuvah, because of the enormity of his sin. Such sinners are:

a) He who leads a community to sin; included in this class

of sinners is the man who hinders a community from fulfilling a commandment.

b) He who turns his fellow from good to evil ways, such as "the seducer and enticer" (cf. Deut. 13).

c) He who seeing his son acting viciously, does not prevent him by force. Since his son is under his government, if the man were to check his son, he would leave off sinning. Hence, he is considered as leading his son to sin. Included in this class of sinners is every man who can possibly check sinners, be they individuals or a community, and does not, but rather allows them to stumble on.

d) He who says, I will sin and then repent. Included in this class is the man who says, I will sin and Yom Kippur will make atonement for me.

2. Of the twenty-four, there are five sins that close Teshuvah in the face of those who commit them. Such sinners are:

a) He who separates from a community; for when they are doing Teshuvah he will not be with them, and not share the benefit of the merit they acquire.

b) He who opposes the dicta of the sages. For his opposition will cause him to separate from them, and he will not know the ways of Teshuvah.

c) He who mocks the commandments. For, since the commandments are despicable in his eyes, he will not seek them out and perform them. Then how shall he acquire merit?

d) He who despises his teachers; for that causes him to be cast out like Gehazi (II Kings 5:27). Then when he becomes an outcast, he will find no teacher and no one to instruct him in the path of truth.

e) He who hates being admonished; for he leaves himself no way for Teshuvah, admonishment being the cause of Teshuvah. For when a man is told his sins, and made to feel ashamed of them, he turns in Teshuvah. . . . God also com-

manded that the sinners be admonished, as it is said, "Cry
aloud, spare not" (Isa. 58:1). All the prophets, as well, admonished Israel until they turned in Teshuvah. Therefore,
it is necessary to appoint a man in every congregation who
is a great sage, and old, and has been in awe of heaven from
his youth, and is beloved by the people, in order that he may
admonish them and make them turn in Teshuvah. But the
man who hates being admonished neither goes to the admonisher nor listens to his words. Therefore he will continue in his sins, which are good in his eyes.

3. Of the twenty-four, there are five sins, which committing, a man finds it impossible to turn in complete Teshuvah,
because they are iniquities committed in his relationship with
his fellow man and the sinner cannot tell to whom to make
restitution or whose forgiveness to ask. Such sinners are:

a) He who curses the people in general, and not any
known individual in particular, so that he cannot ask forgiveness of any particular man.

b) He who shares with a thief. He cannot return the theft,
not knowing whom it belongs to, since the thief steals from
many people, and brings the theft to him, which he receives.
He commits still another sin in that he encourages the thief
and leads him into sin.

c) He who finds a lost article and does not keep announc-
ing it publicly until he can return it to its owner. After a
time, when he does Teshuvah he does not know to whom to
return the lost article.

d) He who despoils the poor and the orphaned and the
widowed. These poor folks are constantly emigrating from
city to city. Since they are not well known anywhere, the man
cannot tell to whom the goods belong, and cannot return
them to their owner.

e) He who accepts a bribe in order to pervert justice does

not know how far justice has been corrupted, and how powerful its effects are, in order to make amends. For he will find excuses for his conduct. The man commits still another sin in encouraging the briber, and leading him into sin.

4. Of the twenty-four, there are five sins for which the sinner may be assumed not to do Teshuvah, because they are trivial in the eyes of most men. The result is that the sinner imagines he has committed no sin. Such sinners are:

a) He who eats at a meal where there is not enough for the host; this act is a minor form of theft. The guest imagines that he has not sinned, and says to himself, But I ate with his permission!

b) He who makes use of a poor man's pledge, which may be merely an ax or a plow. The borrower will generally say in his heart, They have not lost their value. Why, I have stolen nothing from him!

c) He who looks at a woman he may not marry imagines to himself that he has done nothing wrong. For he says, Did I lie with her, or even come near her? He does not know that even eying a woman lustfully is a serious iniquity, for it leads to the act of lust itself, as it is said, "And that ye go not about after your own heart and your own eyes" (Num. 15:39).

d) He who tries to gain honor through disparaging another. He says in his heart that what he has done is not a sin, since the other person was not there at the time, and could not suffer from any shame. Moreover, he thinks he only contrasted his own good deeds and wisdom with the deeds and lack of wisdom of his fellow, so that people might gather that he was to be honored and the other to be despised.

e) He who is suspicious of innocent people says in his heart, I am committing no sin, because (he says), What harm have I done to him? I only suspect him; perhaps he is guilty, and perhaps he is not. This man does not realize that thinking of an innocent person as a possible transgressor is an iniquity.

5. Of the twenty-four, there are five sins toward which the sinner will always be drawn, and which he will find it very hard to leave off. Therefore, every man should beware of becoming dependent on them, for they are all very vicious habits. They are: talebearing, and gossip, and temper, and evil thought, and bad company. Bad company because the man who keeps bad company learns their ways, which become imprinted on his heart. That is what Solomon meant when he said: "But the companion of fools shall smart for it" (Prov. 13:20). We have already explained in our section on moral dispositions what the qualities are that every man ought always to cultivate. How much more, then, do they apply to the person who is doing Teshuvah.

6. Yet all these sins and those like them, despite the fact that they hinder Teshuvah, do not altogether prevent it. For if a man sincerely does Teshuvah and turns from his sins, he is considered penitent and has a share in the world to come. [Maimonides, Hilkhot Teshuvah IV]

FREE WILL

1. Every man is given free will. If he wishes to turn to the good way and to be righteous, he has the power to do so. Or if he wishes to turn to the evil way and to be wicked, he has that power, too. Thus it is written in the Torah: "Behold, the man is become as one of us, to know good and evil" (Gen. 3:22). That is to say, this species, man, has become unique in the world, there being no species like him in the respect that, of himself and from the exercise of his own knowledge

and reason, he knows good and evil. He can do whatever he wishes, and there is no one to hinder him from doing good or evil. This being so—"lest he put forth his hand" (*ibid.*).

2. Do not believe what the fools among the nations of the world and most of the blockheads among the children of Israel say: to wit, that the Holy One, blessed be he, decrees whether a man will be righteous or wicked at the moment of his creation. It is not so. But every man may become righteous like Moses our master, or wicked like Jeroboam, wise or foolish, compassionate or cruel, miserly or generous, and so with all the other qualities. There is no one to coerce a man, and no one to determine his actions, and no one to draw him into either one of the two ways; he himself of his own free will turns to whatever way he wills. That is what Jeremiah meant when he said, "Out of the mouth of the Most High proceedeth not evil and good" (Lam. 3:38). That is to say, the Creator does not determine that a man will be good or that he will be evil. Since this is so, the sinner is responsible for any injury he does to himself. Therefore, it is fit for him to cry and to bewail his sins and what he has done to his soul and the evil he has brought upon it. This is expressed in the next verse: "Wherefore doth a living man complain?" (Lam. 3:39). Jeremiah continues, saying as it were, "Since we have free will and committed all these evils knowingly, it is fit that we turn in Teshuvah and forsake our wickedness, since we have the power to do so." This is expressed in the next verse: "Let us search and try our ways, and return to the Lord."

3. And this is an important principle, the pillar of the Torah and of the commandment, as it is said, "See, I have set before thee this day life and good" (Deut. 30:15), and "Behold, I set before you this day a blessing and a curse"

(Deut. 11:26). That is to say, you have the power, and whatever a man wishes to do he can do, whether it be good or bad. And because he has this power, it is said, "Oh that they had such a heart as this alway . . ." (Deut. 5:26), implying that the Creator does not coerce the sons of man, nor decree that they are to do either good or evil, but all they do is in their own discretion.

4. If God had decreed whether a man were to be righteous or wicked, or if there were some force inherent in his nature that irresistibly drew him to a particular course, or a special science, or a particular view, or a special action, as the stupid astrologers pretend, how could He have commanded us through the prophets, "Do thus and do not thus, better your ways and do not follow your wicked impulses"—if from the moment of a man's creation his destiny had already been decreed, or if his nature irresistibly drew him to that from which he could not free himself? What place would there be for all of the Torah, and by what right or justice would the wicked be punished or the righteous rewarded? "Shall not the Judge of all the earth do justly?" (Gen. 18:25).

But you must not wonder: How can a man always do whatever he wishes, and his actions be at his own discretion—can he ever do anything without the permission of his Master and his Master's will? The Writ itself says (Ps. 135:6): "Whatsoever the Lord pleased, that hath He done, in heaven and in earth."

Know then that everything is done according to His will, despite the fact that our actions are in our power. How? Just as the Maker wishes it that fire and air ascend and water and earth descend, and the sphere revolve in a circle, and that the rest of the world's creations be as he wishes them—so he wishes man to have freedom of will, and all his deeds to be at

his discretion, and for man to be under no coercing or attract-
ing force, but that, of himself and from the exercise of the
intelligence God gave him, he do whatever he wishes. Therefore, man is judged by his deeds. If he does good, good is
done to him; and if he does evil, evil is done to him. So the
prophet says, "This hath been of your doing" (Mal. 1:9),
and, "According as they have chosen their own ways" (Isa.
66:3). It was on this subject that Solomon said, "Rejoice. O
young man, in thy youth . . . but know thou, that for all
these things God will bring thee into judgment" (Eccles.
11:9). That is to say, know that what you do is in your power,
and you must give a reckoning.

5. Should you say, "Either the Holy One, blessed be he,
knows everything that is to be before it happens, and knows
before a man comes into being whether he will be righteous
or wicked, or He does not know. If God knows that a man
will be righteous, it is impossible that he should not be righteous; and should you say that God knows that he will be
righteous, and yet it is possible for him to be wicked—then
God does not know the matter clearly." Should you ask thus,
you must know that the solution to this problem is "longer
than the earth, and broader than the sea" (Job 11:9). Many
important principles of the highest sublimity are connected
with it. But you must know and understand in this connection only what I am about to say. We have already explained in the second chapter of "Laws Relating to the
Fundamentals of the Torah" that the Holy One, blessed be
he, does not know with a knowledge external of himself,
like the human beings, whose knowledge and self are two
distinct things. But He, exalted be his Name, and his knowledge are one, and the mind of man cannot comprehend this
clearly. And, just as the mind of man cannot apprehend or

discover the real essence of the Creator, as it is said, "for man shall not see me and live" (Exod. 33:20), so it is not in the power of man to apprehend or discover the knowledge of the Creator. So the prophet said (Isa. 55:8): "For My thoughts are not your thoughts, neither are your ways My ways." [Maimonides, Hilkhot Teshuvah V]

TESHUVAH

Teshuvah makes atonement for all transgressions; even if a man has transgressed all the days of his life, if he does Teshuvah at the end, nothing of his wickedness is remembered unto him, as it is said (Ezek. 33:12): "And as for the wickedness of the wicked, he shall not stumble thereby in the day that he turneth from his wickedness." [*Ibid.* I.3]

And what is Teshuvah? It occurs when the sinner forsakes his sin, and removes it from his thoughts, and concludes in his heart not to do it again, as it is said, "Let the wicked forsake his way, and the man of iniquity his thoughts" (Isa. 55:7). Let him also regret what has happened, as it is said, "Surely after that I was turned, I repented" (Jer. 31:19). And let the sinner call to Him who knows all hidden things to witness that he will never return to sin that sin again. [*Ibid.* II.2]

TESHUVAH FOR EVIL THOUGHTS

Do not say that one does Teshuvah only for transgressions that involve an act, such as whoring, theft, and robbery. But, just as a man must turn in Teshuvah from these, so he must search out his evil thoughts and turn from anger, and from hostility, and from jealousy, and from quarreling, and from the pursuit of money or honor, and from the greed for food and such like matters—for all these a man must turn in Teshuvah. These iniquities are more serious than those which involve an act, for when a man is addicted to them, it is difficult for him to leave off doing them. And thus it is said (Isa. 55:7): "Let the wicked forsake his way, and the man of iniquity his thoughts." [*Ibid.* VII.3]

THE RUNG OF TESHUVAH

How exalted is the rung of Teshuvah! The night before he did Teshuvah this very man was separated from the Lord God of Israel, as it is said, "But your iniquities have separated between you and your God" (Isa. 59:2); he cried out and was not answered, as it is said, "Yea, when ye make many prayers, I will not hear" (Isa. 1:15); he performed the commandments, and they were thrown back in his face, as it is said, "Who hath required this at your hand, to trample my courts?" (Isa. 1:12); "Oh that there were even one among you that would shut the doors" (Mal. 1:10); and today, after doing Teshuvah, that same man clings to the Divine Presence, as it is said, "But ye that did cleave unto the Lord your God are alive everyone of you this day" (Deut. 4:4); he cries out and is immediately answered, as it is written, "And it shall come to pass, that before they call, I will answer" (Isa. 65:24); he performs the commandments and they are accepted with pleasure and joy, as it is said, "For God hath already accepted thy works" (Eccles. 9:7). Yes, even more—they are much desired, as it is said (Mal. 3:4): "Then shall the offering of Judah and Jerusalem be pleasant unto the Lord, as in the days of old, and as in ancient years." [*Ibid.* VII.7]

DEAR ARE THOSE WHO DO TESHUVAH

And let not the man who is doing Teshuvah imagine that he is kept far from the rung of the righteous, because of the iniquities and sins he has sinned. It is not so; rather he is as beloved and desirable to the Creator, as though he had never sinned. Yes, even more—his reward is great, for lo, having tasted sin, he has forsaken it, and conquered his impulse. The sages said, "Where those who do Teshuvah stand, the completely righteous cannot stand" (Berakhot 34b). That is to say, the rung they stand on is higher than that of those who have never sinned, because they have had to labor harder to conquer their passions. [*Ibid*. VII.4]

THE WAY OF THOSE WHO DO TESHUVAH

The right way is for those who do Teshuvah to be very lowly and modest. If fools insult them by reminding them of their past actions, saying, "Last night you used to do such and such, and last night you said thus and thus"—they ought not to be affected by them, but listen, and rejoice in the knowledge that this will be accounted their merit. For once they are ashamed of their past actions and humiliated for them, their merit is greater and their worth increases. It is a great sin to say to one who has done Teshuvah, "Remember your past actions," or to recall them in his presence in order to shame him, or to recall similar actions and matters, in order to remind him of what he used to do. These practices are forbidden under the general injunction against vexing others with words which the Torah warns us against, as it is said (Lev. 25:14): "ye shall not wrong one another." [*Ibid*. VII.8]

TESHUVAH BRINGS REDEMPTION NEAR

All of the prophets commanded Teshuvah, and Israel will only be redeemed through Teshuvah. And the Torah has already promised that Israel will do Teshuvah at the last period of their Exile and be redeemed at once, as it is said (Deut. 30:1–3): "And it shall come to pass, when all these things are come upon thee . . . and shalt return unto the Lord thy God . . . that then the Lord thy God will turn thy captivity." [*Ibid*. VII.5]

A LETTER ON TESHUVAH

(Rabbi Nathan of Bratzlav to His Son)

With the help of God, the eve of the Sacred Sabbath of Return, 5591 [1830].

To my beloved son, Rabbi Isaac, may his light shine bright:

I have this hour received your letter and there is no time to reply to it as it deserves. May God strengthen your heart and waken you on the great and awesome day approaching in peace, that one day of the year, that you may merit to be renewed from that time on. And do not let a day be lost without secluding yourself and thinking of the meaning of your life. Into every day get as much of Torah and prayer and good deeds as you can, as much as you can steal from this passing shadow, this vanity of vanities, this vanishing cloud. . . . Remember well that all our days are vanity, yet every man on whatever level he may stand can attain eternal life. There is no time now for any more.

The words of your father, who seeks your welfare and prays in your behalf, Nathan of Bratzlav. [Alim li-Terufah]

II. The Laws and Customs of the Ten Days of Teshuvah

PENITENTIAL PRAYERS AND OTHER PRAYERS

One rises early for penitential prayers on every one of the ten days of Teshuvah.

During all the days between Rosh ha-Shanah and Yom Kippur, one engages in much prayer and supplication, inserting in the prayer of benedictions the passages beginning, "Remember us for life," "Who is like unto thee," "Inscribe for life," and "In the book of life." [Tur Orah Hayyim, No. 602]

LIKE THE WEEKDAYS OF A FESTIVAL

It is cited in "The Beginning of Wisdom," in the name of Rabbi Moses Cordovero [16th cent.] that the days between Rosh ha-Shanah and Yom Kippur are like the intermediate days of a festival, and work is forbidden. But one ought to seclude oneself and engage in Torah and Teshuvah. [Shem Tov Katan]

Despite the fact that these days are days of prayer and supplication, one feels the same awakening of love as during other holidays. [Divre Yehezkel]

LAW BELOW, COMPASSION ABOVE

It is a widespread custom from the earliest days, from the time of our saintly rabbi [Judah ha-Nasi, 2nd cent.] on, that, beginning with the months of Nisan and Tishri, no cases are tried and no trials are held, so that no man may bring suit against his brother and friend—except for those matters which the Court cannot dismiss, because of their great urgency. [Teshuvot ha-Geonim]

Nor does any man take an oath in the Court until after Yom Kippur [Rema, Orah Hayyim, No. 602, quoting the Maharil] for fear of bringing down the punishment of God upon the world because of swearing. [Ture Zahav]

But Rabbi Mordecai Jaffe [16th–17th cent.] wrote:

It seems to me that it is very much better to judge and give decision in human affairs, that there may be peace among

men on Yom Kippur. For another reason: Lo, our sages, of
blessed memory, have said (Deut. Rabbah V.5): "Where
there is justice, there is no judgment; and where there is no
justice, there is judgment. That is to say, if we do justice on
earth below, there is no judgment in heaven above; but if
there is no justice below, there is judgment above." This
being true, if we do not judge below, lo, the quality of divine
justice will be directed toward us, God forbid! Therefore, it
seems to me that it is better to judge below and to silence the
judgment above. [Levush]

And those who tremble at the word of God are careful to
pay whatever debts they owe to their fellows before Yom Kippur, even if it is not demanded of them, so that the Accuser
will find nothing to complain about. [Yosif Ometz, No. 983]

THE BLESSING OF THE NEW MOON

We do not recite the blessing of the New Moon until after
Yom Kippur. [Rema, Orah Hayyim, No. 602]

But it is the Sephardic custom in the holy city of Jerusalem,
as well as in the holy city of Hebron, to recite the blessing of the New Moon before Yom Kippur. [Sede Hemed]

RACHEL'S GRAVE AND THE GRAVES OF THE RIGHTEOUS

Many of the inhabitants of Jerusalem, men, women and children alike, at this time usually go to pray at the grave of
Rachel, our mother, and at the graves of the righteous on the
Mount of Olives, and at other graves of the righteous near
the city, and there pour out their speech to God like water, for
themselves and for their brothers and their families in the
Exile, praying that God may inscribe them in the book of
good life on the coming Day of Judgment. [Yerushalayim I]

WEDDINGS

It is customary not to perform weddings during these Days of Awe [Siddur Rabbi Yaabetz] but there is no support for this practice anywhere in the words of our early rabbis. [Responsa, Melamed le-Hoil III]

CITRONS

In places where citron sellers are to be found, pious men are accustomed to buy themselves citrons, palm leaves, and myrtle branches during the Days of Awe for use during the Feast of Booths. [Mateh Efrayim]

THE BLESSING

People bless one another during the period between Rosh ha-Shanah and Yom Kippur with the blessing, "May your judgment in the book of life be completed and sealed for your good."

ACTIVE TESHUVAH

Since the ten days of Teshuvah are days of good will, let every man coming from the House of Prayer in the morning seek at once to do good deeds [Aspeklariah ha-Meirah], for though everyone does Teshuvah on Rosh ha-Shanah, that is Teshuvah in thought alone, and active Teshuvah, which is impossible on Rosh ha-Shanah, is needed. Therefore, this need for active Teshuvah is filled during those of the ten days of Teshuvah which are weekdays. [Shem mi-Shmuel]

It is a fine thing to give gifts of charity. That is what Rabbi Moses ben Maimon, of blessed memory, wrote [Hilkhot Teshuvah III.4], and such is the practice of all the house of Israel, who give more gifts of charity and do more good deeds

and observe more commandments between Rosh ha-Shanah
and Yom Kippur than during the rest of the year.

OUR LIFE AND THE LENGTH OF OUR DAYS

After having performed a good deed, let every man sit and
study Torah. If the Torah is our life and the length of our
days at all times, how much more is that true during these
Days of Awe, when Moses our master, peace be upon him,
waited to receive the Torah for the last time.

During these Days of Awe, many people make it a practice
to study all twenty-four books of the Holy Writ, which is
particularly proper for those who know only the Holy Writ
and are bound to read through all the twenty-four books
every year.

But it is fitting and proper to read them through not simply
to pass over them, but one ought to understand their meaning. Let not the reader think in his heart, They are only
stories; what is the use of reading them? But they are called
sacred writings and were spoken in the sacred spirit; men of
understanding will find a use and matter for study at every
reading, and in every subject they examine closely. For these
stories contain mysteries of Torah, and were written down
for us not for their own sake, that is, not as the story of visible
events, but for the principles behind them, that is, their inner
secret. They may be compared to angels, who because of their
great sanctity put on the dress of this world when they descend to visit the earth, that the world may be able to endure
them. How much truer this is of the Torah, which is the
foundation of all the world, and which, because of its great
sanctity, the world would not be able to endure. Therefore,
the Torah descended to earth in the dress of these stories, and

its essence is covered by mysteries. The fool looks only at the
dress; but those who understand a little of the inwardness of
the Torah, which is the body under the dress, and those who
have merited knowledge and understanding of their Master
and his divinity, gaze more deeply into the mysteries of the
Torah, which are the soul; and in the world to come when
these people are souls, they are destined to understand even
more of the soul. . . . Indeed, the man who has been careful
to read the scriptural portion once and the Aramaic Targum
once every week, need not read through all twenty-four books
a second time, but may begin with the prophets and proceed
slowly, that he may understand the Writ. [Hemdat Yamim]

So it is fit and proper during these Days of Awe to study
the admonitory books of the early and later moralists, which
awaken a man's heart to Teshuvah. One ought not to make
them all of his study, for they lose their effect on the soul
when one has concentrated too much on them. For as it is
with cures of body ailments, so it is with soul ailments. One
ought rather to study admonitory books a little every day,
until he feels himself that the words have come into his innermost parts and turned him to his Father who is in heaven.

One ought to make the principal part of his study the tractate Yoma and its commentaries, to understand the service of
Yom Kippur as it was in the Temple. Our sages, of blessed
memory, have said, "Whoever engages in Torah is considered
as one who has sacrificed a burnt-offering" (Menahot 110a).
One ought also to study the Shulhan Arukh and its commentaries, in order to know how he must act according to the
law. He who has been allowed to reach the level of true concentration, and is able to interpret the laws and rules—and
there is no need to add, one who regularly teaches worthy
students—ought not to stop studying. There is no greater

commandment than that. "For, from the day when the Temple was destroyed, the Holy One, blessed be he, has had only the four cubits of law in his world" (Berakhot 8a). What Raba said to his students (*ibid*. 35b): "Please do not show yourselves to me during the days of Nisan and Tishri" —he said because they used to prepare their maintenance for the entire year during those months.

It is also necessary to study the meaning of the prayers and liturgical poems and penitential prayers during the Days of Awe that one may know the meaning of what one is saying. This is especially true of the Reader.

If one is spiritually secure, and has come into the mystery of God, let him study the hidden knowledge as well. A humble demeanor and seclusion are powerful aids to comprehension. But it has been tested and proven that he who studies the words of Kabbalah as publicly as though they were words of Torah will not merit the vision of its light. [Mateh Efrayim]

SELF-EXAMINATION

Let every man examine his actions and turn from those of them that are evil; that which is a questionable transgression requires more Teshuvah than that which is certain transgression, for a man regrets his actions more when he knows them than when he does not [Rema, Orah Hayyim, No. 603]. Rabbi Hayyim Vital [16th–17th cent.], in his book "The Gates of Sanctity," wrote: "The roots of transgression are pride and desire, forbidden conversation and melancholy; these are the prime causes of uncleanliness, from which secondary issues result." A scholar needs to be particularly careful (Sukkah 52a): "For every man who is greater than his comrade has a stronger inclination as well, and his accidental faults are considered deliberate sins." [Mahazik Berakhah]

MEASURE FOR MEASURE

Let the living take the events and misfortunes that occur to the sons of man to heart, and know that they come because of sins they have committed. The Holy One, blessed be he, punishes men measure for measure for their deliberate sins. Now the man who is in awe of the terror of the Lord and the glory of his majesty will seclude himself for one hour every day during the Days of Awe, and gaze deeply into the transgressions that a man generally carelessly neglects, and quietly gather strength to understand the commandments. Our master Rabbi Jonah [Gerondi, 13th cent.] wrote in his book "The Gates of Teshuvah" that the sinner who is late in turning in Teshuvah makes the punishment even heavier. For he knows that he is in disfavor, and that he has a refuge in Teshuvah, but stands by his rebelliousness, though he has the opportunity to escape ruin.

Children of Israel, do not make of falsehood your trusted refuge. If your heart pursues after lust, look closely into yourself, lest your end be bitter, as it is written: "There is a way which seemeth right unto a man, but the end thereof are the ways of death" (Prov. 14:12). Children of Israel, know that the soul will not be at ease in this world though it come into all the kingdoms of the earth, knowing that there is a world to come where it will be at ease and rest. So it is written (Jer. 6:16): "Thus saith the Lord: 'Stand ye in the ways and see, and ask for the old paths, where is the good way, and walk therein, and ye shall find rest for your souls.'" [Iggeret Rav Saadia Gaon]

None of the souls has a resting place in this world, nor any security, though it attain the greatest of kingdoms and the highest of heights. It is not in its nature. For, knowing there is a dwelling place more to be honored than any other, the soul longs after it and yearns for it. [Emunot ve-Deot IX.1]

III. The Fast of Gedaliah

THE FAST

On the third of Tishri falls the Fast of Gedaliah, which, coming at the close of Rosh ha-Shanah, is also called the Fast of the Seventh, after the seventh month, when Gedaliah the son of Ahikam was killed and the last ember of Israel was extinguished; and this was the cause of the ultimate Exile. [Maimonides, Hilkhot Taanit V.2], which was the cause of all their troubles. The death of a righteous man is as hard for the Holy One, blessed be he, to bear, as the day when the Temple was destroyed. As the fast on the Ninth of Av was instituted in memory of the Destruction, so a fast was instituted in memory of Gedaliah the Righteous. And all the laws that are in practice during the other public fasts are practiced during the Fast of Gedaliah as well. [Mahzor Bene Roma]

CONSCIENTIOUS READERS

Conscientious Readers go into seclusion for seven days beginning with the Fast of Gedaliah until Yom Kippur, and study the order of the service and mend their deeds and seclude themselves to be alone with their Maker night and day in solitude and piety, as the High Priest used to do. [Moed lekhol Hai]

IV. The Sabbath of Return

WHY IT IS SO CALLED

The Sabbath between Rosh ha-Shanah and Yom Kippur is

called the "Sabbath of Return," because then the portion from
the prophets beginning "Return, O Israel, unto the Lord thy
God" (Hos. 14:2) is read. The common people call it the
"Sabbath of Teshuvah," because it falls during the days of
Teshuvah.

THE ORDER OF THE PRAYER

The order of the prayer is the same as on other Sabbaths,
and almost the same prayers are added as during the ten days
of Teshuvah.

THE READING OF THE TORAH

The reading of the Torah on this Sabbath consists sometimes
of the portion beginning "And Moses went" (Deut. 31), and
sometimes of that beginning "Give ear" (Deut. 32).

Regardless of which of the two portions is read, the portion at the end of Hosea beginning "Return, O Israel" (Hos.
14:2) is the reading from the prophets. Then the congregation passes to the book of the prophet Joel, where they read
from "Blow the horn in Zion, sanctify a fast," up to "And my
people shall never be ashamed" (Joel 2:15–27). There are
those who read from the eleventh verse, "And the Lord ut-
tereth his voice," and others who conclude with the verses at
the end of Micah, "Who is a God like unto thee" (Mic. 7:18–
20). No youth is ever called to read the portion from the
prophets, but a man of importance is called up for that reading. [Mateh Moshe; Mateh Efrayim]

MAKING AMENDS

We have already said above that if a man passes each of the
ten days in Teshuvah, he makes atonement for all the faults
he committed on the corresponding days of the week all year
long. The man whose heart is wholly God's must make
amends on this Sabbath for all the sins that he committed
during other Sabbaths by profane conversation, or idle mat-

ters, or strong emotion. Let him meditate Teshuvah all day, and speak only when absolutely necessary; and let him study from morning till night, so that the entire day will be sacred and sanctified to God; let every man do as much as he is able.

That is not the way of many of the common people, who after having prayed a quick Afternoon Prayer on Sabbaths and holidays spread out over the courtyards in the cool of the day and begin to sadden the Sabbath Spirit with laughter and light-headedness, things which are bad and bitter as hemlock for the body and soul and besmirch everything sacred. Instead, as is fit, of greeting the Sabbath Spirit with words of Torah, which are more pleasant and more sweet than honey, by studying the laws of the Sabbath and its regulations, they greet her with the bitter food of idle matters and mockery and laughter and light-headedness, until they bring the Sabbath Spirit, the darling daughter of God, to the verge of tears. She cries that there is none to lead her, and none to take her by the hand.

Woe to the poor daughter exiled from her father's table! Her face is blacker than soot, her glow has waned, her glory passed away, and she is as one who flees with her hand to her head, dressed in black and swathed in black, crying, "Where shall I take my shame from before my Father who is in heaven?" Woe to those who act thus! Alas for them, for the Spirit will scream in her pangs to her Father who is in heaven, crying, "I have been zealous of the honor of your Name, because the house of Israel has deserted the Sabbath of your sanctity. I shall not continue to see their faces; I shall go and return to my first place, for it was better for me then than now." Now if the portion of the light-headed is bad and bitter on the other Sabbaths, how much worse is it on the "Sabbath of Return"! For the Sabbath will rise to accuse, rather then

to defend them; it will recall their early and late iniquities,
and will awaken the harsh quality of divine justice, and will
bring no remedy. He who guards his soul will stay far from
these men, and will sanctify this Sabbath more than all other
Sabbaths, in the Torah of God and in the pure fear of God
all the day. Then the Sabbath will defend him, that he may
issue innocent in the judgment and be inscribed in the book
of good life and of peace. [Hemdat Yamim]

YOUR RIGHTEOUSNESS IS EVERLASTING

There are some who say that one ought not to recite the
prayer beginning "Your righteousness is everlasting" during
the Afternoon Prayer, because it contains the phrase "your
judgments are a great abyss," and we are pleading with God,
"Do not enter into judgment with us"—asking him to judge
us with more than justice. [Maharil]

There are others [Rema, Orah Hayyim, No. 602, Biure
Hagra] who say that, on the contrary, one ought to recite this
prayer, as it is said in the Talmud (Arakhin 8b): "Were it
not for your righteousness like a mighty mountain, who
could stand before your judgments?" Such is the Ashkenazic
custom, even when the eve of Yom Kippur falls on the day
after "the Sabbath of Return." Neither the Sayings of the
Fathers, nor the series of Psalms beginning "Bless the Lord,
O my soul" are recited, because the rabbi expounds at that
time, and one must be free to listen to his sermon. [Siddur
Rabbi Yaabetz, Shaar ha-Matarah]

SERMON

It is the custom in all the Diaspora of Israel for the rabbi of
the city to expound in the main House of Prayer on the laws
and legends, the morality and the subjects of Teshuvah on

that Sabbath, in order to tell the folk the punishment for transgression, and to set their hearts to meditating Teshuvah.

The admonisher must choose his words so as not to attack Israel, and certainly not to disparage them. Let him take to heart the fact that Gideon saved Israel because he spoke in their behalf. Our sages, of blessed memory, said the same when they said that the Blessed One does not wish Israel to be accused, nor have it said they are iniquitous. Isaiah the prophet, peace be upon him, was punished for saying, "And I dwell in the midst of a people of unclean lips" (Isa. 6:5). Further, it is said in the Midrash Tanhuma on Genesis 32:4: "You may blame yourself, not Israel, who said 'We will do,' before they said 'We will hear,' at Mount Sinai, and who declare the unity of My name twice every day." [Devash le-Fi]

For this reason, let the admonishers who come to admonish Israel be careful to speak softly, and indirectly and respectfully, so as not to arouse the quality of divine justice against the people of Israel, lest his judgment fall on the clean and the unclean alike, and cause loss and harm, God forbid! [Kav ha-Yashar XLIII]

There is a tale about an admonisher who came to Tiktin and spoke words of admonition. The Gaon Rabbi Meir of Tiktin burst into tears and said to the admonisher, "Why have you shamed me publicly, and broken the rule against shaming one's fellow man in public?"

Said he to him, "God forbid, rabbi! I was not speaking of you."

Cried the rabbi, "But *they* are all righteous! And who of them could have sinned if not I?" [Shemen ha-Tov]

When the Maggid Rabbi Yehiel Mikhal of Zlotchov [18th-

19th cent.] used to preach and admonish the folk, he would cover his face and turning toward the Ark would say, "Master of the universe, lo, your folk are perfect and worthy, and eager to do your will. Now the reason why I am speaking against them is for the sake of the honor of your Name— that they be even stronger in keeping your commandments." [Agra de-Khallah]

Just as the admonisher is commanded to say nothing in his sermon to shame the transgressors, so he is commanded not to speak boastfully lest he grow proud, God forbid!

A TALE

It is related of Rabbi Heshel [18th–19th cent.] that he had an admonisher who stood watch over him even during his sermon, and when he would recognize anything at all unseemly in any sentiment of Rabbi Heshel's, he would admonish him in the presence of the entire congregation. Rabbi Heshel would accept the admonition and stop in the middle of his sermon. [Tikkun Hatzot, No. 112]

A SERMON

Once the righteous Rabbi Ezekiel of Shenyava [19th cent.] happened to be in the city of Ohel. He ordered the announcement made that he would deliver a sermon in the House of Prayer. All the city gathered and came. He ascended the pulpit and said: Listen, my masters: Once I delivered a sermon in this very place, and did not have heaven altogether in mind. Now it is a great sin to mix unseemly intentions into a sermon, and I wish to do Teshuvah. Our sages, of blessed memory, have said, "The sign of complete Teshuvah is when the same transgression comes to the hand of the transgressor in the same place where he first committed it, and he avoids

it" (Yoma 86b). Therefore, I have come to do Teshuvah in
this very place. And I beg the Holy One, blessed be he, to
forgive me.—They say there was a great self-awakening
among the folk because of this sermon, because people saw
how far Teshuvah extends. [Mekor Hayyim]

IT IS GOOD FOR THE PREACHER

It is good for the preacher to pray a short prayer before the
sermon, so that he will not feel self-satisfied, and so fall into
the sin of pride [Kav ha-Yashar XLIII]. Such was the custom
of Rabbi Heshel, of blessed memory, who when he rose to
preach publicly used first to recite verses from the Book of
Job (20:6–9) which subdue a man's heart: "Though his ex-
cellency mount up to the heavens, and his head reach unto
the clouds; yet he shall perish for ever like his own dung;
they that have seen him shall say: 'Where is he?' He shall
fly away as a dream, and shall not be found; yea, he shall be
chased away as a vision of the night. The eye which saw him
shall see him no more; neither shall his place any more behold him."

THE TORAH OF TRUTH

Once the righteous Rabbi Berish of Oshpitzin [Auschwitz;
18th–19th cent.] expounded on the "Sabbath of Return" in
the House of Prayer. There was a visitor there from Moravia.
Now it is the custom of the Ashkenazim to dispute with the
rabbi during his sermon; a custom which has been done
away with in the country of Poland, because it is an en-
couragement to the will to evil. For lo, if the disputant wishes
to clear up a matter he can follow the rabbi home and dispute with him there, and not dispute with him here in public. The visitor interrupted the rabbi with a question during
his sermon, and the rabbi replied. Then the rabbi lowered

his face to the prayer stand, and stood so for a short while. Afterward, he raised his head and said, "He who does not study Torah for its own sake can be pushed over by a fly. But he who studies Torah for its own sake cannot be moved by all the kings of the East and the West. For lo, all his words declare that the Lord is God, and that is the absolute truth." [Seva Ratzon]

HOMILIES FOR THE SABBATH OF RETURN

"Return, O Israel, unto the Lord thy God; for thou hast stumbled in thine iniquity" (Hos. 14:2); "Shall the horn be blown in a city, and the people not tremble? Shall evil befall a city, and the Lord hath not done it?" (Amos 3:16)—like a country that was suffering under an invasion of troops. But there was one old man who kept warning all the inhabitants of that country; all who listened to him were saved, and all who did not listen were killed by the troops. Thus it is written: "So thou, son of man, I have set thee a watchman unto the house of Israel; therefore, when thou shalt hear the word at My mouth, warn them from Me. When I say unto the wicked: O wicked man, thou shalt surely die, and thou dost not speak to warn the wicked from his way; that wicked man shall die in his iniquity, but his blood will I require at thy hand. Nevertheless, if thou warn the wicked of his way to turn from it, and he turn not from his way; he shall die in his iniquity" (Ezek. 33:7–9). Thus it is said: "Shall a horn be blown in a city?"—on Rosh ha-Shanah—"and the people not tremble?"—the people being Israel. "Shall evil befall a city, and the Lord hath not done it?"—the Holy One, blessed be he, does not desire the death of the wicked, as it is said: "Say unto them: As I live, saith the Lord God, I have no pleasure in the death of the wicked, but that the wicked turn

from his way and live" (Ezek. 33:11). My people, what do
I beseech of you, except to "turn ye, turn ye, from your evil
ways; for why will ye die, O house of Israel?" (*ibid*.). There
are some who derive the same sense from the text: "For thus
saith the Lord unto the house of Israel: Seek ye Me, and live"
(Amos 5:4). My people, what do I beseech of you, says God,
but to seek me and live. Therefore, Hosea (14:2) warns
Israel and says to them, "Return, O Israel, unto the Lord thy
God." [Pesikta de-Rav Kahana, Shuvah]

Wisdom was asked: The sinner, what of his punishment?
Said she to those who asked: "The soul that sinneth, it shall
die" (Ezek. 18:20). The Torah was asked: The sinner, what
of his punishment? Said she to those who asked: Let him
bring a guilt-offering, and he will be atoned for;—as it is
written, "And it shall be accepted for him to make atonement
for him" (Lev. 1:4). The Holy One, blessed be he, was asked:
The sinner, what of his punishment? Said he to those who
asked: Let him do Teshuvah, and he will be atoned for;—as
it is said, "Good and upright is the Lord; therefore, doth He
instruct sinners in the way" (Ps. 25:8). My children, what
do I beseech of you, says God, but to seek me and live. Said
Rabbi Phineas: Why is he good? Becaues he is upright. Why
is he upright? Because he is good. "Therefore, doth He instruct sinners in the way." That is, he instructs them in the
way to do Teshuvah. Therefore, Hosea warns Israel and says,
"Return, O Israel." [*Ibid*.]

Rabbi Judah bar Simon said: "Return, O Israel, unto the
Lord thy God," even if you have denied the principle of God's
existence.

Rabbi Eleazar said: It is the way of the world that when
a man insults his fellow in public and after a time wishes to
be reconciled with him, the latter says, You insulted me in

public, and now wish to be reconciled when we are alone.
Get the men before whom you insulted me, and I will be
reconciled with you.—But not the Holy One, blessed be he.
For though a man stand and blaspheme and revile him in
the market place, the Holy One, blessed be he, says to him:
Do Teshuvah when we are alone, and I shall accept you.
[*Ibid.*]

Another interpretation: "Return, O Israel, unto the Lord
thy God." A king's son was at a distance of a hundred days'
journey from his father. Said his friends to him, "Return to
your father." He said to them, "I cannot." His father sent to
him and said, "Go as far as you are able, and I shall come the
rest of the way to you." Thus, the Holy One, blessed be he,
said to Israel (Mal. 3:7): "Return unto Me, and I will return
unto you." [Pesikta Rabbati, Shuvah Yisrael]

Another interpretation: "Return, O Israel." Teshuvah is
dear to the Holy One, blessed be he, for he abrogates his own
words for the sake of Teshuvah. How? He wrote in the
Torah: "When a man taketh a wife, and marrieth her, then
it cometh to pass, if she find no favor in his eyes, because he
hath found some unseemly thing in her, that he writeth her
a bill of divorcement, and giveth it in her hand, and sendeth
her out of his house, and she departeth out of his house, and
goeth and becometh another man's wife, and the latter husband hateth her, and writeth her a bill of divorcement, and
giveth it in her hand, and sendeth her out of his house; or if
the latter husband die, who took her to be his wife; her
former husband, who sent her away, may not take her again
to be his wife, after that she is defiled" (Deut. 24:1–4). But
the Holy One, blessed be he, does not do so. Despite the fact
that Israel deserted him and served another, "and they for-
sook the Lord, and served Him not" (Judg. 10:6), he said to

them: Do Teshuvah and come to me and I will accept you. Jeremiah makes it explicit: "If a man put away his wife, and she go from him, and become another man's, may he return unto her again? Will not that land be greatly polluted? But thou hast played the harlot with many lovers; and wouldest thou yet return to Me? Saith the Lord" (Jer. 3:1). Come, and I will accept you. "Return, O Israel, unto the Lord thy God." [*Ibid.*]

Another interpretation: "Return, O Israel." If a man has done complete Teshuvah, the transgressions he formerly committed are not held and mentioned against him. Whence do we learn this? Isaiah makes it explicit: "And the former things shall not be remembered, nor come into mind" (Isa. 65:17). Teshuvah is dearer even than sacrifices. Samuel the prophet says (I Sam. 15:22): "Behold, to obey is better than sacrifice, and to hearken than the fat of rams." [*Ibid.*]

Rabbi Abba bar Yudan said: Whatever makes an animal ritually unfit makes a man ritually fit. The Torah declares ritually unfit that animal which is "blind or broken, or maimed, or having a wen" (Lev. 22:22). But the Torah declares fit the man who has "a broken and a contrite heart" (Ps. 51:19).

Rabbi Alexandri said: If a common man uses a broken vessel, it is considered a disgrace. But not the Holy One, blessed be he. All his vessels are broken. "The Lord is nigh unto them that are of a broken heart" (Ps. 34:19); "Who healeth the broken in heart" (Ps. 147:3); "A broken and a contrite heart" (Ps. 51:19). Therefore, Hosea warned Israel, and said to them, "Return, O Israel." [Pesikta de-Rav Kahana, Shuvah]

Another interpretation: "Return, O Israel." Five things bring about redemption: A man is redeemed by troubles: "In thy distress, when all these things are come upon thee. . . ." (Deut. 4:30). And by the end: ". . . in the end of

days. . . ." And by Teshuvah: ". . . Thou wilt return to the
Lord thy God. . . ." And by compassion: ". . . for the Lord
thy God is a merciful God. . . ." And by the aiding merit
of the patriarchs: ". . . nor forget the covenant of thy fathers." Now Teshuvah brings about both compassion and the
aiding merit of the patriarchs, for the Torah says, "thou wilt
return to the Lord thy God, and hearken unto his voice"
(*ibid.*) and, immediately afterward, "for the Lord thy God
is a merciful God." Come, let us return to him, for we have
no God like him, who accepts us when we turn from sin.
[Pesikta Rabbati, Shuvah Yisrael]

THY GOD

"Return, O Israel, unto the Lord thy God." The meaning
is, return *until* the Lord, that is, the Creator, becomes "thy"
that is, *your own* God. [Avodat Yisrael]

v. The Thirteen Qualities

PENITENTIAL PRAYERS

The eighth of Tishri, which is the eighth of the ten days of
Teshuvah, is called the "Thirteen Qualities," after the hymn
which Rabbi Amittai [ben Shefatiah, ca. 900] composed on
the thirteen divine qualities. People rise earlier to pray on
that day than at other times.

The reason why we rise slightly earlier on that day than
at other times and recite the Thirteen Qualities and many
penitential prayers is because on that day Abraham, our
father, peace be upon him, departed to sacrifice Isaac, his son.
For, lo, "on the third day," which was Yom Kippur, "Abraham lifted up his eyes, and saw the place afar off" (Gen.

22:4). Thus, he left the day before the eve of Yom Kippur and on that day much compassion is awakened on high because of the merit of the Binding of Isaac. We rise early in order to bring up the remembrance of the early rising of Abraham. We mention the Thirteen Qualities of compassion, and recite many prayers, for that day is a day of good will for the Omnipresent. [Nehmad mi-Zahav]

There are places where people are careful to recite the penitential prayers, the Thirteen Qualities, on a day on which there is a reading of the Torah. Thus, if Yom Kippur falls on Monday, they recite the Thirteen Qualities on Thursday. If Yom Kippur falls on Thursday, they recite the Thirteen Qualities on Monday.

MAKING CANDLES FOR YOM KIPPUR

It is the custom of the women of Germany to prepare candles for Yom Kippur and for the House of Prayer on the eighth of Tishri, the anniversary of the first day of the dedication of the Temple. [Kippur Tamim]

It is the women's custom to measure the graveyard with thread that is made into wicks. Then they dip the thread in wax and make large heavy candles, to burn twenty-four hours, from one evening to the next. Those who can, make their candles out of white wax, which is finer and more decorative, and burns well. While they are making the candles they recite many prayers and supplications and mention the names of dead kinsmen and kinswomen over every thread, especially if they were pious, they being able to plead for those who are still alive. If the eve of Yom Kippur falls on Sunday, they make the candles on Thursday because they cannot make the candles on the eve of the Sabbath out of respect for the Sabbath. [Mateh Efrayim]

Why was the making of the candles entrusted to the women? In order that they should engage in the good deed, to make amends for the harm they originally caused, for by eating of the Tree of Knowledge Eve brought death unto the world, and put out the light of the world. [Shaar ha-Melekh]

TWO KINDS OF CANDLES

There are two kinds of candles, "candles of health" and "candles of the soul." "Candles of health" are for those who are alive and, according to custom, only for those who are married, one candle for each couple. It is not the custom to make separate candles for sons and daughters, even if they are grown up, so long as they are not married. The "candles of the soul" are for dead parents, whether both are dead or only one—only one candle for both. A woman too can make this candle.

The "candles of health" are large and the "candles of the soul" are small. But they must be so made as to burn until the close of Yom Kippur. There are some whose custom it is to burn "candles of health" in the House of Prayer, and "candles of the soul" at home. But that is not the proper way, because they are ceremonial candles, and the place for them is the House of Prayer. [Mateh Efrayim]

THE RITUAL OF CASTING

It is the custom of many pious men in Galicia to go to a river to recite the Casting ritual on this day, and not on Rosh ha-Shanah [Devar Yom be-Yomo], since it is hard for them to walk at that time because of their physical weakness.

I have observed that it was the custom of my master, the mighty one in Israel, Rabbi Abraham Jacob of Sadagora

[19th cent.], to wait with the Casting ritual until the seventh of the ten days of Teshuvah, and on the night of the eighth, after the Casting ritual, he would recite the Thirteen Qualities. As I understood it, he did so because the first six days were still in the domain of Rosh ha-Shanah, and those from the seventh on in the domain of Yom Kippur. So he saw to it that he generally recited the Casting on the first day which was in the domain of Yom Kippur. [Binyan Shelomo]

THE COVENANT OF THE THIRTEEN QUALITIES

"And the Lord passed by before him, and proclaimed: The Lord, the Lord, God, merciful and gracious, long-suffering, and abundant in goodness and truth; keeping mercy unto the thousandth generation, forgiving iniquity and transgression and sin; and he will clear the guilt" (cf. Exod. 34:6–7). Said Rabbi Yohanan: If this were not a Writ, it would be impossible to say it—teaching us that the Holy One, blessed be he, wrapped himself in a robe like a Reader and showed Moses the order of the prayer. He said to him, "Whenever Israel sins, let them perform this service before me, and I shall forgive them."

"The Lord, the Lord"—I am he who is the Lord before a man sins, and I am he who shall be the Lord after a man sins and does Teshuvah.

"God, merciful and gracious." Said Rav Judah: God made a covenant with the Thirteen Qualities, that they are never to be rejected, as it is said (Deut. 34:10): "Behold, I make a covenant. . . ." [Rosh ha-Shanah 17b]

Rabbi Hama bar Rabbi Hanina said: What is the meaning of the Writ, "After the Lord your God shall ye walk" (Deut. 13:5)? Could a man really walk after the Divine Presence, when it has been said, "For the Lord thy God is a devouring fire" (Deut. 4:29)? But the meaning is: Walk in the way of the qualities of the Holy One, blessed be he. As he is gracious and compassionate, so you must be gracious and compassionate. [Sotah 14a; Shabbat 133b]

When Moses rose to heaven, he found the Holy One, blessed be he, seated writing the words "long-suffering" in the Torah. Moses said to Him, "Master of the universe—do you mean long-suffering toward the righteous?" Said He to him, "Even toward the wicked as well." Said Moses to Him, "Let the wicked perish." Said He to him, "You shall see which you desire."

When Israel sinned, the Holy One said to Moses, "And did you not say to me 'long-suffering toward the righteous only'?" He said to Him, "Master of the universe, and did you not tell me, 'Even toward the wicked as well.'" [Sanhedrin 111a]

"Forgiving iniquity and transgression." Raba said: Every man who passes over the right to retaliate—all his sins are passed over, as it is said, "That pardoneth the iniquity and passeth over the transgression" (Mic. 7:18). Whose iniquity is pardoned? His who passes over the transgression against himself. [Rosh ha-Shanah 17a]

"Forgiving iniquity." Rabbi Huna said, in the name of Rabbi Abbahu: There is no forgetting by the Holy One, blessed be he, as it were, but he assumes forgetfulness for the sake of Israel. What is the reason for thinking so? It is written (Exod. 34:6): "forgetting iniquities"; and David said the same (Ps. 85:3): "Thou hast forgotten the iniquity of Thy people, Thou hast pardoned all their sin." [Yerushalmi, Sanhedrin X.1]

"Forgiving iniquity and transgression." Moses said to the Holy One, blessed be he, "Master of the universe, when

Israel sin before you, and do Teshuvah, reckon their deliberate sins as errors." [Yoma 36b]

"He will clear the guilt." It has been taught: Rabbi
Eleazar says: It is impossible to say, "He will clear the guilt,"
for it also says, "He will not clear the guilt" (cf. Exod. 34:7);
and it is impossible to say, "He will not clear the guilt," for
it also says, "He will clear the guilt." How explain this? He
clears the guilt of those who turn in Teshuvah, but does not
clear the guilt of those who do not turn. [*Ibid.* 86a]

"Teaching us that the Holy One, blessed be he, wrapped
himself in a robe like a Reader" (Rosh ha-Shanah 17b).
Rabbi Moses ben Maimon [12th cent.] wrote: "This is
an allusion to the hidden and inscrutable quality of God.
For, although man knows God, be blessed, from the point of
view of his actions, alluded to in the Thirteen Qualities,
nevertheless, his essence cannot be perceived by any living
thing." [Midreshe ha-Torah, Ki Tisa]

"Whenever Israel sins, let them perform this service before me and I shall forgive them" (Rosh ha-Shanah 17b).
Rabbi Moses Alshekh [16th cent.] wrote in the name of the
author of "Livnat ha-Sappir": "It was not said, 'Let them
say this service before me' but 'Let them *perform* this service
before me'; for forgiveness does not depend on words alone,
but on performance as well. If a man makes his qualities
resemble the qualities of the Holy One, blessed be he—his
iniquities are forgiven him." [Etz Yosef on En Yaakov]

"The Lord, the Lord." I am he who is the Lord before a
man sins, and I am he who shall be the Lord after a man sins
(Rosh ha-Shanah 17a). Rabbi Samuel Eliezer Edels [16th–
17th cent.] raised a question: "What need is there for compassion before a man sins?" But it is cited in the "Duties of
the Heart" [11th cent.] that one of the righteous said to his

disciples: If you had no sin, I should be afraid of that in you which is greater than sin, pride. For pride, which is more serious than sin, is to be found in the man who thinks he has not sinned.—From which we learn that even before he sins a man certainly needs compassion to atone for a proud heart. [See Hekhal ha-Berakhah, Kedoshim]

vi. The Eve of Yom Kippur

PENITENTIAL PRAYERS

The order of the eve of Yom Kippur is as follows: There are places where many penitential prayers are recited, as on the eve of Rosh ha-Shanah. This is the Ashkenazic custom. There are other places where only three penitential prayers are recited; all according to the local custom. [Maharil]

In Aden it is customary to blow the ram's-horn on the eve of Yom Kippur. [Even Sappir, Bet Aden]

THE CUSTOM OF KAPPAROT

Immediately after the penitential prayers, before daylight, the order of Kapparot is performed; and there are some who perform the order of Kapparot during the night.

It is the custom for men to take roosters and women to take hens. Pregnant women take both roosters and hens, since they may bear male children. White fowls are preferred, in keeping with the saying (Isa. 1:18): "Though your sins be as scarlet, they shall be as white as snow." [Rema, Orah Hayyim, Magen Avraham, No. 605]

At any rate, one ought not to try to obtain white fowls, for that is a heathenish practice. But, if there happens to be

a white fowl in the lot, it ought to be preferred. [Bayit
Hadash]

THE ORDER OF KAPPAROT

One takes the Kapparah in his right hand and recites, "A
life for a life," and then reads the passage in the prayer book
beginning, "The sons of man who sit in darkness and in the
shadow of death"; then one holds the Kapparah in one's left
hand, and lays one's right hand on the head of the fowl, and
swings it around one's head, and says, "This is my substitute,
this is my exchange, this is my atonement. This fowl will go
to death, and I shall enter upon a good and long life and
peace." One repeats the ceremony three times, and lays his
hand on the head of the fowl, and has it slaughtered at once.

IMMEDIATE SLAUGHTER

The slaughter of the Kapparah ought to take place immediately after one has swung and laid one's hand on the
fowl, like a sacrifice in the Temple. [Rema, Orah Hayyim,
No. 605]

The intestines are thrown onto a roof, or into a courtyard,
where the birds can reach them [Rema, Orah Hayyim,
No. 605], for it is the way of fowls to scavenge and eat worms
and creeping things [Levush], and their intestines are the
first receptacles for the scavenged food; hence, one ought
not to eat them [Elef ha-Magen]. Rabbi Simeon, the son of
Zemach Duran [14th–15th cent.], wrote: The reason why
people make it a custom to throw away the intestines of their
Kapparot on the eve of Yom Kippur is to show compassion
to the birds.—For it is fitting to show compassion to dumb
creatures, that we in turn may be shown compassion by
heaven [Ture Zahav]. The same is said in the Midrash:
"Take this for your guiding mark: If you show compassion

to your fellow, you will be shown compassion in turn." And it has been explained [Bayit Hadash]: Show compassion not only to your fellow, but to dumb creatures as well, as it is said (Ps. 145:9): "And His tender mercies are over all His works."

REDEEMING THE KAPPAROT

It is the custom to sell the Kapparot, and to give the money received for them to the poor. [Siddur Derekh ha-Hayyim]

Rabbi Jacob ben Moses ha-Levi [14th–15th cent.] expounded: There are places where the Kapparot themselves are given to the poor. But the custom in the Rhine district, where the price of the Kapparah is given to the poor, is a better one, for the poor man is not ashamed to accept the money. But when the poor man is given the fowl itself, he says to himself: First this man cast his iniquities onto this fowl, then he humiliated me by giving it to me. [Maharil]

CUSTOMS FAR AND NEAR

The custom of Kapparot is not the same everywhere, and has not been the same at all times, nor has it always been performed with living animals.

It was the custom in olden times to braid baskets for each of the small children in the house, about fifteen or twenty days before Rosh ha-Shanah. The baskets were filled with dirt and animal manure and sowed with wheat, barley, Egyptian beans and peas. The plants grew about half a foot. Then each of the children would take his basket [on the eve of Rosh ha-Shanah] and swing it around his head seven times, and say, "This is instead of me, this is my exchange, this is my substitute," and throw it into a stream. [Otzar ha-Geonim, Yoma]

There are places where Kapparot is not known. Such is the case in Aden, and all the cities of Yemen [Nahlat Yosef II], where they know nothing of the custom. There is a story about Rabbi Jacob Saphir ha-Levi [19th cent.] who asked the householder with whom he was staying to buy him a fowl for Kapparot, and the latter did not know what he meant, because they do not practice this custom in Yemen [Bet Aden]. For the Yemenites do not accept any custom and law which Rabbi Moses ben Maimon [12th cent.] did not favor. Nor is this true only of Yemen, for the majority of the inhabitants of Constantinople do not practice this custom, either. [Sede Hemed]

Some of the great early sages cried out against the custom of Kapparot and wished to do away with it. Rabbi Moses ben Nachman[13th cent.]forbade it as a heathen practice [Orhot Hayyim, Hilkhot Erev Yom Kippurim] and Rabbi Joseph Karo [16th cent.] wrote to the same effect in the Shulhan Arukh [Orah Hayyim, No. 605]: The custom of performing the ritual of Kapparot by slaughtering fowls on the eve of Yom Kippur to represent the males, and by reciting verses, is a practice that ought to be prevented.

Despite the fact that the early sages inveighed against Kapparot and wished to abolish it as a heathen practice, it has continued strong, being viewed as of great antiquity. [Rema, Orah Hayyim, No. 605]

The man who does not observe the custom of Kapparot ought to make atonement by giving a sum of money to charity equal to the value of the Kapparot. [Orhot Hayyim, quoting Yafe la-Lev]

After the act of Kapparot, the Morning Prayer is said.

CHARITY FOR THE LIVING AND THE DEAD

After leaving the House of Prayer, it is customary to visit the graveyard, there to distribute charity to the poor.

LESS STUDY

It was said of Rabban Yohanan ben Zakkai that in all his days he never spoke of secular things, and never walked four cubits without studying Torah and without wearing phylacteries, and no one ever came to the House of Study before him, and he never fell asleep in the House of Study for a long or a short period, and never meditated in the filthy alleys, and never left the House of Study while any other person was there, and never was found sitting silent, but was always sitting and studying. No one but he ever opened the door for his disciples, and he never said anything that he had not heard from the mouth of his master; and he never said, "The time has come to leave the House of Study," except for the eve of Passover, and the eve of Yom Kippur. [Sukkah 28a]

It was said of Rabbi Akiba that never in all his days did he say in the House of Study, "It is time to stop studying," except for the eve of Passover, and the eve of Yom Kippur. He wished to leave early on the eve of Passover for the sake of the children, so that they would not fall asleep before the Seder; and on the eve of Yom Kippur, to feed the children. [Pesahim 109a]

EATING AND DRINKING ON THE EVE OF YOM KIPPUR

"And ye shall afflict your souls in the ninth day . . . " (Lev. 23:32). But do we fast on the ninth? Do we not fast on the tenth? But the purpose of this verse is to tell us that he who eats and drinks on the ninth and fasts on the tenth [Sheiltot, Vezot ha-Berakhah], is considered by the Writ as fasting on both the ninth and the tenth days. [Rosh ha-Shanah 9a]

The Writ says: "And ye shall afflict your souls in the ninth day" (Lev. 23:32). I call eating on the ninth fasting. That being so, that man is best who eats and drinks a great deal [Rashi, *ad loc.*] to show that he accepts, delights and rejoices in Yom Kippur, because it was given to Israel as an occasion to make atonement. For since it is impossible to honor Yom Kippur proper by eating and drinking as other holidays are honored, it must be so honored the day before. [Bet Yosef, Tur Orah Hayyim, No. 604]

My brother, Rabbi Benjamin [de Pietosi, 13th cent.] interpreted the talmudic text: "He who eats and drinks on the ninth is considered by the Writ as fasting on both the ninth and the tenth days" (Yoma 81b)—as directed against the opinion held by the Sadducees, who fasted on the ninth day as well. For the Scripture was given to be interpreted only by the sages, and the sages interpreted fasting on the ninth day to mean eating and drinking. [Shibbole ha-Leket, No. 307]

"And ye shall afflict your souls." The Torah uses the word "souls"; the meaning is that the affliction is laid on the soul, and not on the body, for the affliction of the soul is eating and the affliction of the body is fasting; the which are opposites. Therefore, the Writ says, "Ye shall afflict your souls," meaning to include both soul and body in one phrase. There is to be affliction for the body and for the soul (as it says soon after, "in your souls," meaning both body and soul), for the affliction of the soul consists in eating on the ninth, and the affliction of the body and its submission in fasting on the tenth.

The secret behind all this is that the man who is happy and of good heart in complete faith that the next day will be a day of forgiveness and atonement for the community of Israel and that his iniquities will be atoned for among theirs—happy in this faith, he eats and drinks. It is fitting to consider his feast as much of a virtue as though he had fasted, for he obtains as much merit from his joy in observing the commandment of eating as from his fasting on the next day. [Yesh Sakhar]

Our sages, of blessed memory, said: "He who eats and drinks on the ninth is considered by the Writ as fasting on both the ninth and the tenth days" (Yoma 81b). The explanation is that the man who can eat and drink on the ninth, after having considered the fact that he must stand before the Holy One, blessed be he, and give an accounting to him of all his acts and thoughts during the entire year—yet, believing that God in truth pardons and forgives, and that on this day shall atonement be made—with the strength of that confidence he eats on the eve of Yom Kippur—such a man, it was said in the Talmud, was considered as fasting on both the ninth and the tenth days. [Or Yesharim, quoting Moses of Kobrin]

THE SECRET BEHIND THE EATING AND DRINKING

It is known that eating is called a sacrifice, as it was said, "A man's table makes atonement for him" (Hagigah 27a), and fasting too is called a sacrifice, because a man sacrifices his fat and his blood when he fasts. But eating comes under the category of an ascending sacrifice; one, that is, which raises the lower rungs and the holy sparks and the sacred quality in the food. For, by taking into himself the power of food and its vital spirit, man can serve God with greater devotion. In this way, the holy sparks which are clothed in the dress of

food ascend, when a man is completely devoted to the name
of heaven, as it is written, "In all thy ways acknowledge
Him, and He will direct thy paths" (Prov. 3:6)—informing
us that nothing is remote from the service of the Blessed One.
On the contrary, by such eating man clings the more closely
to God; such eating is considered a sacrifice to God, because
he who does so raises the fragments of the inferior holiness to
their superior root, and adds devotion to the divine share
that is in him. The Creator, be blessed, takes great pleasure
in this, for the lower rungs draw nearer to him.

The secret behind the fast is that it comes under the category of a sacrifice and the superior realm's approach to the
inferior realm. For, by a man's having a broken heart and
one subdued to God, the root of the superior sanctity is
aroused to draw man near to God. But not every man merits
the ascent to such a rung. For lo, some people only eat to
satisfy their desire, and are left with their own vital spirit
unaffected by the vital spirit which they receive from the
food of the inferior realm, and they add no sanctity to their
souls by such eating. Besides, it is possible, yes almost certain,
that their eating further removes them from the Creator, be
blessed. On the other hand, he devises means so as not to
reject those who deserve being rejected, in order that every
superficial food eaten by all Israel may ascend to the superior
realm. For this purpose, he has set one day in the year aside,
the eve of Yom Kippur, as a day on which eating and drinking is considered to be doing a good deed. Even if a man's
eating should come under the category of superficial eating
simply to satisfy his desire, he is considered on the eve of Yom
Kippur as doing a good deed. By means of this superficial
eating, the superficial eatings of the entire year are enabled
to ascend to the superior realm.

Afterward comes Yom Kippur, which is the only day of fasting commanded by the Torah, a day of self-awakening when Teshuvah comes down from the superior realm to each and every one in Israel. For, even those who do not have the strength to awaken themselves without being awakened from on high, because they are on a very low rung and have not the virtue in themselves of awakening to Teshuvah—Teshuvah contracts itself, and comes down to them from the superior realm, in order to cause them to awaken and raise their fragments of divinity to the Creator, be blessed. That is the secret behind the descending of the sacrifice; by virtue of the drawing near of the Teshuvah from the superior realm, man is brought nearer to God, be blessed. Because the Teshuvah from the superior realm needs to contract itself on Yom Kippur in order to draw near to all Israel, we were commanded to fast on that day, fasting coming under the category of an approach by the superior to the inferior realm. For the superior realm to draw near to the inferior, it is necessary for the inferior to draw near to the superior. Therefore, the Holy One, be blessed, commanded us to eat on the eve of Yom Kippur, eating coming under the category of the inferior's approach to the superior. By both these means, that is to say, by eating on the eve of Yom Kippur and fasting on Yom Kippur, all the elements of both realms unite and all Israel are sanctified and draw near to their Creator. [Meor Enayim; see Derekh Hasidim]

THE ORDER OF THE NOON MEAL

There are some whose custom it is to break bread as on a holiday and to recite the blessing [Kaf ha-Hayyim; see Shene Luhot ha-Berit]. It is a custom [Sefer ha-Matamim] to shape the loaves in the form of wings, because Israel are like angels on Yom Kippur, as the Midrash expresses it; and it is written of the angels that they each had six wings (Isa. 6:2).

In Lithuania it is the custom on the eve of Yom Kippur to decorate the loaves with the figure of a ladder, as an allusion to the ascent of the prayers, after the hymn beginning, "Let our supplication ascend." The piece of bread over which the blessing is recited is then dipped in honey, and the same is true at the beginning of the Concluding Meal.

It is right to eat fish. [Tur Orah Hayyim, No. 603]

Despite the fact that eating on the eve of Yom Kippur has been praised as a virtue, one ought to eat only light dishes that are easy to digest, so as not to be full and in high spirits during the prayer on Yom Kippur [Levush; Ture Zahav]

Every man ought to sit down to this meal with great humility, and not allow himself to become angry at anything, in order not to come into temptation. Rather, one ought to prepare calmly for the holy day, and beseech compassion and help from the Holy One, blessed be he; for if he does not help, one cannot succeed.

APPEASING ONE'S FELLOW

Yom Kippur makes atonement for transgressions committed in man's relations with the Omnipresent; Yom Kippur does not make atonement for transgressions in men's relationships with one another, until the transgressor has appeased his fellow. This was expounded by Rabbi Eleazar ben Azariah, who said, "It is written, 'From all your sins before the Lord shall you be clean' (Lev. 16:30). Yom Kippur makes atonement for transgressions committed in man's relations with the Omnipresent. But Yom Kippur does not make

atonement for transgressions in men's relationships with one
another, until the transgressor has appeased his fellow."
[Mishnah Yoma VIII.9]

Rabbi Isaac said: He who has caused his comrade vexation,
even if only by speech, must appease him, as it is said, "My
son, if thou art become surety for thy neighbor, if thou hast
struck thy hands for a stranger—thou art snared by the words
of thy mouth . . .—do this now, my son, and deliver thyself, seeing thou art come into the hand of thy neighbor; go,
humble thyself, and urge thy neighbor" (Prov. 6:1-3). The
meaning is: If he has a money claim on you open the palm
of your hand to him, and if not, send many friends to speak
to him for you.

Rav Hisda said: He ought to appease his fellow before
three rows of three men each, as it is said (Job 33:27): "He
cometh before men, and saith: I have sinned, and perverted
that which was right, and it profited me not."

Rabbi Yose bar Hanina said: He who beseeches his injured
fellow to pardon him ought not to beseech him more than
three times, as it is said, "I *pray* thee, *forgive*, I *pray* thee now,
the transgression of the servant of the God of thy father"
(Gen. 50:17). If his fellow has died, he shall bring ten men
and stand them at the grave, and say, "I have sinned to the
Lord, the God of Israel, and to this man [so and so] whom
I have injured." [Yoma 87a]

Rabbi Eleazar said in the name of Rabbi Hoshaya: "From
all your sins shall ye be clean before the Lord" (Lev. 16:30).
Yom Kippur makes atonement for the sin which only God
can recognize. [Keritot 25b]

Blessed be his Name and exalted the remembrance of him
who holds Israel dear, and who gave them the ten days of
Teshuvah. For even the Teshuvah which an individual does

during that period is accepted as a community Teshuvah. Therefore, all Israel must employ Teshuvah and make peace with and pardon one another on the eve of Yom Kippur, that their Teshuvah and their prayer may be accepted by the Holy One, blessed be he, in peace and with affection. For we find that great is the power of peace; for even the Holy One, blessed be he, paraphrased for its sake, as it is said, "And Sarah laughed within herself, saying; 'After I am waxed old shall I have pleasure, my lord being old?'" (cf. Gen. 18:12). "And the Lord said unto Abraham: Wherefore did Sarah laugh, saying: Shall I of a surety bear a child, who am old?" (Gen. 18:12–13). She said "my lord being old," and the Holy One, blessed be he, paraphrased: "I . . . who am old." He said this in order not to cause enmity between Abraham and Sarah.

Rabbi Eleazar said: Great is peace, for even if Israel is worshiping idols, if they keep the peace and are united, the quality of divine justice will not touch them, as it is said, "Ephraim is a company of idolators, let them alone" (Hos. 4:17). Rabbi Eleazar also said: Great is peace, for even the blessing of the priests concludes with peace, as it is said, "And give thee peace" (Num. 6:26). Even in the world to come, when the Holy One, blessed be he, will return to Jerusalem and will return all the exiled into her midst, he will return them for peace, as it is said, "Pray for the peace of Jerusalem" (Ps. 122:6). The Writ also says (Isa. 68:12): "Behold, I will extend peace to her like a river."

See how great is the reward of him who makes peace between men. It is written, "Thou shalt build the altar of the Lord thy God of unhewn stones" (Deut. 27:6). Now, if stones that cannot hear and cannot see and cannot smell and cannot speak are saved by the Writ from the sword, because they make peace between men through the sacrifices which are offered upon them, and it is proclaimed of them, "Thou shalt lift up no iron tool upon them" (Deut. 27:5)—how much more is this true of man, who can hear and see and smell and speak, when he makes peace among his fellow men! [Pesikta Rabbati, Shuvah Yisrael, addendum]

Let our master teach us: If one has quarreled with his comrade, how can he make atonement on Yom Kippur?

Thus have our masters taught (Mishnah Yoma VIII.9): "Yom Kippur makes atonement for transgressions committed in man's relationship with the Omnipresent; Yom Kippur does not make atonement for transgressions in men's relationships with one another, until the transgressor has appeased his fellow." Now if a man goes to appease his fellow, and his fellow will not be appeased, what shall he do? Rabbi Samuel bar Nahman said, Let him bring ten men, and stand them in a line, and say before them, "There was a quarrel between so and so and myself, and I have tried to appease him, but he has obstinately not wished to be appeased. I now beg his pardon." And whence do we learn that this is what he has to say? From the verse: "He cometh before men, and saith: I have sinned, and perverted that which was right, and it profited me not" (Job 33:27). Then the Holy One, blessed be he, seeing him humble himself, makes atonement for his transgressions. For as long as a man continues in his wilfulness he is not pardoned. You must know that so long as Job held out against his comrades, and his comrades against him, the quality of divine justice was directed against him. We find that Job said to them, "But now they that are younger than I have me in derision" (Job 30:1). And they said to him, "With us are both the gray-headed and the very aged men" (Job 15:10). But when he appeased them and besought compassion upon them, the Holy One, blessed be he, returned to him in that hour, as it is said, "And the Lord returned the fortune of Job" (Job 42:10). When? "When he prayed for his friends" (*ibid.*). Thus says the verse (Deut. 13:18): "And He will show thee mercy, and will have compassion upon thee."

Rabbi Yose ben Durmaskit said: Take as your guiding sign: Whenever you have compassion on your fellow, the Holy One, blessed be he, has compassion on you. Abraham, because he sought compassion for Abimelech and prayed in his behalf, at once took his reward, as it is said: "And Abraham prayed unto God; and God healed Abimelech, and his wife, and his maid-servants; and they bore children" (Gen. 20:17). And what was the reward he took? That his wife was remembered and gave birth to a son, as it is said (Gen. 21:1): "And the Lord remembered Sarah as He had said, and the Lord did unto Sarah as He had spoken." [Pesikta Rabbati, Harninu]

All Israel must appease one another, for if they do not, the Holy One, blessed be he, will not forgive them. For lo, we have learned: Despite the fact that he brought his fellow all the sheep of Kedar, he will not be forgiven until he appeases him. If his fellow will not forgive him, he is called cruel, as it is said (Gen. 20:17), "And Abraham prayed unto God" (Baba Kamma 92a). We know that Abraham was a compassionate man, and he who does not act as Abraham did does not come of Abraham's seed, and, not being of Abraham's seed, is a cruel man in truth, as it is said, "And He will give thee mercy, and will have compassion upon thee" (Deut. 13:18). That is to say, when God will give you mercy so that you will have mercy on his creatures, he will have mercy on you, "as He hath sworn unto thy fathers" (*ibid.*), who were merciful men. And every man must further appease his fellow after his fellow has forgiven him, beseeching him to pray before the Creator, be exalted, to forgive him, as Abraham did for Abimelech. [Sefer ha-Minhagot]

"Yom Kippur does not make atonement for transgressions committed in men's relationships with one another." Our teacher, Rabbi Samuel Garmison [18th cent.], wrote that the Omnipresent shares in the transgressions that men commit in their relationships with one another which are also in part transgressions against the Omnipresent. For example, if a man insults his fellow, lo, he has transgressed against the commandment, "Thou shalt love thy neighbor as thyself" (Lev. 19:18). There are many such examples. So long as a man has not appeased his fellow, even that part of the transgression which is a transgression in his relationship with God is not atoned for. [Birke Yosef]

The Kabbalists wrote: "The prayer of him who does not banish hatred on Yom Kippur is not heard." [Kaf ha-Hayyim, Jerusalem]

Let not this matter be light in the eyes of any man in Israel, for it is the cornerstone of atonement on Yom Kippur, and of the acceptance of prayers, and of our own speedy redemption. The same is true of its opposite, God keep us from it, enmity, that is, which is like gall and wormwood. For, there is no doubt that this quality, enmity, hinders the coming of our Messiah, and is the reason why our prayers are not accepted, while we remain in exile, where there is no peace in our midst. For in truth, it is because of our iniquities which are great that many evils and misfortunes daily fall on our heads, there being none who seek to know why God acted thus to his preferred people whom he chose for his inheritance. It is because of this that we pass from downfall to downfall, and every day is more accursed than that which comes before it. There is no doubt that God is righteous and it is we who have done wickedly; our sufferings proceed from our own hand, and not God's. For every man walks after the stubbornness of his own heart and does what is right in his own eyes, the righteous and the wicked, the great and the small alike. The divisions and cleavages that exist among us are public and well known.

For we do not behave like members of one nation, having one tongue, as we should; for indeed do we not all have one Father, and did not one God create us all? Then why are we not united, all the seed of Israel? How much more ought we to be one, dwelling as we do in the land of our foes, literally like one lamb among thousands and tens of thousands of wolves! Is it not enough that all the peoples hate us—why should we hate one another too? Now a fire doth issue from the rock of our division, and there is none to extinguish. On the contrary; every man hastens to add fuel to it until it grows into a great consuming fire. May God who is good make atonement for us and remove our heart of stone and renew a steadfast spirit in our midst and remove hatred and contention from us, until we be united in the land. [Hemdat Yamim]

It is the custom to go to visit one's friends on the eve of Yom Kippur to beseech their forgiveness, though there is generally no need to do so, for one has not sinned against one's friends, and even if one has sinned against them, it was unintentional, and love covers all sins; their enmity must certainly have left them already. Yet being an ancient custom, it is worthy of respect, for there is no knowing what feelings are stored up in the hearts of one's friends.

I do not say that one ought not to go to visit one's friends, but rather that people ought not to neglect an act that is both proper and an obligation, to wit, that of visiting the person whom one knows for a certainty one has sinned against. And if he will not do so, you ought to send many friends to plead with him. Even if it is the other person who has sinned, one ought to go to that person and make peace with him.

But people who turn what is nonessential into the essential, and repudiate the essential, the forgiving and being forgiven by one's enemies, are, I think, in the wrong. [Yosif Ometz]

IMMERSION

It is a fine custom to immerse oneself on the eve of Yom Kippur, in order to be clean on Yom Kippur both within and without; within, by doing Teshuvah and confessing one's sins, in order to be acceptable before our Father who is in heaven, and without, by washing and bathing, as it is said (Isa. 1:16), "Wash you, make you clean, put away the evil of your doings from before mine eyes" [Israel al-Nakawa, Menorat ha-Maor, Hilkhot Yom ha-Kippurim]. We have already learned in the Zohar [III. 214b] that we must bathe in a stream on the ninth of the month to purify ourselves.

Those who believe that the essential purpose of the ritual bath is purity do not require a confession before immersion, but those who believe that the purpose is Teshuvah do require such confession. Rabbi David ben Samuel ha-Levi [17th cent.], the author of Ture Zahav, wrote that it is the custom to do as Rabbi Isaac Luria [16th cent.] did, and make confession in the ritual bathhouse before immersion.

AT THE AFTERNOON PRAYER

After having immersed, one returns home, and puts on one's Sabbath clothes, and goes to the House of Prayer to pray the

Afternoon Prayer while it is still early. It is the custom for everyone to take with him the candles he made in honor of the day. They are brought to the Afternoon Prayer, despite the fact that they are not kindled until just before nightfall. This is done in order to be able to place them properly so that they will not fall, which is not possible after the Afternoon Prayer when everything is done in haste, in which one might place the candles hastily and they might fall and cause one to disturb his prayer on the holy day. It is customary to make long boxes and fill them with sand and stick the candles into them.

CHARITY

In most places it is the custom to distribute charity to the poor on the way to the House of Prayer for the Afternoon Prayer.

There are some places where charity platters are placed on the table where the Torah is read, and everyone gives as much as he can.

In the holy city of Jerusalem, it is our custom to go to the Wailing Wall to pray a special prayer in honor of the day, and the poor folk and the charity wardens stand there and everyone who comes to the Wall gives them a contribution.

PEACE IN HIS HIGH PLACES

The giving of charity on the eve of Yom Kippur during the time of the Afternoon Prayer does much to make peace between Israel and their Father who is in heaven. It is said in the Talmud, "Every charity and deed of kindness that Israel do in this world does much to make peace and is an important intercessor between Israel and their Father who is in Heaven" (Baba Batra 10a). How much more is this true on the eve of Yom Kippur when, after making peace with his fellow, a man still seeks to make peace between the poor man and his Father who is in heaven. How? By charity and deeds of kindness to the poor.

It is said in the Midrash (Lev. Rabbah XXXIV): Rabbi Judah bar Rabbi Simon said: The poor man sits and complains: Why am I worse than any other man? Yet he lives in his house, and I live here. He sleeps in a bed and I sleep on the ground! If you come and give to him—by my life [says God] I shall consider it as though you made peace between him and me. As it is written (Isa. 27:5): "Or else let him take hold of My strength, that he may make peace with Me; yea, let him make peace with Me."

vii. The Afternoon Prayer for the Eve of Yom Kippur

THE PRAYER

A Reader is chosen for the Afternoon Prayer who has all the qualities that were listed as necessary for the Reader for Yom Kippur. The Reader wraps himself in a prayer shawl, even in places where it is the practice to pray the Afternoon Prayer at other times without wearing prayer shawls. [Mateh Efrayim]

Then the Afternoon Prayer is prayed, and the Confession recited, as we have learned (Yoma 87b): "Confession on the eve of Yom Kippur is at nightfall; but the sages say, One ought to make confession before eating and drinking, lest one become upset during the feast."

The Eighteen Benedictions are recited just as they are all the week, but when one reaches the phrase "who makes peace," one recites the Confession beginning "Our God and God of our fathers, let our prayer come before you."

STRIPES

After the Afternoon Prayer, all the congregation receive forty stripes less one, as a reminder to turn from the transgressions they have committed. It is the custom for the person receiving the stripes to recite the Confession while being flogged, and for the flogger to recite the verse, "And, being compassionate, he will forgive the iniquity" (Ps. 78:38) three times; for this verse contains thirty-nine letters in Hebrew, corresponding to the thirty-nine stripes. It is the custom to be flogged with any kind of whip, for the stripes are only a memorial of the original lashes. But one may use a lash of calf leather, after the saying (Isa. 1:3) "The ox knoweth his owner." [Rema, Orah Hayyim, No. 607]

A TALE

A tale is told of a certain hasid who went to see his rabbi. Before entering the house he thought to himself, It might be worth while to receive the "forty stripes," so that the zaddik will find no defect in me. He was still thinking of this when the door opened, and he entered. Greeting him, his rabbi said, "What is the reason why the sages, of blessed memory, took one from the forty stripes, making them thirty-nine, when it is written in the Torah, 'Forty stripes he may give him'? (Deut. 25:3). Yet the sages commanded that only thirty-nine stripes be given. The reason is that when a man commits a transgression and is flogged, perhaps if he received a full forty stripes according to the letter of the Torah he might think that he had wiped away his iniquity. Therefore, the sages, of blessed memory, went and took one from the forty (Makkot 22a), in order that the sinner might know that he had not yet received all his punishment, and had still to better his ways." [Haaretz, 25 Tishri 5696 (1935)]

ON THE TORAH

I heard the Gaon Rabbi Meir Arik, of blessed memory, the head of the Court of Buczacz, say that he had heard the Gaon Rabbi Joseph Saul Nathanson [19th cent.], the head of the Court of Lwow, say of himself that he was not diligent in Torah study. But the Gaon of Vilna [18th cent.] was really diligent in Torah study, and if·he lost a minute of his study, he would write in his notebook that on such and such a day he had lost so many minutes of Torah study. On the eve of Yom Kippur he would take his notebook and reckon up the minutes he had lost during the course of the whole year, and would cry and make confession for his iniquity in wasting time that he should have devoted to the Torah. It was further said of the Gaon of Vilna that the minutes he lost during the course of a single year never added up to more than three hours. [Dor Deah]

VIII. Final Preparations for Yom Kippur

CONCLUDING MEAL

On leaving the House of Prayer following the Afternoon Prayer, one hurries home to eat the Concluding Meal. It is customary for the women to set the table before the worshipers return from the House of Prayer.

Besides the fact that eating and drinking are the commandment of the day, this feast is in preparation for the next day's fast, in order that the fasters may be healthy and strong to do Teshuvah.

ONE'S TABLE

One should invite poor men who are worthy to his table, for as long as the Temple stood, the sacrifice made atonement, while now a man's table makes atonement for him (Hagigah 27a). Rashi interprets "makes atonement for him" as meaning "is his hospitality." This is especially true of this meal at a time when one is asking for atonement.

One ought during this meal to sit with fear and trembling. One ought not to think of any extraneous matter, and not become vexed with one's household, lest he become upset and be unable to eat the Concluding Meal.

THE MEAL

It is customary during this meal to eat neither fish nor any spicy dish, because they heat the body; nor does one eat sesame seeds for fear of their coming up again. No intoxicating drinks are taken, lest one become drunk and the prayer be an abomination. It is the custom to eat fowl. If one does not have fowl, he may eat beef. But one ought to be careful to eat at least the prescribed amount of bread, so that the Grace will not be said in vain. For on the eve of Yom Kippur there are some who eat quickly, and some who eat very little, so that the fast will not be hard on them; but one has to beware of eating less than the required amount. [Mateh Efrayim]

One ought to hurry to finish one's meal before sunset, because it is necessary to "add to the sacred from the profane," by adding to the beginning and close of Yom Kippur, as it is said, "And ye shall afflict your souls in the ninth day of the month at even" (Lev. 23:32). That is to say, begin to fast and afflict yourselves at that part of the ninth day which is adjacent to the tenth. One ought also to hurry in order to have time to bless one's children and then go to the House of Prayer, because it is the custom to say Kol Nidre while it is still daylight. There are places where a sage expounds before

Kol Nidre, and there are other places where the practice is to take a ritual bath after the Concluding Meal, before entering the House of Prayer. [Mateh Efrayim]

When one has finished the Concluding Meal, one ought to wash his hands. Even if one has not been careful to observe the washing of hands after the meal all the year, one ought to wash one's hands at this time, to add cleanliness and purity. One ought to recite Psalm 126, beginning: "A Song of Ascents. When the Lord brought those that returned to Zion, we were like unto them that dream." One ought to recite it with devotion and tears, for our misfortunes are frequent, and the hour is pressing, and the persecutions many, and God has not yet returned the exile of his people.

And one says the Grace after Meals with great devotion. At the recital of the blessing ending "Builder of Jerusalem," as well as of the verses that refer to Jerusalem, one ought to awaken one's heart to Teshuvah, for our city was desolated because of our many iniquities, and with Israel doing Teshuvah, the Holy One, blessed be he, is destined to rebuild Jerusalem.

THIS IS THE TABLE THAT IS BEFORE THE LORD

After the Concluding Meal, a fine cloth is spread over the table, and many books are arranged in place of the loaf of bread. The books are covered by another cloth, and left thus until the close of Yom Kippur, as an allusion to the fact that this day is mighty and awesome, and we must honor it not with food and drink, but with Torah and prayer. [Sede Hemed]

WHITE CLOTHING

After the Grace after Meals, one puts on clean clothing, for so it is said in the Talmud (Shabbat 119a): "The Exilarch said to Rav Hamnuna: What is the meaning of the Writ, 'And the holy of the Lord honorable' (Isa. 58:13)? Said he to him: That is Yom Kippur, on which there is no eating and no drinking. The Torah said, Honor it with a clean cloak."

It is preferable to put on white clothing, to resemble the ministering angels. [Rema, Orah Hayyim, No. 610,4]

THE GARMENT OF THE DEAD

It is also customary to put on a kittel, which is white and clean, and the garment worn by the dead, as well. With this example before him, a man's heart becomes submissive and broken. [Rema, *ibid.*]

Once, before Kol Nidre, the pious Rabbi Moses Teitelbaum [18th–19th cent.] said: Brothers, children of Israel, consider that in these garments which we are now wearing we shall go to the world above, to give a reckoning before the King over all kings, the Holy One, blessed be he. Therefore let us imagine that we are standing in these garments before the throne of glory to give our reckoning. Let us wholly regret our sins, for in the hour when one stands before the throne of glory he really does regret them. No regretting helps after death—but it does help now. Therefore let us wholeheartedly regret our sins, and let us truly take it upon ourselves never to sin again. Let us beseech pardon and forgiveness from the King who pardons and forgives. [Taame ha-Minhagim, quoting Yismah Moshe]

The kittels are not to be decorated with gold, nor their collars adorned with gold. For gold is a reminder of the iniquity of the golden calf, and "an accuser cannot also serve as a defender." Thus it was said in the Talmud (Rosh ha-Shanah 26a): "Why does not the High Priest wear gold garments when he enters the Holy of Holies to perform the service? Because an accuser cannot serve as a defender."

But the kittels may be decorated with silver, and with silver collars; for silver is white, and white is a symbol of grace. [See Mateh Efrayim]

It is not the custom of the inhabitants of Jerusalem to wear kittels on Yom Kippur, the way people outside of Palestine do. For if they were to wear kittels in order to resemble the ministering angels, why, most of the inhabitants of Jerusalem wear white cloaks over their clothing every day, and the resemblance would not be apparent. If they were to wear them because they resemble the garments worn by the dead—the dead are not dressed in kittels in Jerusalem.

THE PARENTS' BLESSING

Before he goes to the House of Prayer, the father blesses his children. We find that the patriarchs blessed their children before their death; and Moses our master, too, peace be upon him, blessed Israel before his death. For at their deaths they were raised to a peak of holiness. So, on the eve of Yom Kippur, before going to the House of Prayer, when one is free of the cares of the world and is about to purify oneself with an extreme holiness, one blesses his children, and the Holy One, blessed be he, heeds the blessing.

It is written of the patriarchs of old, when they were about to bless their children: "And it came to pass, that when Isaac was old, and his eyes were dim, so that he could not see" (Gen. 27:1), and "Now the eyes of Israel were dimmed for age, so that he could not see" (Gen. 48:10). This informs us that when a man comes to bless his children, he ought to shut his eyes, so as not to see their flaws. [Kol Dodi]

What is the blessing? The blessing is that they may be

sealed for a good life, to be worthy to serve God with a perfect heart, and to walk in the way of the righteous and make their hearts strong for the study of the Torah. For at that hour the fear of the Day of Judgment is upon the children, and the words of the blessing imprint themselves upon their hearts.

The formula we use for the blessing is as follows: "May God make thee as Ephraim and Manasseh. May it be the will of our Father who is in heaven to place his love and fear in your heart. May the fear of God be before you all the days of your life, so that you will not sin; and may your delight be in the Torah and in the commandments. May your eyes look straight ahead. May your mouth speak wisdom, and your heart contemplate fear. May your hands be engaged in keeping the commandments, and your legs run to do the will of your Father who is in heaven. May he give you sons and daughters who are righteous and engage in the study of the Torah and in keeping the commandments all their days. May your spring be blessed; and may God allow you to find your rightful sustenance in ease and with plenty, beneath his broad hand, and not through the gift of flesh and blood. May your livelihood be one which will set you free for the service of God; and may you be inscribed and sealed for a good life and a long, in the midst of all the righteous of Israel. Amen." [Hayye Adam]

THE ESSENCE OF BLESSING

The year my grandfather [Rabbi Zevi Hirsh of Liska; 18th cent.] died, all his sons and daughters entered to receive his blessing on the eve of Yom Kippur. He stood up and fixed every one of us with his clear eye. We at once encircled him, and he, of blessed memory, put on his robe and wound the sash around his waist, turning as he wound, and looking at us. I could see that he wanted to speak, but his lips were locked, and it was not in his power to open his holy mouth, because of his awesome fear. Finally, he opened his mouth, and trembling said only these words, "My children, if you cling to God, it will be good for you." [Rabbi Zev Wolf, Darkhe ha-Tov veha-Yashar]

Many people go to their relatives, too, to be blessed on the eve of Yom Kippur, if they are worthy people and pious and saintly. They beseech them to pray in their behalf on the holy day, and to mention them in their prayers. [Mateh Efrayim]

It is best to do so early while it is still daylight, for at night it is fitting that we be prepared to receive the holy day in a quiet and composed frame of mind. [Kitzur Shulhan Arukh]

GOING TO THE HOUSE OF PRAYER

Rabbi Zev Wolf, the grandson of Rabbi Zevi Hirsh of Liska [18th cent.], said: I often saw my grandfather walking to the House of Prayer on the eve of Yom Kippur, his very earlocks trembling with fear. Before going to the House of Prayer, he would stand before his bookcase and ask the holy volumes for forgiveness. [Darkhe ha-Tov veha-Yashar]

It is customary to put on one's kittel at home before going to the House of Prayer, so that one goes to the House of Prayer in fear and awe to welcome the holy day.

There are some who take off their shoes and walk barefooted to the House of Prayer. [See Shibbole ha-Leket]

THE REGIONS OF LIGHT

In places where it is the custom to kindle a candle on the eve of Yom Kippur, it should be kindled; but in places where that is not the custom, it should not. But if the eve of Yom Kippur falls on a Sabbath, it *must* be kindled. At any rate, a candle is kindled in Houses of Prayer and in Houses of Study, and in dark alleys, and at the bedsides of the sick. [Orah Hayyim, No. 610]

In places where it is the custom to light the candles at home, the women recite the blessing ending, "who sanctified us by his commandments and commanded us to light the candle of Yom Kippur," and some women also recite the blessing with the phrase, "who has kept us alive," as on a holiday. If Yom Kippur falls on a Sabbath, they recite "to light the candle of Sabbath and Yom Kippur," and the blessing with the phrase, "who has kept us alive." In places where it is not the custom to kindle candles at home, if Yom Kippur falls on a Sabbath, the candles are kindled, but the phrase, "of Yom Kippur" is not recited in the blessing, and the phrase, "the candle of Sabbath" is; nor is the blessing with the phrase, "who has kept us alive" recited. [Mateh Efrayim]

It is the custom to have many candles burning in the Houses of Prayer. [Shulhan Arukh, Orah Hayyim, No. 610]

CONGREGATIONAL PRAYER

Congregational prayer is always heeded, and even if there are sinners in the congregation, the Holy One, blessed be he, does not reject the prayer of the group. Therefore, a man should join a congregation, and not pray alone if he can pray with a group [Maimonides, Hilkhot Tefillah VIII.1]. This was said of the other days during the year. How much more is it true of Yom Kippur, which is a day when we beseech compassion and pardon and forgiveness for all our iniquities, as well as redemption, as it is written (Ps. 55:19; see Berakhot 8a): "He hath redeemed my soul in peace from the battle that was against me; for I was with many."

Two men carrying a load would not be able to carry it as
well separately as together. Two men raising their voices
are more apt to be heard than if they cry separately. So it is
with Yom Kippur: because all folk, great and small, afflict
themselves together, even if a few have sinned, the many do
not lose the good that has been decreed for them, such as
rain and plenty. [Sefer Hasidim, No. 276]

One enters the House of Prayer with fear and trembling,
"for great is the day of the Lord and very terrible; and who
can abide it?" (Joel 2:11). For at that time the books of the
living and the dead are open before Him. Nevertheless, one
ought not to despair, God forbid. For the Holy One, blessed
be he, rewards the faith that Israel show in their Father who
is in heaven, who wishes their acquittal, by assembling and
coming to prayer; he hears their prayer and accepts their
Teshuvah.

"For great is the day of the Lord"—that is Rosh ha-Shanah.
"And very terrible, and who can abide it"—that is Yom
Kippur, when the books of the living and the dead are open
before Him. It is written, "A Prayer of David. Hear the
right, O Lord, attend unto my cry; give ear unto my prayer
from lips without deceit. Let my judgment come forth from
Thy presence; let Thine eyes behold with equity" (Ps. 17:1-
2). The people of Israel say to the Master of the universe:
"Now you are sitting to judge us, while our accusers and
defenders stand before you. May it be your will that your
eyes shall behold with equity." He says to them, "By your
lives, I will do so, for I wish to acquit you; as it is said (Isa.
42:21): 'The Lord desires to acquit.'" [Pesikta Hadata, Bet
ha-Midrash VI]

THE MERITS OF ISRAEL

Rabbi Levi Isaac of Berditchev [18th cent.], holy and awe-some as one of the seraphim, whose holiness and self-denial was a wonder of wonders, used to pray with fear and trembling. Because of his fear of the God of hosts, he could never stay in one place, and a man would leave him at one corner of the room, and find him in another. Everyone who saw him at prayer and heard his voice felt his hair stand on end and his heart melt and all the crookedness of his heart straightened.

It was the rabbi's holy way to fall to the earth on the eve of the holy day, on the way to the House of Prayer. And when he would say the phrase, "Magnified and sanctified be His great Name," all those who heard him would lose their sense of reality and would be afire with God's Name. All his days he spoke in defense of Israel, and particularly on the eve of the holy day. He would say, "You have given us the tenth day of Tishri for affliction and atonement, and the ninth day to eat and to drink. Yet see your people Israel: every one of them is here in the House of Prayer, not a person missing. There is not a single drunkard drowsy with wine among them, and there is not one of them lying sick at home from overeating. They are all standing here bare-foot. Have you another nation like this?" [Seder ha-Dorot he-Hadash; Eser Orot]

A LITTLE SANCTUARY

"The hallowed stones are poured out at the head of every street" (Lam. 4:1). When the Temple was destroyed, the Holy One, blessed be he, scattered its stones over all the world, and every place where a stone fell, a House of Prayer was built. [Aggadat Eliyahu, quoting a midrash]

It is for this reason that a House of Prayer is called a little sanctuary, because it has a little of the Temple, a stone of the Temple, which is sunk into every House of Prayer. [*Ibid.*]

The sages said: "And not a man said to his fellow: There is no place for me to lodge in Jerusalem" [Sayings of the Fathers V.5]. Of the pilgrims it was said, despite the fact that all the tribes went up to Jerusalem "not a man lodged outside of the entrance to the city" [Avot de-Rabbi Natan]. For where love and brotherhood rest, it is not crowded, and on Yom Kippur, when all of Israel unite their hearts for their Father who is in heaven, and peace and fellowship dwell among them, the place of the Omnipresent contains them all. I have been told that all the congregation enter the House of Prayer in Jerusalem and it becomes full, and then when the pilgrims from all the surrounding places are added, there are over three hundred people more; yet they can all be there, without being pressed for room. [Magen Avot]

This is especially true on Yom Kippur, when every man in Israel is on a high spiritual level, since spiritual objects take up no room. We have found the same to be true of the Temple: "They would stand crowded together, but have room when they prostrated themselves" [Sayings of the Fathers V.5]. For everyone who entered the Temple rose to an extreme spiritual level and occupied no space. [Aggadat Eliyahu]

TENTH MAN FOR A QUORUM

Let me tell you, O children of the living God, about the wonderful thing that happened in Hebron on Yom Kippur. Now you must know that there are not always ten men in Hebron to worship publicly; it is only on Sabbaths and holidays that people from the villages assemble there so that they can pray with a quorum of ten and more; but all the inhabitants of Hebron are very pious.

Now it came to pass one Yom Kippur eve that there were only nine men in Hebron, and the inhabitants of Hebron waited for the villagers to come, but no one of them came. For they had all gone to Jerusalem the holy city, may it be rebuilt and re-established speedily in our days, since it is nearby, being only a distance of a quarter of a day's travel away. So they were in great sorrow, lest they each be forced to pray alone on Yom Kippur, and they wept bitterly.

Now the sun had already sunk, and it was very late. And it came to pass that they lifted their eyes, and, lo and behold, an old man coming from the distance; and they rejoiced exceedingly when they saw him. Now when he had come up to them they set the Concluding Meal before him that he might eat; but he blessed and thanked them, and said that he had already eaten on the way. So they prayed on the holy day, and honored the man highly. At the close of Yom Kippur they fell into a dispute, for every one wanted to take the guest to his home. Finally they decided to cast lots, and the guest fell to the lot of the cantor, who was a pious man and related wonderful dreams and visions of night. So the cantor went homeward, the guest following after him. When the cantor came near his home, he turned around to honor the guest and allow him to enter the house first—and he looked, and, lo and behold, he was gone. They sought him but could not find him anywhere about. Then they were all greatly saddened, for they thought that he had gone on his way in the night, because he had not wished to partake of their hospitality.

But on that night the old man visited the cantor in a dream, and told him that he was our father Abraham, peace be upon him, who had come to complete their quorum, for he saw they were in great sorrow, lest they should each have to pray alone. And they rejoiced greatly and blessed the great God for having done wondrous deeds. Amen, and so be His will. [Emek ha-Melekh]

ENDED IS THE SECOND BOOK WHICH IS THE BOOK OF THE DAYS BETWEEN ROSH HA-SHANAH AND YOM KIPPUR.

BOOK THREE

Yom Kippur

1. The Significance of the Day

And the Lord spoke unto Moses, saying: Howbeit on the tenth day of this seventh month is the day of atonement; there shall be a holy convocation unto you, and ye shall afflict your souls; and ye shall bring an offering made by fire unto the Lord. And ye shall do no manner of work in that same day; for it is a day of atonement, to make atonement for you before the Lord your God. For whatsoever soul it be that shall not be afflicted in that same day, he shall be cut off from his people. And whatsoever soul it be that doeth any manner of work in that same day, that soul will I destroy from among his people. Ye shall do no manner of work; it is a statute for ever throughout your generations in all your dwellings. It shall be unto you a sabbath of solemn rest, and ye shall afflict your souls; in the ninth day of the month at even, from even unto even, shall ye keep your sabbath. [Lev. 23:26–32]

And on the tenth day of this seventh month ye shall have a holy convocation; and ye shall afflict your souls; ye shall do no manner of work; but ye shall present a burnt-offering unto the Lord for a sweet savor: one young bullock, one ram, seven he-lambs of the first year; they shall be unto you without blemish; and their meal-offering, fine flour mingled with oil, three tenth parts for the bullock, two tenth parts for the one ram, a several tenth part for every lamb of the seven lambs; one he-goat for a sin-offering; beside the sin-offering of atonement, and the continual burnt-offering, and the meal-offering thereof, and their drink-offerings. [Num. 29:7–11]

And it shall be a statute for ever unto you: in the seventh

month, on the tenth day of the month, ye shall afflict your souls, and shall do no manner of work, the home-born, or the stranger that sojourneth among you. For on this day shall atonement be made for you, to cleanse you; from all your sins shall ye be clean before the Lord. It is a sabbath of solemn rest unto you, and ye shall afflict your souls; it is a statute for ever. And the priest, who shall be anointed and who shall be consecrated to be priest in his father's stead, shall make the atonement, and shall put on the linen garments, even the holy garments. And he shall make atonement for the most holy place, and he shall make atonement for the tent of meeting and for the altar; and he shall make atonement for the priests and for all the people of the assembly. And this shall be an everlasting statute unto you, to make atonement for the children of Israel because of all their sins once in the year. And he did as the Lord commanded Moses. [Lev. 16:29-34]

AN EVERLASTING STATUTE

On the seventh day after the ten commandments were given, Moses ascended the mountain, as it is said, "And the glory of the Lord abode upon Mount Sinai, and the cloud covered it six days" (Exod. 24:16)—in order to cleanse Moses. "And the seventh day He called unto Moses out of the midst of the clouds . . . and [Moses] went up into the mount; and Moses was in the mount forty days and forty nights" (Exod. 24:16-18). On the seventeenth of Tammuz he descended and broke the tablets: "And it came to pass on the morrow, that Moses said unto the people: Ye have sinned a great sin; and now I will go up unto the Lord, peradventure I shall make atonement for your sin" (Exod. 32:30). He ascended on the eighteenth of Tammuz and besought compassion for Israel, as it is said, "So I fell down before the Lord the forty days and

the forty nights that I fell down; because the Lord had said
He would destroy you. And I prayed unto the Lord, and
said: O Lord God, destroy not Thy people and Thine inheritance . . . that Thou hast brought forth out of Egypt
with a mighty hand" (Deut. 9:25). In that hour, the Holy
One, blessed be he, was appeased with Israel, and told Moses
to hew the second set of tablets and to ascend Mount Sinai,
as it is said, "Hew thee two tables of stone like unto the first,
and come unto me into the mount" (Deut. 10:1). He descended on the twenty-eighth of Av and hewed two tables,
as it is said, "And he hewed two tables of stone like unto the
first; and Moses rose up early in the morning, and went up
unto Mount Sinai, as the Lord had commanded him, and
took into his hand two tables of stone" (Exod. 34:4). Then
he ascended on the twenty-ninth of Av and the Torah was repeated to him a second time; as it is said, "Now I stayed in
the mount as at the first time, forty days and forty nights;
and the Lord hearkened unto me that time also; the Lord
would not destroy thee" (Deut. 10:10). The second days were
favorable, like the first. From this we may learn that the days
between were days of disfavor. Moses descended on the tenth
of Tishri, which was Yom Kippur, and brought the people
the news that he had been acceptable to the Omnipresent, as
it is said, "Pardon our iniquity and our sin, and take us for
Thine inheritance" (Exod. 34:9). Therefore, this day has remained as a statute and remembrance for generations, as it
is said (Lev. 16:34): "And this shall be an everlasting statute
unto you." [Seder Olam Rabba VI]

Yom Kippur will never be done away with, as it is said
(Lev. 16:34): "And this shall be an everlasting statute unto
you, to make atonement for the children of Israel, because of
all their sins, once in the year." [Midrash Mishle IX]

ETERNAL JOY

"Days were fashioned, but for Him one" (cf. Ps. 139:16). That is Israel's Yom Kippur, which was a day of great rejoicing for "Him who spoke and the world came into being," a day which He gave to Israel out of his great love for them. . . . Even more: When he pardons the iniquities of Israel, he is not sad at heart, but rejoices exceedingly, saying to the mountains and the hills, to the springs and the valleys, "Come and rejoice greatly with me, for I am forgiving the iniquities of Israel." Therefore, let every man remember all that has happened from the day the Holy One, blessed be he, chose Abraham, until this very hour. And let every man remember all the good and righteous things that He has done for Israel at every hour, as it is said, "Remember these things, O Jacob . . ." (Isa. 44:21), and it is said, "I have swept aside like a cloud thy transgressions" (Isa. 44:22). As clouds that are swept aside by the wind, so the transgressions of Israel are swept aside in this world and will not rise again in the world to come, as it is said, "I have swept aside like a cloud." What does the phrase, "for I have redeemed thee" (*ibid.*) teach us? "I have redeemed thee from the book of death and put thee in the book of life." Therefore, it was said, "For I have redeemed thee." That is why following it we find the verse: "Sing joyfully, O ye heavens, for the Lord hath done it." [Seder Eliyahu Rabbah I]

AS A NUT

"I went down into the garden of nuts" (Cant. 6:11). A nut tree does not thrive if its roots are covered at planting time. So it is with Israel: "He that covereth his transgressions will not prosper" (Prov. 28:13). As a nut which if it falls into filth, can be picked up and wiped and rinsed and washed and then can be eaten—so it is with Israel: however much they besmirch themselves in iniquity all the days of the year, Yom Kippur comes and makes atonement for them, as it is said (Lev. 16:30): "For on this day shall atonement be made for you, to cleanse you; from all your sins shall ye be clean before the Lord." [Cant. Rabbah VI]

THE DAY MAKES ATONEMENT

Says Rabbi Judah the Prince: Yom Kippur makes atonement for all transgressions against the commandments in the Torah, whether one does Teshuvah or not; except for the man who casts off the yoke, and is contemptuous of the Torah, and destroys the covenant of the flesh [attempts to remove the evidence of his circumcision]. For if one does Teshuvah for these things, Yom Kippur makes atonement; but if one does not do Teshuvah, it does not. [Keritot 7a]

THE CLASSES OF ATONEMENT

Rabbi Mattiah ben Heresh asked Rabbi Eleazar ben Azariah: Have you heard the four classes of atonement which Rabbi Ishmael expounded? Said Rabbi Eleazar to him: There are really three classes, but Teshuvah refers to each of them. It is written, "Return, ye backsliding children" (Jer. 3:22). It is also written, "For on this day shall atonement be made for you" (Lev. 16:30). It is also written, "Then will I visit their transgression with the rod, and their iniquities with strokes" (Ps. 89:33). And it is written, "Surely this iniquity shall not be expiated by you till ye die" (Isa. 22:14). How is that? If a man has transgressed against an affirmative commandment and has done Teshuvah at once, he is pardoned before he moves. Of him the Scripture says, "Return, ye backsliding children." If a man has transgressed against a prohibitive commandment and does Teshuvah at once, judgment is suspended and Yom Kippur makes atonement. Of him the Writ says, "For on this day shall atonement be made for you." If a man has deliberately committed transgressions which are punishable by a divine visitation or death, Teshuvah and Yom Kippur make atonement for half of his transgressions, and his sufferings during the rest of the year make atonement for the other half. Of him it is said, "Then will I visit their transgression with the rod, and their iniquities with strokes." But it is not in the power of Teshuvah to suspend, or of Yom Kippur to make atonement for, or sufferings to wipe away, the judgment against him who profanes the name of God. But Teshuvah and Yom Kippur make atonement for a third, sufferings make atonement for another third, and the death of the sinner with its suffering wipes all away. Of him the Scripture says, "Surely this iniquity shall not be forgiven unto you till ye die,"—teaching us that death wipes all away. [Yerushalmi, Yoma VIII. 7; Babli, Yoma 86a]

A SABBATH OF SABBATHS

Someone asked the pious Rabbi Zevi ha-Kohen of Rymanov, of blessed memory: Wherein lies the superiority of Yom Kippur, that it is called "a Sabbath of Sabbaths"? Is not the Sabbath also written of as "a Sabbath of Sabbaths unto the Lord" (Exod. 35:2)?

He replied to him who asked: I see that you do not read the portion of the week with care. Indeed, of the Sabbath it is written, "A Sabbath of Sabbaths unto the Lord," but of Yom Kippur it is written, "A Sabbath of Sabbaths unto you" (Lev. 23:32). For on Yom Kippur we draw the sanctity of the superior realm down nearer to us. [Taame ha-Minhagim]

The ten days of Teshuvah are a process of drawing upward from earth to heaven; on Yom Kippur the Holy One, blessed be he, draws down from heaven nearer to Israel. [Shem mi-Shmuel]

WHATSOEVER SOUL

During the ten days of Teshuvah, a man can find out the extent of his love and fear of God, for his soul will awaken to turn to God during the holy days according to the extent of his fear. He who is fearful of God will be moved to Teshuvah from the eve of Rosh ha-Shanah, as our sages, of blessed memory, said: "On the eve of Rosh ha-Shanah great men begin to afflict themselves, lesser men during the days between the Days of Awe, and still lesser on Yom Kippur." Indeed the person in whose eyes even Yom Kippur is like other days has no part in the soul of Israel. For it is said, "For whatsoever soul it be that shall not be afflicted in that same day, he shall be cut off from his people" (Lev. 23:29). The meaning is that the soul which is not afflicted even during the sacred and sanctified day is no longer a member of the community of Israel. [Siddur ha-Minhagim]

WHEN YOM KIPPUR CAN FALL

Yom Kippur never falls on Sunday or on Tuesday or on Friday, but always on Monday, Wednesday, Thursday, or on the holy Sabbath. Rabbi Isaac Eisik of Koretz, author of Berit Kehunat Olam wrote: We have learned in the Mishnah (Kelim XVII.14) that some of the things created on the first, third, and sixth days can become ritually unclean, while nothing created on the second, fourth, and fifth days can become ritually unclean.

On the first day of Creation, the earth and water were

created, and earthenware vessels and liquids can become ritually unclean. On the second day, the firmament, in which there is no ritual uncleanliness, was created. On the third day, the trees were created and wooden vessels can become ritually unclean. On the fourth day, the lights were suspended in the sky; they have no ritual uncleanliness. On the fifth day the birds and fish were created, and vessels made from them cannot become ritually unclean. On the sixth the beasts and the animals and the creeping things and man were created; and vessels made of their bones and of their skin can become ritually unclean. Therefore Yom Kippur, which is all purity, falls only on one of the days of cleanliness and purity. [Otzrot Hayyim, Metzora]

II. Restrictions

FIVE AFFLICTIONS

On Yom Kippur it is forbidden to eat and to drink, and to wash, and to anoint oneself, and to put on shoes, and to have sexual intercourse. [Mishnah Yoma VIII.1]

These five afflictions correspond to the five books of the Pentateuch which were completed on that day, and to the five senses by which we keep the commandments or commit transgressions. [Eliyahu Zutta on Levush, quoting a responsum of the Maharil]

HOLIER THAN THE HOLY

The next feast held after the "Trumpets" is the Fast. Perhaps one of the perversely minded who are not ashamed to censure things excellent will say, What sort of a feast is this in which there are no gatherings to eat and drink, no company of entertainers or entertained, no copious supply of strong drink

nor tables sumptuously furnished nor a generous display of
all the accompaniments of a public banquet, nor again the
merriment and revelry with frolic, nor dancing to the sound
of flute and harp and timbrels and cymbals, and the other
instruments of the debilitated and invertebrate kind of
music which through the channel of the ears awaken the
unruly lusts? For it is in these and through these that men,
in their ignorance of what true merriment is, consider that
the merriment of a feast is to be found. This the clear-seeing
eyes of Moses the ever wise discerned and therefore he called
the fast a feast, the greatest of the feasts, in his native tongue
a Sabbath of Sabbaths, or as the Greeks would say, a seven
of sevens, a holier than the holy. He gave it this name for
many reasons.

First, because of the self-restraint which it entails; always
and everywhere indeed he exhorted them to shew this in all
the affairs of life, in controlling the tongue and the belly
and the organs below the belly, but on this occasion especially
he bids them do honor to it by dedicating thereto a particular
day. To one who has learned to disregard food and drink
which are absolutely necessary, are there any among the
superfluities of life which he can fail to despise, things which
exist to promote not so much preservation and permanence
of life as pleasure with all its powers of mischief?

Secondly, because the holy day is entirely devoted to
prayers and supplications, and men from morn to eve employ
their leisure in nothing else but offering petitions of humble
entreaty in which they seek earnestly to propitiate God and
ask for remission of their sins, voluntary and involuntary,
and entertain bright hopes looking not to their own merits
but to the gracious nature of Him who sets pardon before
chastisement.

Thirdly, because of the time at which the celebration of

the fast occurs, namely, that when all the annual fruits of the earth have been gathered in. To eat and drink of these without delay would, he held, shew gluttony, but to fast and refrain from taking them as food shews the perfect piety which teaches the mind not to put trust in what stands ready prepared before us as though it were the source of health and life. For often its presence proves injurious and its absence beneficial. Those who abstain from food and drink after the ingathering of the fruits cry aloud to us with their souls, and though their voices utter no sound, their language could hardly be plainer. They say, "We have gladly received and are storing the boons of nature, yet we do not ascribe our preservation to any corruptible thing, but to God the Parent and Father and Saviour of the world and all that is therein, Who has the power and the right to nourish and sustain us by means of these or without these. See, for example, how the many thousands of our forefathers as they traversed the trackless and all-barren desert, were for forty years, the life of a generation, nourished by Him as in a land of richest and most fertile soil; how He opened fountains unknown before to give them abundance of drink for their use; how He rained food from heaven, neither more nor less than what sufficed for each day, that they might consume what they needed without hoarding, nor barter for the prospect of soulless stores their hopes of His goodness, but taking little thought of the bounties received rather reverence and worship the bountiful Giver and honor him with the hymns and benedictions that are his due."

By order of the law the fast is held on the tenth day. Why on the tenth? As has been shewn in our detailed discussion of that number, it is called by the learned the all-perfect, and embraces all the progressions, arithmetical, harmonic and geometrical, and further the harmonies, the fourth, the

fifth, the octave and the double octave, representing respec-
tively the ratios 4:3, 3:2, 2:1, and 4:1, and it also contains the
ratio of 9:8, so that it sums up fully and perfectly the leading
truths of musical science, and for this reason it has received
its name of the all-perfect. In ordaining that this privation
of food and drink should be based on the full and perfect
number 10, he intended to prescribe the best possible form of
nourishment for the best part of us. He did not wish anyone
to suppose that as their instructor in the mysteries he was
advocating starvation, the most intolerable of sufferings,
but only a brief stoppage in the influx which passes into the
receptacle of the body. For this would ensure that the stream
from the fountain of reason should flow pure and crystal-
clear with smooth course into the soul, because the constantly
repeated administrations of food which submerge the body
sweep the reason away as well, whereas if they are checked,
that same reason stoutly fortified can in pursuit of all that
is worth seeing and hearing make its way without stumbling
as upon a dry firm causeway. Besides, it was meet and right
when everything has shewn abundance as they would have
it, and they enjoy a full and perfect measure of goodness, that
amid this prosperity and lavish supply of boons, they should
by abstaining from food and drink remind themselves of
what it is to want, and offer prayers and supplications on
the one hand to ask that they may never really experience
the lack of necessities, on the other to express their thank-
fulness because in such wealth of blessings they remember
the ills they have been spared. [Philo of Alexandria, The
Special Laws II]

ABANDONING NATURAL FUNCTIONS

And they fast on this day to approach a resemblance to the
angels, inasmuch as the fast is consummated by humbling

themselves, lowering their heads, standing, bending their knees, and singing hymns of praise. Then all the physical powers abandon their natural functions and engage in spiritual functions, as though having no animal nature. [Kuzari III.5]

BAN ON MATERIAL PLEASURE

The purpose of the fast of atonement is also explainable by the fact that it gives a sense of·Teshuvah. It is the day on which the master of the prophets descended with the second set of tablets and announced that the people's great sin had been forgiven; that day became forever a day for Teshuvah and the perfect service of God. For that reason, every material pleasure and every labor for the benefit of the body was banned on that day. My meaning is: Every man ought to confess his sins and turn from them on that day. [Guide to the Perplexed III.43]

A SERMON ON THE FIVE AFFLICTIONS

On Yom Kippur, God, be exalted, commanded that the body and the soul be afflicted with five afflictions, in order to keep the soul from being at home in the body and to send it off to withdraw from corporeality like an angel. Because the soul has five names, which are: soul, wind, spirit, the only one, and the living one; and has five elements, there are five afflictions to lessen and remove the corporeality.

The soul is called the living one because it is the essence of vitality. There is a corresponding prohibition against eating and drinking, leading to a lessening of the body's vitality. Then when the body's vitality is lessened, the soul is not at home in the body.

The prohibition against sexual intercourse corresponds to the quality of singleness. For the soul is a unity and is at home only in a body where there is unity, and there is only unity of body when a man and a woman are joined together, as it is said, "and they shall be one flesh" (Gen. 2:24). When we keep from intercourse, the body's unity is lessened and the soul is not at home in the body.

The prohibition against washing corresponds to the quality of spirit, after the phrase "the spirit of man is the lamp of the Lord" (Prov. 20:27). For the spirit shines with the light of God; in the course of washing, the body freshens and shines and the spirit is at home in the body. When one does not wash one's body, the spirit is not at home in the body.

The prohibition against anointing corresponds to the quality of soul. For the quality, soul, refers to an object that is unchangeable, since the soul is not lessened or polluted, but remains pure, as our sages, of blessed memory, said, "the soul which Thou didst give me pure is" (Berakhot 60b). Anointing removes the filth from the body, and the body becomes pure; then the soul is at home in the body. When a man afflicts himself by not anointing his body, his soul is not at home in his body.

The prohibition against wearing shoes corresponds to the quality of wind. The soul is called wind because it is a light, spiritual substance, lacking matter. For, the reason why the wind can carry others as mentioned in the verses: "then a wind lifted me up" (Ezek. 3:14), and "that the wind of the Lord will carry thee" (I Kings 18:12), is because the wind itself is lifted from the earth. When a man is wearing shoes on his feet, he is raised above the earth and the soul is at home in the body. But if he is barefoot and his feet stumble on the earth and are not lifted above the earth, the soul is not at home in the body.

These are the five afflictions mentioned in the Torah. They are all intended to lessen the corporeality of the soul, until the soul separates from the body and becomes completely holy, as is fitting. Thus the whole purpose of Yom Kippur is to withdraw from and lessen the importance of the body. Therefore, on this particular day the High Priest is permitted to go into the innermost part of the Temple, for on Yom Kippur the Holy of Holies is completely sanctified and clean of all materiality. Only the Ark stands there, containing the tablets, the spiritual Torah; for the Torah, being spiritual, has no relation to the material. On the contrary, when the body is weakened and its strength lessened, the spiritual grows stronger. [Derush Naeh]

EATING AND DRINKING

Yom Kippur is the day when the superior light from which the other lights emanate is revealed. It contains the secret of the world to come, where, according to the sages, there is no eating and drinking. Therefore, we were commanded to afflict ourselves on Yom Kippur, as an allusion to the light to be revealed on that day. For when it is revealed, all manner of joy and happiness and atonement will appear. The day is called the Day of Atonement, for it removes all manner of filth, as it is written (Lev. 16:30): "For on this day shall atonement be made for you, to cleanse you." [Tolaat Yaakov]

The pious Rabbi Abraham Joshua Heshel of Apt [18–19th cent.] used to say: If it was in my power, I would do away with all the afflictions, except for the afflictions on the bitter day, which is the Ninth of Av—for who could eat on that day?—and the afflictions on the holy and awesome day, Yom Kippur; who needs to eat on that day? [Sifran shel Zaddikim]

WHEN YOM KIPPUR FALLS ON A SABBATH

When the holy Sabbath has a worthy guest like the New Moon, it surrenders one prayer. [For when the New Moon falls on a Sabbath, the Additional Prayer for the New Moon is said, and not that of Sabbath.] When the Sabbath has a guest who is even greater than the New Moon, it surrenders all its prayers [for when a holiday falls on a Sabbath all the prayers of the holiday are said, and not that of Sabbath], but it does not surrender any of its feasts. But when the Sabbath has a guest who is very great, than whom is none greater, that is the holy day, Yom Kippur—lo, it surrenders all its prayers and all its feasts too. [Sippurim u-Maamarim Yekarim]

The pious Rabbi Leib, called "the Sabbath observer," used to walk behind his servant with his eyes shut when he had to pass through the market on the Sabbath. On Friday he used to go to buy all the Sabbath necessities himself. When he would come to the flour vendor, he would say to him, "Give Leib the best flour in honor of the holy Sabbath." And when he would come to the butcher he would say to him, "Give Leib the best meat in honor of the Sabbath." And he said the same when he bought fish and all the other necessities for the Sabbath.

When Yom Kippur would fall on a Sabbath, he would prepare all the Sabbath necessities according to his custom for every other Sabbath during the year, and set the table. When he came home after the prayer of Kol Nidre, he would sit down at table and say, "Master of the universe, the obstacle to observing the Sabbath is not on my part. I would like to delight in the Sabbath, as you have commanded. But you have said that we must afflict ourselves on this day, and so, since that is your will, Leib is leaving everything on the table, according to your holy will." [Or ha-Meir]

CARING FOR THE SICK

A sick person is fed at the word of experts. If there are no experts present, he is fed if he wishes, until he says, Enough! [Mishnah Yoma VIII.5]

In the case of a sick person who needs food, if there is a recognized doctor present, even a Gentile, who says, "If he is not fed, his illness may become more serious," we are careful to feed him, lest his life be in danger. The same is also true when the doctor is a woman. Even if a Jewish doctor says that there is no need to feed him, and others say there is, the other doctors are heeded, and the sick man is fed.

If a sick man says, I do not need to eat, and the doctor says he does, we rely on the doctor. This is true even if the sick man is a recognized doctor himself; we consider that his illness may have caused him to lose his sense of judgment. If a sick man says, I need to eat, though a hundred doctors say he does not need to eat, we take his word for it. Though the doctors say that food will injure him, we take the word of the sick man. Even if he says simply that he needs to eat, though he does not say that if he is not fed his life will be endangered, he is fed. That is the case when he knows that it is Yom Kippur. If he does not know that it is Yom Kippur, he is told of it. If he says, I do not need to eat, and later changes his mind and says, I do need to eat, he is fed, for his condition is not always the same. Therefore, even if the sick man does not say, I need to eat, until he is asked, but eats when given food, it seems to be permissible to ask and feed him.

If one doctor says the sick man must eat, and another says he does not need to eat, or if there are two against two and the sick man says nothing, he is fed. If the sick man and one of the doctors say he need not eat, and one doctor says he must, or if the sick man says nothing and one doctor says he must eat, while two others say he need not, he is not fed. But if the doctor who says he must eat is famous for his skill, his words are heeded, even if two other doctors are against feeding the sick man.

Where the law allows a sick man to eat, and he does not wish to, that is a foolish kind of piety, of which it was said, "And surely your blood of your lives will I require" (Gen. 9:5). It is also said, "Be not righteous overmuch" (Eccles. 7:16); so the sick man is fed against his will. [Mateh Efrayim]

The Gaon Rabbi Hayyim of Brisk [19th cent.] used to be lenient with the sick in the matter of eating on Yom Kippur. He was asked, "How is it that the master is so lenient when it comes to Yom Kippur?" Said he, "Not that I am lenient when it comes to Yom Kippur, but that I am strict when it comes to saving a life." [Oral communication by Rabbi Samuel Bialoblotzki]

DURING A CHOLERA EPIDEMIC

When there was a cholera epidemic in 1848, Rabbi Israel Salanter posted announcements in all the Houses of Prayer of Vilna on the eve of Yom Kippur, urging the people not to fast on that holy and awesome day, and to cut short the recitation of the liturgical poems of the day, and to go walking in the fresh air. After the Morning Prayer on Yom Kippur he took a roll in his hand and stood on the pulpit and after making the blessing ending "who creates various kinds of foods," ate the roll before the eyes of the entire congregation, that the people might see him and follow his example; for much is permitted where there is mortal danger, and the life of a single person was dearer in his eyes than all the wealth in the world. [Ir Vilna]

During the epidemic, God preserve us, the pious Rabbi Shalom of Belz [19th cent.] announced that all who felt faint ought to eat and drink as much as they needed. [Rav of Spinka, Orhot Hayyim]

HOLY GROUND

Why is the wearing of shoes prohibited on Yom Kippur? Because all the worlds are elevated on Yom Kippur when Israel does complete Teshuvah; the earth upon which we live is elevated too, and is called holy ground. Therefore, it is forbidden to step upon the earth wearing shoes, as it is written (Exod. 3:5): "Put off thy shoes from off thy feet, for the place whereon thou standest is holy ground." [Mena-hem Zion]

Rabbi Moses Hagiz [17th–18th cent.] in his book "The Learning of the Sages," wrote in the name of the masters of allusion that the actual reason why men have taken to wear-ing shoes is that the flesh may not touch the earth, for the earth was cursed because of the sin of Adam. Thus we keep a distance between our foot and the earth. But in holy places where it is holy ground and the earth is in the blessed category and no longer in the cursed, there we must go barefoot. That is the meaning of the verse (Exod. 3:5): "Put off thy shoes from off thy feet, for the place whereon thou standest is holy ground."

There is still another reason for the prohibition against wearing shoes on Yom Kippur. Rabbi Moses Isserles wrote [Orah Hayyim, No. 223]: It is the custom to say to a person

putting on a new garment, May you wear it out and get a
new one! There are some who write that one ought not to
say this about shoes or clothing which are made from the
skins of animals (even if unclean), for if that were the case,
it would seem as though the animal were being killed to
make a garment, and it is written, "And His tender mercies
are over all His works!" (Ps. 145:9). Rabbi Moses Isserles
also wrote [Yoreh Deah, No. 25] that he who is slaughtering
an animal for the first time ought to recite the blessing
ending "who has kept us alive" when he covers the blood
of the animal, not when he slaughters it; for he is injuring
a living thing. Therefore, how can a man put on a garment
for which it is necessary to kill a living thing, on Yom Kippur, which is a day of grace and compassion, when it is
written, "And His tender mercies are over all His works"?
[Siddur ha-Minhagim]

CHILDREN ON YOM KIPPUR

Small children ought not be made to fast on Yom Kippur,
but ought to be trained a year or two before they reach the
age of maturity, to become accustomed to keeping the commandments. [Mishnah Yoma VIII.4]

Said Abbayi, My nurse told me that a child of six is ready
to study the Holy Writ, a child of ten the Mishnah, a child
of thirteen can fast for twenty-four hours, and a girl can
fast at twelve." [Ketubot 50a]

At what age ought a child be trained to fast? A child who
is fully ten years old and even one who is fully nine years
old may be trained for a couple of hours. How? If he was
used to eating at the second hour of the day [eight o'clock],
he is fed at the third hour [nine o'clock]. If he was used to
eating at the third hour, he is fed at the fourth. He ought to

be made to fast according to his strength. The same is true
of both boys and girls. [See Maimonides, Shevitat Asor II. 10–
11]

They followed a fine practice in Jerusalem when they
trained their sons and daughters to fast on the fast day;
eleven-year-old children fasted until midday, and twelve-
year-olds the entire day. Thirteen-year-old children were
led around and presented before all the elders, that the
elders might bless and encourage and pray for them, and
the child might merit the study of the Torah and good deeds.
Every man went before his superior in knowledge and piety
and bowed down to him, that he might pray in his behalf,
being well-disposed and devout. The inhabitants of Jerusalem did not leave their children behind them at home, but led
them to the House of Prayer to encourage them to keep the
commandments. [See Soferim XVIII.5]

THE BEASTS AND BIRDS

It is necessary to give one's beast whatever it needs to eat on
Yom Kippur, for we must have compassion on the beasts,
that heaven might have compassion on us. [Leket Yosher]

We have heard that pious men used to feed their beasts
and birds on Yom Kippur.

THE PLEASURE OF THE SENSE OF SMELL

All the senses are mentioned in the story of the sin of Adam
(Gen. 3:6–8), save the sense of smell, for all the others
shared in the sin: "And when the woman saw"—the sense
of sight; "she took of the fruit thereof"—the sense of touch;
"and did eat"—the sense of taste; "and they heard"—the
sense of hearing. So we perceive that because the sense of
smell was not defective like the other senses, it has been said
of the Messiah of our salvation, who will be revealed speedily

in our days, "and his scent shall be in the fear of the Lord" (Isa. 11:3). Therefore it was said: "What is that the soul enjoys, but the body does not enjoy? It is the sense of smell" (Berakhot 43b). And that is why the pleasure we receive from the sense of smell is not forbidden on Yom Kippur. [Alumat Yosef, quoting Bene Yisakhar]

There are some whose custom it is to take various spices with them in order, by reciting benedictions over them, to be able to recite a full hundred benedictions on that day.

THE PROHIBITION AGAINST WORKING

All the labors that are forbidden on the Sabbath are forbidden on Yom Kippur. The only difference between the Sabbath and Yom Kippur is in the matter of punishment; for every transgression committed on the Sabbath which is punishable by stoning is punishable by divine visitation when committed on Yom Kippur, as we have learned: "The only difference between the Sabbath and Yom Kippur is that punishments for deliberate violations committed against the former are punished by a human court, and those committed against the latter by divine visitation" (Mishnah Megillah I.5). But in order to save a life one may desecrate on Yom Kippur every commandment that one may desecrate on the Sabbath for the same purpose, and Yom Kippur may not be desecrated for the same causes for which the Sabbath may not be desecrated. [Menorat ha-Maor]

III. Before Kol Nidre

AWAKENING

It is a widespread custom throughout most of the Diaspora for the rabbi of the city to address strong words to the con-

gregation before or after Kol Nidre. He ought not to make
his sermon long, but only speak long enough to awaken the
people to Teshuvah. He ought to raise his voice in weeping,
that, hearing him, they might awaken their own hearts to
Teshuvah.

A SERMON BEFORE KOL NIDRE

We all entered the old House of Prayer fearful and trembling, and the entire hall was filled an hour and a half before
the prayer. When our rabbi [Shmelke of Nikolsburg, 18th
cent.] reached the threshold of the House of Prayer wrapped
in a prayer shawl he went up to the Ark, crying as he went
in a loud voice and with much weeping the verse: "For on
this day shall atonement be made for you, to cleanse you;
from all your sins shall ye be clean before the Lord" (Lev.
16:30); and he quoted Rabbi Akiba (Mishnah Yoma
VIII.9): "Happy are you, O Israel; before whom do you
purify yourselves and who is it that purifies you—if not your
Father who is in heaven."

At once all the people burst into tears. When the zaddik
reached the Ark, he began to recite various verses to awaken
the people to Teshuvah, such as: "Against Thee, Thee only,
have I sinned, and done that which is evil in Thy sight" (Ps.
51:6); "For I do declare mine iniquity; I am full of care
because of my sin" (Ps. 38:19); "Purge me with hyssop, and
I shall be clean; wash me, and I shall be whiter than snow"
(Ps. 51:9); "And I will sprinkle clean water upon you, and
ye shall be clean; from all your uncleannesses, and from all
your idols, will I cleanse you" (Ezek. 36:25). And he expounded them as exhortations; but he wept so loudly we
could not hear his words.

Afterward he began to expound the loftiness of the holy

and awesome day, Yom Kippur, on which every man can
find help and redemption to enable him to redeem his soul
from the pit. This is, he said, like the story about the son of
a lord, on whom one of the officers used continually to in-
form. Once the informer left the city; at once the son ran to
his father and cried and supplicated before him, saying that
he regretted the evil he had done and was ready from that
time on to leave his evil way. At once his father's compassion
was moved, and he drew the son near to himself and rejoiced
greatly over him.

The reference is evident: "On Yom Kippur Satan has no
permission to act as accuser" (Yoma 20a). If we seek God
on this day and purify ourselves of all our guilt by doing
Teshuvah, and with weeping and supplication, he will
certainly listen to us and the verse, "now . . . let the power
of the Lord be great" (Num. 14:17), rather than the verse
"of the rock that begot thee, thou wast unmindful" (Deut.
32:18) will be fulfilled.

Therefore come, my beloved brothers, my heart's com-
panions, let us strengthen ourselves with weeping and supplication before our Father who is in heaven, and let us purify
ourselves before him, for on this Yom Kippur when there is
no Satan or mishap, His compassion will certainly be moved
in our favor. But you must know, my brothers, that the
reciting of, "Hear, O Israel" is one of the principles of Teshuvah. Let us recite, "Hear, O Israel," as though we were giving
our lives for the sanctification of the Name of God. For
indeed Abraham our father offered up his life for the sanctification of the Name of God and threw himself into the
fiery furnace, and Isaac his son offered himself at the Binding.
If we follow their footsteps and do as they did and sanctify

his great Name with love, and cry all together, "Hear, O Israel," with devotion, they will stand and intercede for us on the holy and awesome day.

At once all the people burst into tears and cried, "Hear, O Israel, the Lord our God, the Lord is one."

Then our master and rabbi continued and said: After having merited the sanctification and proclamation of the unity of his Name out of his great love for us, we have no doubt merited the purification of our hearts for his service and for his fear. But we must still fulfil a great principle of Teshuvah, which is the acceptance of the commandment, "Thou shalt love thy neighbor as thyself" (Lev. 19:18).

At once all the people cried after him, "Thou shalt love thy neighbor as thyself."

Then our rabbi continued and said, Since we have merited the sanctification of his Name, be blessed, and the unification of our souls to love our neighbors, God will help us to find pardon, and we shall merit the purification of our thoughts as the Blessed One has commanded us in his holy Torah; the Torah itself will intercede for us. As our master and rabbi said these words, he opened the doors of the Ark and said, But know, my brothers, that shame and disgrace ought to cover us when we face the Torah, after having desecrated its twenty-two letters. Therefore, each and every one of us ought to make a detailed confession of the iniquities that are known to him and weep and supplicate and suffer bitterly for his sins and the sins of his youth.

At once all the people burst into tears and began to make confession of their iniquities.

After they had finished making confession, our rabbi took a scroll and expounded the verse, "Behold, I was brought forth in iniquity, and in sin did my mother conceive me"

(Ps. 51:7). He said, Who can hear these words without his heart being torn to shreds? Even a heart of stone would melt.

Our rabbi also expounded as follows: The principle behind our purification is alluded to in the Mishnah, "Heave-offering seedlings that have become unclean become clean again if replanted, for they do not carry uncleanliness" (Terumot IX.7). That is to say, heave-offering seedlings that became unclean when detached from the earth lose their uncleanliness when replanted. For as long as seedlings are attached to the earth they are clean. When plucked from the earth they can become unclean. But if they are attached to their source again, their uncleanliness stops.

So it is with us. Our souls are hewn from the pure place under the throne of glory, and when our souls come to this world they become unclean because of our iniquities. But when a man attaches his thoughts to the Name of God, be blessed, the soul returns and attaches itself to its source, and is cleansed of its uncleanliness, as the Scripture says, "But ye that cleave unto the Lord your God are alive every one of you this day" (Deut. 4:4). For when a man clings to God with all his soul, he revives his soul by cleansing it of its uncleanliness, as it is said, "are alive every one of you this day." It is also said, "Light is sown for the righteous, and gladness for the upright in heart" (Ps. 97:11); for when we have cleansed our soul like a seedling that returns to its source, there will be "gladness for the upright in heart."

Our rabbi continued and said: But you must know that the weeping on this day will not avail if there is sadness in it, for "the Divine Presence does not rest . . . in the midst of sadness . . . but in the midst of joy at keeping a commandment" (Shabbat 30b). Indeed, this day on which we merit the stripping of all the crookedness from the hearts, and the approach to the King over all kings, the Holy One, blessed be he, and the return of our souls to their source— this day is indeed a day of joy, when his hand is opened to receive those who return, to make atonement for us and cleanse our souls. Therefore, let all the tears we shed on this day be tears of joy, for we have merited the approach and the attachment unto the Lord, we who "are alive every one of us this day." That is the meaning of the verse, "Serve the Lord with fear, and rejoice with trembling" (Ps. 2:11), and of the verse, "and gladness for the upright in heart" (Ps. 97:11). After we have stripped our hearts of all their crookedness and have merited the lofty height of the "upright in heart," our joy will certainly be complete. [Divre Torah]

PEACE-MAKING

If a man has had no chance to appease his fellow on the eve of Yom Kippur, he ought to try to appease him on the night of Yom Kippur, before Kol Nidre. I have heard one of the great scholars say that when it is impossible for a man to make peace with his fellow at any other time, peace will come on this day. [Leket Yosher]

For Yom Kippur is the embodiment of all the days of the year, and it gives life to all the days. It humbles man's heart, making him desire only to cling to the Name of God, be blessed. Thus, all kinds of material and spiritual divisions are abolished and peace is made. Hence joy and gladness remain. [Likkute Etzot]

PRAYER SHAWL

It is a widespread custom through all the Diaspora of Israel to pray in prayer shawls on the night of Yom Kippur. One

must wrap himself in his prayer shawl while it is still daylight, in order to be able to say the benediction over that act.
But there are places where prayer shawls are not worn on the
night of Yom Kippur [see Rashi, Sefer ha-Pardes]. Rabbi
Joseph ben Moses [15th cent.], the author of Leket Yosher,
wrote to the same effect: "I remember that prayer shawls
were not worn in Austria on the night of Kol Nidre."

LIGHT IS SOWN

Before Kol Nidre a great light comes down from on high,
filling all the worlds and the angels and the souls to over-
flowing. They collect because of the tears which we let fall
before the Name of God. [Pinhas of Koretz, manuscript]

Before Kol Nidre the Ark is opened and the Torah Scroll
is taken out. But there are places where it is not the custom
to take out Torah Scrolls, and the Ark is not even opened.
[Likkute Mahariah]

There are places where two Scrolls are taken out, and
other places where all the Torah Scrolls are taken out and
given to the elders of the congregation, who stand on the
platform. Everyone embraces and kisses the Torah Scrolls,
and beseeches their forgiveness and pardon for having dishonored the Torah; they all take it upon themselves to guard
the Torah in their hearts, and to walk in its ways. The verse,
"Light is sown for the righteous, and gladness for the upright of heart" (Ps. 97:11), is recited seven times.

AND GLADNESS FOR THE UPRIGHT OF HEART

It was the holy way of the righteous Rabbi Meir of Apt [19th
cent.] to kindle the hearts of Israel with extreme joy for the
service of the Name of God. One Kol Nidre night many
people were assembled in the House of Prayer. The rabbi

entered the House of Prayer and said with great excitement, "Jews, let us appease our Holy Torah whom we have dishonored all year by not fulfilling the commandments which are written in it." At once all the people were so struck by his words that they burst into weeping which lasted for two hours.

As soon as the rabbi, of blessed memory, had said these words he went home. After two hours he returned to the House of Prayer and saw that they were all weeping. He cried, "Jews, this is not what I desired; I wish you to turn to God in joy." And he began to chant the hymn, "Majesty and faithfulness are His who lives forever," with such enthusiasm and pleasure that they all stopped crying and took one another by the hand and danced for an hour in a great circle. Then they began Kol Nidre. [Kehal Hasidim he-Hadash]

iv. Kol Nidre and the Night of Yom Kippur

THE ORDER OF KOL NIDRE

The Reader takes his stand before the Ark and lowers his prayer shawl over his face.

Two men are stationed, one at the right and one at the left of the Reader, as it is said (Exod. 17:12): "and Aaron and Hur stayed up his hands, the one on the one side, and the other on the other side." [Mordekhai, Yoma, quoting Pirke Rabbi Eliezer]

Each of them takes a Torah Scroll in his hand, one standing on one side of the Reader, and the other on the other side, and says with him three times, "With the knowledge of the Omnipresent, and with the knowledge of the congre-

gation, by authority of the court on high, and by authority
of the court below, we give permission to pray with the
transgressors." For before praying, all the transgressors
are admitted, so that the entire congregation can pray.

Even if the transgressors have not asked for permission
it is given them, for Rabbi Simeon Hasida said (Keritot
6b): "Every public fast in which no sinners of Israel are
present is no fast; for though the odor of galbanum is bad,
yet the Scripture counted it among the spices that make
atonement for the children of Israel." [Menorat ha-Maor]

KOL NIDRE

Then the Reader chants Kol Nidre in the chant handed
down by our fathers from past generations. They begin
the prayer while it is still daylight, and continue into the
night. They all chant Kol Nidre three times. The Reader
begins softly, and raises his voice higher the second time,
and even higher the third, chanting Kol Nidre with trembling and fear and devotion, while the congregation say it
with him in a whisper.

The first time the Reader chants Kol Nidre he ought to
chant in a very low voice, like a man who is amazed at
entering the palace of the king to ask for a favor, and is
afraid of coming close to the king; and so the Reader speaks
softly, like one asking for something. The second time he
ought to raise his voice a little higher than the first time. The
third time he ought to raise his voice higher and higher,
like a man who is at home and accustomed to being a member of the king's household. [Mahzor Vitri, No. 351]

WHY KOL NIDRE

The reason why it is the custom to chant Kol Nidre on the

night of Yom Kippur is because Yom Kippur is a day of forgiveness and Teshuvah, and it is necessary for a man to purify himself of his iniquities. . . . If a man has made a vow during the year and remembers his vow, he must fulfil it; and if he does not fulfil it, Yom Kippur does not make atonement for him. For so we have learned: "Those who are liable for sin-offerings and unconditional guilt-offerings must bring them, even if Yom Kippur intervenes, after Yom Kippur. Those who are liable for suspended guilt-offerings are exempt" (Mishnah Keritot VI.4). This teaches us that Yom Kippur does not make atonement for the sin-offering and the unconditional guilt-offering; and vows are like sin-offerings. It is necessary to fulfil the vows if they are remembered, for a man is under obligation to fulfil a vow from the time he makes it, for Yom Kippur does not make atonement for vows. For this reason, the Geonim of the academies instituted the practice of saying Kol Nidre on the night of Yom Kippur, for remembered vows are fulfilled and the vower is exempt, but what if he does not remember them? What is he to do then, that he may be atoned and be pure on Yom Kippur? So the Geonim instituted the practice of making public annulment of vows that were not remembered. [Rashi, Likkute ha-Pardes]

Rav Natronai [9th cent.] said: "It is not the custom either in the two academies or in these parts to annul vows; neither on Rosh ha-Shanah, nor on Yom Kippur is Kol Nidre recited, though we have heard that it is recited in other lands. But we never saw or heard the like from our fathers. We have already revealed our opinion, and explained explicitly why Kol Nidre ought not to be recited at all. Of what use is an annulment to a man who makes the condition after he has taken a vow that it is to be void? Hence, we do not think and practice thus."

Rav Hai Gaon bar Nahshon Gaon [9th cent.] wrote to
the same effect: "We do not annul vows either on Rosh ha-
Shanah or on Yom Kippur, and we have not heard that our
rabbis ever did so. You too ought to be strict like us, and not
depart from the practice of the academies." [Kol Bo; see
Tur Orah Hayyim, No. 619]

The same is true of Rabbi Isaac Alfasi [11th cent.] and
Rabbi Moses ben Maimon [12th cent.], who omitted any
discussion of Kol Nidre from their decisions, for it seems
they thought it ought not to be said at all.

Rabbi Isaac ben Sheshet Barfat [14th cent.], too, wrote
in a responsum on the subject of Kol Nidre that it is best
not to say Kol Nidre at all, and that such was the custom
in Catalonia. [Bet Yosef, Tur Orah Hayyim, No. 619]

But since the custom had become rooted in the people
and it was hard to uproot it, a few of the sages changed the
version slightly, so that the prayer might be less like an
annulment than a plea for pardon and forgiveness from the
Holy One, blessed be he, in which we plead with him to
forgive us for the iniquity of our vows. Such is the version
[Shibbole ha-Leket, No. 317] quoted by Rav Hai Gaon
[10th–11th cent.]. Rabbi Jacob Tam [12th cent.] also introduced changes in the popular version.

The custom of reciting Kol Nidre has already spread into
every country. It is the Ashkenazic and Sephardic custom
to say it in Aramaic, and the custom in the Balkans and in
Italy to say it in Hebrew.

After reciting Kol Nidre three times, the congregation
cries out with the Reader: "And all the congregation of the
children of Israel shall be forgiven, and the stranger that
sojourneth among them; for in respect of all the people it

was done in error" (Num. 15:26)—in order that the Holy
One, blessed be he, will consent to forgive all the sin of
Israel [Mordekhai, Yoma]. It is the custom for the Reader
to recite the verse three times, and when he finishes, the
congregation says it three times; it is the custom to recite the
verse in a loud voice.

I HAVE PARDONED

Then the Reader recites once, "Pardon, I pray Thee, the
iniquity of this people according unto the greatness of Thy
lovingkindness, and according as Thou hast forgiven this
people, from Egypt even until now (Num. 14:19). And
there it is said. . . ." Then the congregation recites three
times in a loud voice, "And the Lord said: 'I have pardoned
according to thy word'" (Num. 14:20). Then the Reader
recites after them, "I have pardoned according to thy word."

The pious Rabbi Isaac of Neskhizh, of blessed memory,
related in the name of the pious Rabbi Levi Isaac of Berditchev [18th cent.] that once on the night of Yom Kippur
Rabbi Levi Isaac said: Master of the universe, we do not
have the strength to say, "And the Lord said, I have pardoned." Say Thou, "I have pardoned." [Zikhron Tov]

WHO HAS KEPT US ALIVE

Then the Reader recites the benediction with the phrase
"who has kept us alive," and everyone recites the benediction
in a whisper, giving praise and acknowledgment to the
Creator, be blessed, for having allowed us to merit life, and
to be able to fulfil his commandments on that day by fasting
and abstaining from work, and by prayer. The congregation finishes before the Reader so as to be able to respond,
Amen.

The women who have already recited the benediction with the phrase, "who has kept us alive," while lighting the candles at home ought not to recite the benediction again in the House of Prayer, but ought to listen to the Reader and respond, Amen. [Mateh Efrayim]

If Yom Kippur falls on a Sabbath, the Ninety-second Psalm is recited. Then the Scrolls are returned to the Ark, and everyone returns to his place.

REMINISCENCE: AN AMERICAN FARMER

I will never forget the beautiful scene that took place during Kol Nidre. The quorum assembled in the house of one of the farmers. The house was surrounded by trees; the windows were open, and a soft, refreshing breeze was blowing. The menfolk looking very healthy stood in one room, wrapped in their prayer shawls, while the women stood in the other with sunburnt faces and white dresses. The sad and pleasant Kol Nidre melody flowed into the silence of the night. It seemed as though nature itself was listening to the song of the eternal wanderer, who had at last found a place to rest his head. I remembered the Kol Nidre that my forefathers had chanted hiding in dark cellars in Spain. There they poured forth their hearts before their God. Their groaning and moaning were contained in the damp, cold earth, until such time as the Inquisitors came and drew the miserable folk out of the bowels of the earth into the beautiful sunshine—and cast them into the fire. Only then could a Jew freely cry the powerful words, "Hear, O Israel."

The cantor lifted his voice and chanted Kol Nidre for the third time. I seemed to awake from a terrible dream. I saw a beautiful world lying before me. The birds under the window were assisting the cantor with their song, and the

heaven and the earth, those witnesses of all that had happened
to the people of Israel, were joining in song.

Our Creator, thou art eternal, and thy folk Israel is
eternal. [Shishim Shenot Hayyim]

THE EVENING PRAYER ON YOM KIPPUR

The order to be found in our festival prayer books is followed
in reciting the Evening Prayer. The Confession is recited
before the prayer beginning, "O my God, guard my tongue
from evil."

THEY SHALL CONFESS . . .

If a man has transgressed against any of the commandments
in the Torah, whether affirmative or prohibitive, whether
deliberately or accidentally, when he does Teshuvah and
turns from his sin, he is under obligation to confess before
God, be blessed, as it is said, "When a man or woman shall
commit any sin that men commit, to commit a trespass
against the Lord, and that soul be guilty; then they shall
confess their sin which they have done" (Num. 5:6–7).
This is verbal confession and is an affirmative commandment. What is the confession?

The sinner says, "Pray, O God, I have sinned, I have done
iniquitously, trespassed before you and done such and such
things; indeed, I am sorry and ashamed of my actions, and
I will never return and do this act again." That is the essence
of confession. The more the sinner confesses and enlarges
on his sin, the more praiseworthy he is. [Maimonides,
Hilkhot Teshuvah I.1]

THE POINT OF CONFESSION

The point of confession is to recognize that one has committed a sin, and before whom the sin was committed, and

to be heartily ashamed of it, and to regret it; and He who knows all the hidden things will bear witness that the sinner will not sin again, nor return to his folly. [Devash le-Fi]

Just as a sacrifice without Teshuvah is called an abomination—"The sacrifice of the wicked is an abomination" (Prov. 21:27)—so a confession without the heart's agreeing not to sin again is called an abomination. [Meil Shmuel]

A NEW CREATURE

The commentators undertook to comprehend how confession and regretfulness could help the person who is doing Teshuvah, for the law is that a speech cannot void an act. The sinner is guilty of many evil actions, so how can confession, which is a form of speech, help him? But our rabbis, of blessed memory, said that the Holy One, blessed be he, makes a new creature of the man who does Teshuvah (Pesikta Rabbati), and the result is that his speech of confession is the cause of a powerful and great act of creation, and of course all his evil actions are voided. [Midbar Kedemot]

JUDGMENT ACCORDING TO THE MAN

I found this story in a manuscript by Rabbi Hayyim Saragossi, "the great miracle worker," of blessed memory, who heard it from the great Rabbi Abraham Skandari [17th cent.] who heard it from the scholars, who received it in a direct oral line from Rabbi Moses ben Maimon, of blessed memory.

A certain pious man said to Rabbi Moses ben Maimon that he did not need to make the usual confession on Yom Kippur, for he knew that he had not committed any of those sins, and he ought not tell a lie to the King.

Rabbi Moses replied to him, "If you only knew, O wise one,

how difficult is the service of God, be blessed, and how much one ought to serve God, you would certainly know that no day passes during which you do not do everything that is mentioned in the confession, and many other things as well. Every man is judged according to the greatness of his wisdom. So we find that David, peace be upon him, was considered guilty of adultery, although Bathsheba was divorced from Uriah, and considered guilty of his murder, although Uriah deserved death, and considered guilty of iniquity because he cut off the tail of King Saul's robe, even though Saul was pursuing him. For a man's judgment and punishment depends on what he is. Now, for these very words which you have spoken, you, too, are destined to render an account."

Those were the words of the holy man. [Midbar Kedemot]

THE ORDER OF CONFESSION

The sages of old, who knew the sorrow of the sinner who is truly turning to his God but has no words to tell his sins, composed many confessions. Some of them are arranged alphabetically, to make amends for the sinner's marring of the twenty-two letters in which the Torah is written; others are arranged to correspond to the tractates of the Talmud, to make amends for a sinner's defections from the Babylonian and Palestinian Talmuds; others are arranged to correspond to the limbs of the body, to make amends for the sins men commit with each and every limb of their bodies, either in this state or any of their other manifestations.

The order of the confessions in our prayer books and festival prayer books is alphabetical; everyone recites them. The man who knows that he has committed one particular sin ought to cry as he mentions that sin and confess to it

with particular emotion. And if he has committed a sin that
is not mentioned in the confession, he says that sin in a
whisper to himself, and confesses to it from the depths of
his heart and cries over it. But he ought not to raise his voice,
for one does not confess for a personal sin loudly, as it is
said, "Blessed is he whose transgression is forgiven, whose
sin is covered" (Ps. 32:1). But if his sin is well known, he can
confess to it loudly, if he wishes.

WHY THE CONFESSION IS ALPHABETICAL

An alphabetical confession was instituted because the sinner
is destroying the world which God created using the letters of the Torah. [Asarah Maamarot]

There is another reason why the confession is alphabetical:
It may be compared to a king who became displeased with
his wife, and banished her far away. When she had been
away for a long time, she grew very unhappy. What did
she do? She appeared before the king, and, taking the same
violin that had been played at their wedding, played it again,
saying as she played, "Such and such was my offense against
you." She went on confessing and crying until the king's
compassion was moved, as he remembered his love for her
during his youth and at their wedding.

Now the king referred to is the King over all kings, the
Holy One, blessed be he. The wife is the assembly of Israel,
whom he sanctified on Mount Sinai, when he gave us the
sacred Torah; but we rebelled against his word, and he
banished us to alien lands.

Now in the Exile we remember the sanctity that was ours
during the time of the Temple, and that we are now in the
midst of uncleanliness. We say in our hearts: Let us take
the violin on which they played during our wedding—that

is, the alphabet in which the sacred Torah was given—and let us play on it and confess to and cry out our sins alphabetically, until the compassion of God will be moved, when he remembers the love he felt for us in his youth at our wedding—that is, the day when the Torah was given; perhaps he will redeem us speedily in our time, Amen, so be his will. [Tiferet Uziel]

ALL ISRAEL RESPONSIBLE FOR ONE ANOTHER

Why was the Confession composed in the plural, so that we say, We have sinned, rather than, I have sinned? Because all Israel is one body and every one of Israel is a limb of that body; that is why we are all responsible for one another when we sin. So, if one's fellow should sin, it is as though one has sinned oneself; therefore, despite the fact that one has not committed that iniquity, one must confess to it. For when one's fellow has sinned, it is as though one has sinned oneself. [Yesod ha-Teshuvah VI, quoting Isaac Luria]

JOYFUL MELODIES

The Baal Shem Tov, may his merit shield us [18th cent.], once came to a certain city before Rosh ha-Shanah. He asked the inhabitants of the city, "Who is the Reader here during the Days of Awe?" They said to him, "The rabbi of the city." The Baal Shem Tov asked, "How does he conduct the prayers?" They said to him, "He chants all the confessions of Yom Kippur with joyful melodies."

The Baal Shem Tov sent after the rabbi and asked him, "Why do you sing the confessions joyfully?" Said the rabbi to him, "Lo, a servant who is cleaning the courtyard of the king, if he loves the king, is very happy cleaning the refuse from the courtyard, and sings joyful melodies, for he is giving pleasure to the king."

Said the Baal Shem Tov, "May my lot be with yours!"
[Or Yesharim]

OH, LET OUR PRAYER RISE

After the Prayer of Benedictions, the Ark is opened and the
Reader chants the hymn beginning, "Oh, let our prayer
rise."

And why is this hymn chanted in a Wallachian melody?
This was once explained by Rabbi Israel Baal Shem Tov, of
blessed memory, who said that this people have suffered a
great deal but never denied their God, and therefore they
merit the very melody that Israel, who are holy, sing on a
holy day and in a holy place before the Holy One, blessed
be he. [In the Heart of the Seas]

On a Sabbath this hymn is preceded by other prayers related to the Sabbath. Then the congregation and the Reader
recite liturgical poems, penitential prayers and hymns, and
the Ark being opened while some of them are being recited.
Then the Confession is repeated. After the conclusion of the
established Evening Prayer, it is the custom to read from the
Psalms, as well as to read the Hymn of Unity and the Hymn
of Glory. There are some who are accustomed to read the
liturgical poem called, "The Crown of Kingdom," composed
by Rabbi Solomon ibn Gabirol [11th cent.].

THE NIGHT OF YOM KIPPUR

Rabbi Obadiah of Bertinoro [15th-16th cent.] wrote this
about Palermo in his book of travels: On the night of Yom
Kippur and on the night of Hoshanah Rabbah, after the congregation has completed the Evening Prayer, I have seen
trustees of the House of Prayer open the doors of the Ark,
and remain there all night until daylight. The women come
in families to bow and kiss the Torah Scrolls. They enter at

one door and depart at the other across the way. All night they enter and depart, one after another.

It is the custom in Aden and Yemen for every man to approach his fellow after the Evening Prayer, and for them to embrace and to kiss and bless one another. Each man says to his fellow: May you receive tidings of forgiveness and pardon and atonement; may you be inscribed in the book of life and of remembrance. . . . [Nahlat Yosef II]

Thus related Rabbi Jacob Saphir ha-Levi [19th cent.] in the book of his journeys. After the Evening Prayer every man approaches his neighbor in the House of Prayer and they embrace, as is the way of the Ishmaelites on their holidays to this very day. It is an ancient custom, and they bless one another with these words: May your prayers be answered and may you be sealed for a good life. [Even Sappir II, Bet Aden]

PSALMS

It is the custom in many parts of the Exile to recite all the Book of Psalms on the night of Yom Kippur. This is a good custom for those who are conscientious, for there is nothing more important than the Book of Psalms, which contains everything. In it are many Psalms of praise to the Name of God, and many Psalms about awakening to Teshuvah, and many Psalms which are pleas for pardon and forgiveness; and all the Psalms come from the hand of God. King David, of blessed memory, composed them in his wisdom. For he who recites Psalms is like one who prays and like one who engages in Torah study, for King David asked that those who read Psalms should receive the same reward as they would receive if they were engaged in the depths of the Torah. [Shene Luhot ha-Berit, Hilkhot Teshuvah]

PRACTICES FOR THE NIGHT OF YOM KIPPUR

Some people stay awake all night, as a remembrance of the Temple, for thus we learn: "Some of the worthiest men in Jerusalem did not sleep all the night" (Yoma 19b), but sang songs of praise.

There are some whose custom it is to study the tractates of Yoma and Keritot. The kabbalists wrote that it is good to study the secrets of the Torah on that night, because then the gates of understanding are open. [See Or ha-Yashar]

There are some whose custom it is to stand up all the night and all the day of Yom Kippur. But he who does not know for certain that this standing during the prayer will not put him to sleep, or prevent him from praying as he ought—it is a transgression for him to do so, and he ought not to stand even during the day. [Shene Luhot ha-Berit]

Those who sit in the House of Prayer all the night of Yom Kippur ought to be careful not to engage in any conversation at all, for if they do, their loss will be greater than their gain. They ought not to speak even words of the Torah, and to speak only in the Holy Tongue, for that is not the hour and the place to speak in a secular tongue, even words of admonition. Rabbi Isaac Luria [16th cent.] was careful never to speak in a secular tongue in the House of Prayer during the other days of the year, not even when he was delivering a sermon and words of admonition. Would that we could take our cue from him on this holy night! [Moed lekhol Hai, No. 19]

EVERY MAN TO HIS CAMP

A certain rich man once stayed behind in the House of Prayer on the night of Yom Kippur after the prayer, to read through the Book of Psalms. Said the Gaon Rabbi Joseph Dov of Brisk [19th cent.] to him: "A soldier who deserts the army and leaves the country is guilty of the death penalty. But if he should not leave the country, but merely desert one regiment to join another belonging to the same king— for example, if he was assigned to the infantry and deserted to the cavalry, or the other way around—what is the verdict then? Perhaps because he is still serving his king, he isn't considered a deserter? Or perhaps, because he is not serving in the regiment where he was assigned, he is called a deserter anyhow?"

The rich man stood there, wondering what the rabbi was trying to say.

Then the rabbi continued and said, "But I have clear proof that, nevertheless, that soldier is called a deserter. For everyone must serve his king in his own regiment. In the same way, each and every man in Israel must serve the King over all the world with the service that has been laid upon him. The rich man must do charity on the eve of Yom Kippur and give back their pledges to the poor who cannot redeem them; and the poor man who cannot do charity has to do Teshuvah and pray a great deal. Therefore it is the way of the poor to stay in the House of Prayer on the night of Yom Kippur to recite Psalms, and the way of the rich who have given a great deal of charity to go home and sleep.

"Now you, my friend, have deserted your own regiment, and have come to serve your Creator with the service of the poor, thinking to do your duty in that way. You too are called a deserter, for every man must serve his Creator in the camp where he is assigned." [Shemen ha-Tov]

A TALE

The pious Rabbi Meir, the head of the Court of the city of

Karyszczew, author of the book, "Enlightener of the Eyes
of the Wise," was a miracle-worker and a great kabbalist.
Once, after the prayer on the night of Yom Kippur, he lay
down on his bed with his eyes shut and his hands out-
stretched. Every one of the men of the city came and laid
his head under the rabbi's hands, and the rabbi blessed him.

There was a young man who had separated from his
wife because of a quarrel that had come between them, and
had remained away from her for a long time. As soon as he
lowered his head to be blessed, the rabbi sensed who it was
and said, "This man is not living with his wife. I hate such
things. Immediately after Yom Kippur you must make
peace and live together with her again." [Kehal Hasidim
he-Hadash]

v. The Gates of Compassion

THE NIGHT THE SAME AS THE DAY

On Yom Kippur the night is the same as the day. For during
all the days of the year the gates of compassion are open
during the day; during the night they are shut. But on Yom
Kippur, the night is the same as the day; for the gates of
understanding are open from nightfall on, and the night is
the same as the day, to our benefit. [Hemdat Yamim]

PRAYER OF THOSE WHO DWELL IN FIELDS

A certain man took a journey to be able to spend Yom Kippur
with the Baal Shem Tov [18th cent.]. He traveled all the
day and night before Yom Kippur, in order to arrive at his
destination early. The morning of the eve of Yom Kippur
he reached a certain spot near Mezbizh. Said he to himself,
"Here I am near Mezbizh and the horse is very tired, for it

has traveled all night. I'll stop here and pray; meanwhile the horse can graze."

After his prayer, he felt sleep overcoming him. He said to himself, "What difference does it make if I sleep a little? Meanwhile the horse will rest, and afterward I'll be able to travel faster and will certainly come to Mezbizh before noon." So he lay down in the wagon and fell asleep.

When the man awoke he saw it was already dusk of Yom Kippur. He grew very unhappy at the thought that he would be forced to pray in a field near the city after he had tried so hard to be with the Baal Shem Tov on Yom Kippur. He cried loud and bitterly all day and all night.

At the close of Yom Kippur, the man quickly traveled to the Baal Shem Tov. But when he arrived, the Baal Shem Tov made fun of him. For heaven had willed that he was to raise on high the prayer of those who dwell in the fields, by means of his prayer. [Shivhe ha-Besht]

COMBINING LETTERS

A certain countryman, who knew that it is right to eat and drink heartily on the eve of the holy day, said to himself, "I will eat and drink until after the Afternoon Prayer. Then I will get on my horse and will reach the city in a short time." When he concluded his meal, he mounted his horse. But he got lost in the forest, and could not find the way. The sun set and the night of Kol Nidre arrived. He saw that he would have to remain in the forest all the night and all the day of the holy and awesome day. He had no festival prayer book with him, for he had already sent ahead those he had to the city with the members of his household.

The countryman wept long and bitterly and said, "Master of the universe, what shall I do? But there is a verse, 'The word of the Lord can be combined' [cf. Ps. 18:31]. I shall recite the alphabet and you, O Master of the universe, must combine the letters into syllables and words." So he recited all the letters of the alphabet.

Now this recital made a great impression in heaven, for the countryman drew many other prayers to heaven after his. [Devarim Arevim]

THE COMPASSION OF THE RIGHTEOUS

One Yom Kippur, before the pious Rabbi David of Lelov [18th–19th cent.] became a rabbi, he went to the Seer of Lublin to be with him on that day. After the Concluding Meal on the eve of Yom Kippur, Rabbi David went to the ritual bath. When he left the bath, he ran in the direction of the House of Study of the Seer to pray Kol Nidre. On the way he heard an infant crying. He entered the house and found the infant lying alone in his cradle, for its father and mother had gone to the House of Prayer and left the infant without anyone to take care of it. Rabbi David spoke to the child and soothed it and then began rocking it. After the prayer, the father and mother of the infant returned and found the zaddik rocking the infant.

See the compassion the pious feel for Israel! On the night of Yom Kippur, when everybody hurries to pray in the midst of a congregation, that zaddik had pity on an infant in Israel and thought it a very worthy deed to take care of it, despite the fact that by doing so he was forced to pray alone. [Migdal David]

Pious men have compassion not only on Israel, but even on the animals belonging to Gentiles. Once it happened that Rabbi Israel Salanter [19th cent.] was going to the House of Prayer for Kol Nidre. On the way he saw an animal belonging to a Gentile, which was lost. He saw that the animal was in distress, and troubled himself to lead it home over stones and rocks, through fields and gardens. Meanwhile, all the congregation was waiting for him. When he did not come, they went out to look for him. They found him trying to lead the animal into its master's stall.

vi. The Morning Service and the Memorial Prayer

RISING

One rises before daylight for the Morning Prayer. And there are some who say [Keneset ha-Gedolah, Orah Hayyim, No. 619] that one ought not to get up too early, lest sleep overpower him during the Morning Prayer. One washes one's hands up to the joints of one's fingers, and removes the mucus with his fingers before wiping his eyes.

Then one goes to the House of Prayer, and puts on his kittel and wraps himself in a prayer shawl.

The Morning Prayer is recited according to the order to be found in the festival prayer books. The Prayer of Benedictions is recited silently; then the Reader repeats the Prayer of Benedictions, with the addition of many liturgical poems, penitential prayers, and hymns, some while the Ark is open. In Jerusalem the priests ascend to the Ark to "bless the people of Israel with love."

THE ORDER OF TAKING OUT THE TORAH SCROLL

Before taking the Torah Scroll out of the Ark, the prayers beginning, "There is none like unto you" and "Father of Compassion" are recited. Then the leader gives the im-

portant men in the congregation the honor of taking the
Scrolls out of the Ark. If there are any Torah crowns or
other sacred vessels, he gives to certain respected men the
honor of putting them on the Scrolls, while the rest of the
people stand silently by.

Then the Ark is opened, and the verse beginning, "And
it came to pass, when the ark set forward" (Num. 10:35) is
recited, and then the sentence, "Blessed be He who in his
holiness hath given the Torah unto His people Israel." The
Thirteen Qualities are recited three times; then the prayer
beginning, "Master of the universe, fill the needs of our
heart for our good," is recited, and the verse, "But as for me,
let my prayer be unto Thee, O Lord, in an acceptable time; O
God, in the abundance of Thy mercy, answer me with the
truth of Thy salvation" (Ps. 69:14). Then two Scrolls are
taken out of the Ark and the prayer beginning, "Blessed
be the Name of the Master of the universe" is recited.

He who takes the Torah Scroll out of the Ark holds it in
his right arm, and he who receives it, first receives it with
both arms and then moves it over to his right. The Reader
stands with a Torah Scroll in his right arm facing the Ark,
until the congregation has finished the prayer beginning,
"Blessed be the Name." Then he turns to face the congregation and loudly and melodiously calls out, "Hear O Israel,"
and recites the line, "One is our God, great is our Lord,
holy and awesome is his Name" and lifts the Torah Scroll
up high and says, "Magnify God with me and let us exalt
his Name together," to which the congregation replies,
"Yours, O Lord, is the greatness and the might. . . . " Then
he turns to his right and walks to the platform on which
the reading takes place, and the man holding the second
Torah Scroll walks after him. Every one whom the Torah

Scroll passes stands and embraces it with both hands and kisses it, and accompanies the Scroll to the platform. While they are walking, the congregation recite the prayers beginning, "Magnified and sanctified . . . above all things be the name of the King over all kings," and "Father of compassion, have compassion. . . ." As soon as they reach the platform, the Reader places the Scroll in his arm on the reading table, and the other man gives the Scroll in his arm to a responsible boy, who sits on the platform with it until the concluding portion is read from it.

Then the mantle is taken off the Scroll on the table and the Scroll is opened at the place where it is to be read, and the mantle spread over it and the Reader recites, "And may He help and shield and save all those who trust in him." Then he calls out, "Let [so and so] the priest, come forward," and recites, "Blessed is He who in his holiness gave the Torah to his people Israel," and the congregation reply, "But ye that cleave unto the Lord your God are alive every one of you this day" (Deut. 4:4).

He who goes up to the Torah stands at the right of the Reader and holds the "Trees of Life" [handles of the Scroll] with both hands by a cloth or his prayer shawl, and opens the Scroll, and sees the verse where the Reader is to begin, and kisses it with his prayer shawl, and recites silently, "It is a tree of life to them that grasp it." Then he turns his face to the congregation and recites the blessing in a loud voice, "Bless ye the Lord who is to be blessed." All the people respond, "Blessed be the Lord, who is blessed for ever and ever." Then he continues and recites the blessing with the phrase, "who has chosen us" and ending, "giver of the Torah." When the Torah Reader begins to read, the one who has gone up to the reading takes his left hand from the

Scroll and holds the Scroll with his right only throughout the reading, and reads silently with the Reader, word for word. After the reading, he rolls the Scroll shut and recites the blessing, "Blessed art thou, O Lord . . . who has given us a Torah of truth . . . blessed art thou, O Lord, giver of the Torah."

THE READING OF THE TORAH

The section beginning, "And the Lord spoke unto Moses, after the death of the two sons of Aaron" (Lev. 16), is read, because it speaks of the service in the Temple on Yom Kippur.

Rabbi Hiyyah bar Abba said: The sons of Aaron died on the first of Nisan. Then why does the Torah mention their death on Yom Kippur? To teach us that just as Yom Kippur makes atonement for Israel, so the death of the righteous makes atonement for Israel. [Yerushalmi, Yoma I.1; Lev. Rabbah XX]

It is cited in the Zohar on Leviticus 16, that every time righteous men leave the world, judgment leaves the world, and the death of the righteous makes atonement for the iniquities of their generation. Therefore, we read the scriptural section about the death of the sons of Aaron on Yom Kippur in order that it may be an atonement for the iniquities of Israel. Said the Holy One, blessed be he, "Engage in the study of the death of these righteous, and it will be accounted for you as though you were sacrificing on this day and it will make atonement for you." For we have learned that so long as Israel are in Exile and cannot sacrifice two he-goats on this day, the two sons of Aaron may be a memorial of the sacrifice, and we may be atoned through them.

Said Rabbi Yose: It was instituted that this scriptural por-

tion was to be read on Yom Kippur, to make atonement for
Israel who are in Exile, because atonement is the order of
this day, and because the death of the sons of Aaron makes
atonement for Israel. From this we learn that every man
upon whom the sufferings that are chastisements fall is given
an atonement for his sins. Every one who is sorrowful over
the sufferings of the righteous—his own sins are removed
from the world, and he is forgiven. Therefore, the section
about the death of the sons of Aaron is read on this day,
that the people may hear and be sorrowful over the death of
the righteous, and the people's sin may be atoned. For the
Holy One, blessed be he, announces, concerning every one
who is sorrowful for the death of the righteous, or lets tears
fall for them, "And thine iniquity is taken away, and thy
sin expiated" (Isa. 6:7). Besides, the sons of those who are
sorrowful will never die during their lifetime. Of them is
written (Isa. 53:10): "That he might see his seed, prolong
his days." [Zohar III. 56b, 57b]

Then six men are called to the reading of the Torah, the
number corresponding to the subject of the day, which is
atonement for the created world which was created during
the six days of Creation, the number also corresponding to
this world which is compared by our sages to the six days
of the week. If Yom Kippur falls on a Sabbath, seven men
are called to the reading of the Torah. No more than seven
are called up; even if there should be a large gain for charity
[through their donations], it is not the practice to add any
more readers, because the conclusion of every reading from
the Torah refers to the subject of atonement—therefore, one
ought not to make any changes. [Kol Bo; Shaare Efrayim]

The one who has gone up to the reading of the Torah is
blessed with the benediction beginning, "May He who

blessed Abraham, Isaac and Jacob," the phrase, "and may he inscribe him and seal him in the book of pardon and forgiveness" being inserted. He who goes up to the reading promises a donation to charity.

READING FROM THE PROPHETS

After the benediction has been recited by the last one to go up to the Torah, the second Torah Scroll is placed on the table, and the half-Kaddish is chanted with a special melody, and the Reader recites the benediction beginning, "May He who blessed," for the one who is being honored with raising and also the one who is being honored with rolling the Torah Scroll. Then they raise and roll the Scroll together. According to the custom of the Sephardim, the raising takes place before the reading of the Torah. During the rolling, the second Torah Scroll in which the concluding portion is read is uncovered and the scriptural portion beginning, "And on the tenth day" (Num. 29:7–11), is read, and the benediction after reading a portion is recited. Then the Reader recites the benediction beginning, "May He who blessed," for those who raise and roll the Torah Scroll, and they raise and roll the Scroll. When they have finished the rolling, the one who is to read the prophetic portion begins the benedictions before the prophetic portion, and reads the portion in the prophets, beginning, "And He will say: Cast ye up, cast ye up, clear the way," and ending, "for the mouth of the Lord hath spoken it" (Isa. 57:14–58:14). There are some whose practice it is to begin with the verse, "For thus saith the High and Lofty One" (Isa. 57:15).

The reason for reading this prophetic portion is because there are references in it to the subject of the day, such as,

"Is such the fast that I have chosen? The day for a man to afflict his soul?" (Isa. 58:5) and "And the holy of the Lord honorable" (Isa. 58:13), of which the Talmud (Shabbat 119a) said, "That is Yom Kippur." [Tanya]

Then the blessings after the prophetic portion are recited, with special mention of the subject of atonement. If Yom Kippur falls on a Sabbath, special mention is made of the Sabbath day. There are places where the person reading the prophetic portion concludes, "Blessed art thou, O Lord, King who pardons and forgives our iniquities. . . . "

CIRCUMCISION ON YOM KIPPUR

If there is a circumcision on Yom Kippur, it is made between the reading of the Torah and the Additional Prayer. There are some whose custom it is to make the circumcision before the prayer beginning, "Happy are they that dwell in Thy house" (Ps. 84:5), while there are others whose custom it is to circumcise afterward, before the prayer beginning, "Let them praise the name of the Lord." This is the case when the infant is circumcised in the House of Prayer. But if it is necessary to leave the House of Prayer in order to circumcise the infant at its home, the Torah Scroll is first returned to the Ark, because it is improper to lay the Torah Scroll down and go outside.

There are some who say [Peer ha-Dor, No. 63] that the blessing of circumcision is not recited over a cup of wine, for the blessing does not require it. But there are others who say [Ha-Manhig, quoting Rashi] that the blessing is recited over a cup of wine, which is put aside until after Yom Kippur. There are still others who say [Tosafot, Shabbat 139a] that the infant is given a taste of the wine. There are still others who say [Even ha-Ezer, No. 83] that the infant to be circumcised is given a taste of the cup, in addition to that which he is given during the recitation of the ritual prayer containing the phrase, "In thy blood, live" (Ezek. 16:6). The latter indeed is the custom [Mateh Efrayim; Avodat Yisrael]. If the mother must eat, the circumcision is made near her, and she is given the cup to drink from.

MEMORIAL PRAYERS

It is a widespread custom in most of the Diaspora of Israel to recall the souls of one's fathers and relatives who went to their eternal world, on Yom Kippur after the reading from the prophets, and to donate to charity for the recollection of their souls.

Whether he be young or old, everyone whose father and mother are still alive goes outside during the Memorial Prayers, to avoid the possibility of the evil eye, and also that he may not err and say the prayer with the mourners and thus "be bound by a slip of his tongue" [cf. Sanhedrin 102a]. Another reason for his leaving is that if he stayed he would be silent while everybody else was engaged in prayer. [Amude ha-Shulhan]

It is the custom for those whose fathers or mothers have died during the year to go outside during the Memorial Prayers, because they might be reminded of their bitter sorrow and disturb the others with their mourning. [Kerem Shelomo; Orah Hayyim, No. 668]

THE BELOVED AND THE PLEASANT

There are communities where Memorial Prayers are recited for the souls of the rabbis and community leaders who arose in our Exile and, the former with their learning and the latter with their ordinances, strengthened the heart of Israel to bear all their troubles, and to give us singleness of purpose for the sake of God. Memorial Prayers are also recited for the souls of those who were killed for the sanctification of the Name of God, all those men, women, and infants, those who were killed, and whose who were burned, and those who were stoned, and those who were strangled, and those who were slaughtered, and those who were drowned, and those who were hanged, and those who were broken on the wheel, and those who were dragged to bits, and those who were buried alive, and those who suffered the cruelest tortures for the sake of His oneness. Memorial Prayers are also recited for the souls of those who were martyred in the Land of Israel, those who were slain, and those who were slaughtered, and those who were burned alive for the sanctification of the Land, and for the continuance of our people on the land which God promised to our forefathers.

When Memorial Prayers are recited for the souls of relatives, donations are pledged to charity. When Memorial Prayers are recited for the souls of the Geonim and poets and holy community leaders and martyrs, their deeds are mentioned, for their deeds are their charity. Of the Geonim it is said, "they spread the Torah in Israel, and enlightened Israel with their ordinances and their books." Of the poets it is said, "they composed prayers of praise to the Omnipresent and strengthened the heart of Israel with their liturgical poems." Of the community leaders it is said, "they labored in behalf of the congregations and engaged with perfect faithfulness in filling the public needs." And of the martyrs it is said, "in return for their suffering, may their souls be bound in the bond of life."

Many congregations make it a practice for those who go outside for the other Memorial Prayers to return to the House of Prayer for the special memorial prayers, that they may

take the death of the righteous and the martyrs to heart.
The reason why the dead are mentioned is because the
mention of death breaks a man's heart and subdues his
inclination to evil [Kol Bo]. This is particularly true when
the deaths of the beloved and pleasant men who sanctified
the name of heaven in their lives and in their deaths, are
mentioned.

After the Memorial Prayers, the Reader takes a Torah
Scroll in his hand and blesses all those who have donated to
charity on behalf of the souls that were recalled. There are
some who include in the blessing beginning, "May he who
blessed" the phrase "and may he inscribe him, and seal him
for good life on this Day of Judgment"; but there are others
who say [see Maggid Taalumah] that one ought not to
include the phrase "Day of Judgment," for Yom Kippur is
a day of compassion. Then the Reader recites the prayer
beginning, "God full of compassion," and the prayer beginning, "Father of compassion," is recited.

This prayer is not in the prayer books of the Sephardim,
and was instituted during the evil days of the persecutions
of 1096 [Siddur Avodat Yisrael]. It asks the Holy One,
blessed be he, to remember in his compassion "the saintly
and the upright and the wholehearted ones who gave their
souls for the sanctification of the Name of God."

VII. The Additional Prayer: The Service of the High Priest

THE ADDITIONAL PRAYER

The Reader begins the prayer with the fifth verse in Psalm
84 in a loud voice and in the melody of "Happy is the people
that know the joyful shout" (Ps. 89:16), which is recited

before the Additional Prayer of Rosh ha-Shanah. Then he takes the Torah Scroll in which the concluding portion was read and holds it in his hand and says, "Let them praise the name of the Lord; for His name alone is exalted," and the congregation answers after him, "His grandeur is above the earth and heaven," and he recites Psalm 24. If Yom Kippur falls on a Sabbath, Psalm 29 is recited. Then the Scrolls are returned to the Ark, and the verse beginning, "And when it [the Ark] rested . . . " is recited.

Then the Reader takes his stand before the Ark, shaken and fearful, and recites with dread and submission and trembling and awe a special prayer for the Reader, praying that the Holy One, blessed be he, will have compassion on him and will hear his prayer, and praying that those who send him will not be shamed.

The Reader must lay to his heart the thought that in the time when the Temple stood, the High Priest would enter into the Holy of Holies to make atonement for all the people of Israel and to pray for them. Now that we have no Temple and no High Priest, the Reader takes the place of the High Priest, and the prayer is in place of the Temple service; the recollection of these things is an aid to our atonement.

Now, if the High Priest, who was sanctified from the womb and anointed with the anointing oil, and who seven days before Yom Kippur would be secluded from his home, in order to add to his holiness—if he when he entered the Holy of Holies was shaken and fearful, how much more ought the Reader, who has none of all these qualities, to humble his heart and to stand with dread and trembling when he prays and pleads before God to return and have compassion upon us, and to overcome our iniquities, and to return the service to its habitation!

After the Reader has concluded his special prayer, he recites the half-Kaddish loudly and in a traditional melody handed down from the time of the ancient Readers who dedicated their voices to the Omnipresent. Then the Additional Prayer is prayed silently in the order found in the prayer books.

REPETITION OF THE ADDITIONAL PRAYER OF BENEDICTIONS

The Ark is opened, and the Reader recites the repetition of the Additional Prayer of Benedictions. Liturgical poems, penitential prayers, and hymns are inserted, some while the Ark is open. At the words "And we bend the knee, and prostrate ourselves" in the prayer "It is for us to praise the Lord of all," the entire congregation bend the knee and prostrate themselves. The recital of the order of the service of the High Priest in the Temple in Jerusalem is the central theme in the repetition of the Prayer of Benedictions. At the words "And the priests and people . . . when they heard the explicit Name, coming from the mouth of the High Priest, would bend the knee and bow and fall on their faces," the entire congregation bend the knee and fall on their faces. This is repeated three different times during the recital.

These three prostrations are not like the prostration in the prayer "It is for us to praise the Lord of all," for there one bows down in joy at having been found worthy of the portion of the Lord, and here one bows down in sorrow at the glory of the Lord which is absent now. [Yesod ve-Shoresh ha-Avodah]

THE ORDER OF THE TEMPLE SERVICE

At first it was the custom among some of the people to recite

the service of the High Priest on Yom Kippur during all
three prayers. Then the Geonim decided that it ought only
to be recited during the Additional Prayer, for the service
of the High Priest was mainly during the Additional Prayer.
[See Or Zarua, Hilkhot Yom ha-Kippurim, No. 281]

AND THUS HE WOULD SAY

It is told of the pious Rabbi of Apt [18th–19th cent.] that
he came to this world ten times. Once he came as a High
Priest and once as a prince, and once as a king, and once as
an exilarch. We have heard from knowing men that he was
often heard to say with his holy lips during the section
describing the Temple service on Yom Kippur, "Thus *I*
would say" (in place of "Thus he [the High Priest] would
say"), for he was remembering the time when he served as
High Priest in the Temple. [Eser Orot]

A SHORT PRAYER

"And when he [the High Priest] left the Sanctuary, he
would pray a short prayer" (Mishnah Yoma V.1). Is not this
strange, that the High Priest, who underwent many sanctifications before Yom Kippur, yet when Yom Kippur arrived,
the day sanctified above all the days of the year, and he was
found worthy to enter the innermost part of the Temple on
that day of all days in the year—that he should then have
prayed only a short prayer? Indeed, it was fitting for him
there to pour out his prayer and supplication because of the
many needs of Israel. But this is the reason.

When the High Priest came to that sanctified place in
which the light of the Divine Presence, be blessed, rested,
all the material matters of this lowly world were forgotten.
It was only when he left, when he began to part from the

sanctity, only then was he reminded somewhat of the needs
of Israel, and prayed a short prayer. For material matters
were not essential in his eyes, but dross; therefore, he was
brief in his prayer. [Keneset Yisrael, quoting Israel of
Rizhyn]

THE SERVICE OF THE HIGH PRIEST

Seven days before Yom Kippur the High Priest was taken
away from his home and placed in the Chamber of the
Counselors, and another priest was prepared to take his
place, in case something should happen to him and he should
become unfit for the service.

All seven days the High Priest would sprinkle the blood
of the daily sacrifices, and burn the incense, and trim the
lamps, and sacrifice the head and the hind leg of the sacrificial
animal. On all other days if he wished to sacrifice he could;
for the High Priest was the first to sacrifice a portion, and
had first choice in taking a portion.

The High Priest would be given Court elders to read
before him daily for seven days out of the Order of the day.
They would say to him: My lord High Priest, read yourself
with your own mouth; perhaps you have forgotten, or perhaps you did not study.

On the morning of the eve of Yom Kippur, they would
have him stand in the Eastern Gate and have oxen, rams,
and sheep pass before him that he might know and be
familiar with the service.

Neither food nor drink would be kept from him all the
seven days. But he would not be allowed to eat much toward
nightfall of the eve of Yom Kippur, for eating brings about
sleep.

The Court elders would pass him over to the elders of the
priesthood, and they in turn would take him up to the upper

chamber of the House of Abtinas [which prepared the incense], and adjure him, and take their leave, and go their way, saying:

"My lord High Priest, we are the messengers of the Court, and you are our messenger and the messenger of the Court. We adjure you by Him who rested his Name in this house to alter nothing of all that we have said to you." He would turn aside and weep, and they would turn aside and weep.

If the High Priest was a sage, he would expound, and if not, the disciples of the sages would expound before him. If he was familiar with the reading of the Holy Writ, he would read; if not, they would read before him. They would read before him from the Books of Job and Ezra and Chronicles. Zechariah ben Kebutal said: Many times I read before him out of the Book of Daniel.

When the High Priest seemed to be about to fall asleep, the young priests would snap their middle fingers before him and say to him: "My lord High Priest, stand up and drive sleep away by walking on the pavement." They would divert him until the time came for the slaughtering of the daily morning offering. [Mishnah Yoma I.1–7]

It has been taught: They did not entertain the High Priest with their harp or with their lyre, but with the music of their voices. And what they sang was: "Except the Lord build the house, they labor in vain that build it" (Ps. 127:1). Some of the worthiest people in Jerusalem would not sleep all that night, in order that the High Priest might hear the sound of people talking, and sleep might not overtake him. [Yoma 19b]

On ordinary days the altar would be cleared of ashes at cockcrow, or near that time, either before or after it, but on Yom Kippur it was cleared of ashes at midnight, and on the

Three Festivals at the first watch. Before the cock crew the Temple Court would be full of Israelites. [Mishnah Yoma I.8]

The officer would say to them: Go out and see if the time has come for the slaughter of the continual morning offering. If it had come, he who saw it would cry: "Daylight!" Mattiah ben Samuel said: He who saw it would cry: "All the east is lit up!" "As far as Hebron?"—And he would say: "Yes." Now the reason why that question was necessary was because once the moon came up and they imagined that it was the dawn and slaughtered the continual morning offering, which later had to be taken out to the place of burning.

The High Priest would then be taken to the place of immersion. This was the rule in the Sanctuary . . . no one entered the Temple Court for the service until he had immersed himself, even if he was clean. On this day the High Priest would immerse himself five times and make ten sanctifications. . . .

A linen sheet would be spread between him and the people. The High Priest would take off his clothing, go down, and immerse himself. Then he would come up and dry himself. He would be brought the garments of gold and would dress. Then he would sanctify his hands and his feet. The continual offering would be brought to him. He would make the incision and someone else would finish it for him. He would receive the blood and sprinkle it. He went on to burn the morning incense, and to trim the lamps; afterward, to offer up the head, and the limbs, and the pancakes, and the wine-offerings. [Mishnah Yoma III. 1-4]

The morning incense would be burned between the sprinkling of the blood and the burning of the limbs of the sacrificial animal, that of the afternoon between the burning of the limbs and the offering of the drink-offerings. If the High Priest was either old or a weakling, some water would be warmed up and poured into the cold water to dissipate the coldness.

The High Priest would be brought to the Parvah Chamber which was on holy ground. A linen sheet would be spread between him and the people. He would sanctify his hands and his feet and strip. . . . Then he would go down, and immerse himself, and come up, and dry. He would be brought white clothing, would dress, and sanctify his hands and his feet. . . . In the morning he would put on Pelusium linen worth eighteen minas, and in the afternoon Indian linen worth twelve minas, together worth thirty minas, all told. The thirty minas came from the public funds, and if he wished to spend more, he could add some of his own money to the public funds. [Mishnah Yoma III. 5–7]

The High Priest would come to his bullock. His bullock would be standing between the hall and the altar, its head to the south and its face to the west. The High Priest would stand in the east facing the west, and press his two hands upon it, and make confession. And this is what he would say: "O Lord, I have committed iniquities, I have transgressed, I have sinned before you, I and my house. O Lord, forgive, I pray, the iniquities, the transgressions and the sins which I have committed, transgressed, and sinned before you, I and my house, as it is written in the Torah of your servant Moses: 'For on this day shall atonement be made for you, to cleanse you; from all your sins shall ye be clean before the Lord'" (Lev. 16:30). And the priests and people would answer after him: "Blessed be his Name whose glorious kingdom is for ever and ever!"

He would then go back to the east of the Temple court,

to the north of the altar. The Deputy High Priest would be on his right and the head of the family [ministering that week] on his left. There would be two he-goats, and an urn would be there, and in it two lots. They were of box-wood, and Ben Gamala made them of gold, for which he was praised. . . . King Monobaz of Adiabene had all the handles of the vessels used on Yom Kippur made of gold . . . for which he was praised. [Mishnah Yoma III. 8–10; see Tosefta II]

The High Priest would shake the urn and take up the two lots. On one would be written, "For the Lord," and on the other, "For Azazel." The Deputy High Priest would be on his right hand and the head of the [ministering] house on his left. If the lot "For the Lord" came up in his right hand, the Deputy High Priest would say to the High Priest: "My lord High Priest, raise your right hand." And if "For the Lord" came up in his left hand, the head of the [ministering] house would say to him: "My lord High Priest, raise your left hand." Then the High Priest would lay the lots on the two he-goats and say: "A sin-offering to the Lord!" . . . And the people would answer after him: "Blessed be his Name whose glorious kingdom is for ever and ever!"

The High Priest would tie a thread of crimson wool on the head of the he-goat to be sent forth, and stand it [at the gate] where it was to be sent, and stand the he-goat to be slaughtered facing the place where it was to be slaughtered. He would go to his bullock a second time and press his two hands on it and make confession. And this is what he would say: "O Lord, I have committed iniquities, I have transgressed, I have sinned before you, I and my house and the children of Aaron, your holy people. O Lord, forgive, I pray, the iniquities, the transgressions, and the sins which I have committed, transgressed, and sinned before you, I and my house and the children of Aaron, your holy people. As it is written in the Torah of your servant Moses: 'For on this day shall atonement be made for you, to cleanse you; from all your sins shall ye be clean before the Lord' " (Lev. 16:30). And the priests and people would answer after him: "Blessed be his Name whose glorious kingdom is for ever and ever!"

The High Priest would slaughter the bullock and receive its blood in a bowl and give it to the one who was to stir the blood on the fourth terrace of the Sanctuary that it might not congeal. He would take the coal-pan and go up to the top of the altar, and clear the coals on either side, and scoop out some of the glowing cinders at the bottom. Then he would go down and lay the coal-pan on the fourth terrace in the Temple Court.

On every other day he would scoop up the cinders with a coal-pan of silver and pour them into one of gold; but on this day he would scoop up the cinders with a pan of gold, in which he was to bring them [into the Inner Temple]. On every other day he used to scoop up the coals with a pan holding four kabs . . . but on this day he would scoop up the cinders with a pan holding three kabs. On every other day the pan would be heavy, on this day it would be light. On every other day the handle of the pan was short, on this day it was long. On every other day the gold was yellow, on this day it was red. . . . On every other day he would offer up a portion in the morning and a portion in the afternoon, but on this day he would also add his two palmfuls. On every other day the incense would be fine, on this day it would be the finest possible. On every other day the priests would go up on the east side of the ramp and come down on

the west side, but on this day the High Priest would go up
the middle and come down the middle. . . . On every other
day the High Priest would sanctify his hands and his feet
from the laver, but on this day from a golden ladle. . . . On
every other day there were three piles of wood, but on this
day there were four. [Mishnah Yoma IV]

The ladle and the pan would be brought out to him, and
he would take two palmfuls [of incense] and put them into
the ladle. Tall High Priests would take large palmfuls and
short High Priests would take small; that was the measure.
The High Priest would take the pan in his right hand, the
ladle in his left. Then he would go through the Holy until
he would come to the place between the two curtains which
separated the Holy from the Holy of Holies, and there was
a cubit between them. The outer curtain was held back by
a clasp on the south side, and the inner curtain by a clasp on
the north side. He would walk along between them until he
would reach the north side. When he would reach the north
side, he would turn to the south. Then he would go on to
his left along the curtain, until he reached the Ark. When
he reached the Ark, he would put the pan between the two
bars. He would heap the incense upon the coals and the
whole house would fill up with smoke. He would go out
the way he came in, and pray a short prayer in the Outer
House. He would not prolong his prayer, in order not to
disquiet the people.

After the Ark was taken away, a stone from the days of
the Early Prophets was left standing there three finger-
breadths above the ground, and it was called Shetiyah
[foundation stone], and on it the High Priest would place
the pan of glowing coals.

He would take the blood from the one who was stirring

it, and re-enter the place where he had entered [the Holy of
Holies], and stand in the place where he had stood [between
the bars of the Ark], and sprinkle of the blood once upward and seven times downward, but not as though he
wished to sprinkle either upward or downward, but motioning as though he were cracking a whip. And thus he would
count: One, one and one, one and two, one and three, one
and four, one and five, one and six, one and seven. Then he
would come out and lay the bowl on the golden stand in
the Holy.

Then they would bring him the he-goat. He would
slaughter it and receive the blood in a basin. He would then
enter again the place where he had entered [the Holy of
Holies], and stand again in the place where he had stood
[between the bars of the Ark], and sprinkle of the blood
once upward and seven times downward, but not as though
he wished to sprinkle either upward or downward, but
motioning as though he were cracking a whip. And thus he
would count: One, one and one, one and two. . . . Then he
would come out and lay the basin on the second golden stand
in the Holy. . . .

Then the High Priest would take the blood of the bullock
. . . and sprinkle of it on the outside curtain facing the Ark
once upward and seven times downward, but not as though
he wished to sprinkle either upward or downward, but
motioning as though he were cracking a whip. And thus he
would count [see above].

Then he would deposit the blood of the bullock and take
the blood of the he-goat and sprinkle it on the outside curtain
facing the Ark, once upward and seven times downward,
but not as though he wished to sprinkle either upward or
downward, but as though he were cracking a whip. And

thus he would count [see above]. Then he would pour the
blood of the bullock into the blood of the he-goat, thus putting the full basin into the empty one. [Yoma V. 1–4]

"And he shall go out unto the altar that is before the
Lord" [Lev. 16:18]—that is, the golden altar. He would
begin to sprinkle downward . . . from the northeast horn
of the altar, then the northwest, then the southwest, then the
southeast. There where he began the sprinkling of the outer
altar he would finish the sprinkling of the inner altar. And
he would sprinkle every horn of the altar from below upward, except for the horn where he was standing, which he
would sprinkle from above downward. He would sprinkle
on the top of the altar seven times, and the remainder of the
blood he would pour on the western base of the outer altar.
[Yoma V. 4–8]

. . . He would then go up to the scapegoat and press two
hands on it and make confession. And thus he would say:
"Pray, O Lord, your people, the house of Israel, have
committed iniquity, transgressed and sinned before you.
Pray, O Lord, atone, I pray, the iniquities and the transgressions and the sins that your people, the house of Israel
have committed and transgressed, and sinned before you, as
it is written in the Torah of your servant Moses, saying:
'For on this day shall atonement be made for you, to cleanse
you; from all your sins shall ye be clean before the Lord' "
(Lev. 16:30).

And the priests and the people standing in the Temple
Court, when they heard the explicit Name coming from
the mouth of the High Priest, would bend the knee and
bow and fall on their faces and cry: "Blessed be his Name
whose glorious kingdom is for ever and ever."

The scapegoat would be delivered to him that was to lead

it away. Anyone was allowed to lead it away, but the High Priests made it a rule not to allow an Israelite to lead it away. Rabbi Yose said: It once happened that Arsela of Sepphoris led it away, although he was an Israelite. And a special passageway was made for the scapegoat, because of the Babylonians, who used to pull its hair and cry: Take our sins and begone, take our sins and begone!

Some of the worthiest men in Jerusalem would accompany him to the first booth. There were ten booths between Jerusalem and the Peak ninety ris away, seven and a half ris making a mil. At every booth they would say to him: Here is food and water. And they would accompany him from booth to booth except for the last booth, for no one might go up the Peak with him, but might only stand at a distance and watch what he did.

What the priest would do was to divide the thread of crimson wool, tie half of it to the rock and half between the two horns of the scapegoat, and push the scapegoat from behind, and it would fall down the Peak. Its limbs would be smashed to bits before it was half way down the hill. [Mishnah Yoma VI. 2-7]

Then the High Priest would come to the bullock and the he-goat that were to be burned, cut them open and take out the sacrificial parts, put them on a tray and burn them on the altar. He would twist the limbs on poles and have them taken out to the place of burning. . . .

They would say to the High Priest: "The he-goat has reached the wilderness." How would they know that the he-goat had reached the wilderness? They used to set up guards at stations on the way, who would wave cloths; and so it would be known when the he-goat had reached the wilderness. [Mishnah Yoma VI. 7-8]

Then the High Priest would come to read. If he wished to read wearing linen clothing, he could read in that dress. If not, he could wear his own white vestments when he read.

The attendant of the House of Prayer would take the Torah Scroll and give it to the head of the House of Prayer, and the head of the House of Prayer would give it to the Deputy High Priest and the Deputy High Priest would give it to the High Priest, and the High Priest would stand and receive it. And he would read the sections beginning, "After the death of the two sons of Aaron" (Lev. 16) and "How-beit on the tenth day" (Lev. 23:26–32). Then he would roll up the Torah Scroll and lay it in his bosom and say: "There is more written here than I have read to you." Then he would recite by heart the section beginning, "And on the tenth day," which is in the Book of Numbers (29:7–11). Then he would recite the eight benedictions. . . .

Those who saw the High Priest reading would not see the bullock and the he-goat being burned, and those who saw the bullock and the he-goat being burned would not see the High Priest reading. Not that it was not permitted, but because the distance was great and both rites were carried out at the same time.

If the High Priest had read wearing linen clothing, he would then sanctify his hands and feet and strip and go down and immerse himself and come up and dry. He would be brought golden clothing and would put them on and sanctify his hands and his feet. Then he would go out and offer up his own ram and the ram of the people and the seven he-lambs of the first year and without blemish.

The High Priest would then sanctify his hands and his feet and strip and go down and immerse himself and come up and dry. He would be brought white clothing and would put them on and sanctify his hands and his feet. Then he would go in to bring out the ladle and the fire-pan. He would sanctify his hands and his feet and strip and go down and immerse himself. Then he would come up and dry. He would be brought golden clothing and he would dress and sanctify his hands and his feet and go in to burn the afternoon incense and to trim the lamps and to sanctify his hands and his feet, and would strip. Then he would go down, immerse himself, come up and dry himself.

Then he would be brought his own clothing and he would dress. He would be accompanied to his home. There he would make a feast for his friends when he came out of the Sanctuary in peace. [Mishnah Yoma VII. 1–5]

THE INEFFABLE NAME

Ten times would the High Priest pronounce the Name of God on Yom Kippur: six times in connection with the bullock, three times in connection with the he-goat, and once in connection with the lots. Those who were near him would fall on their faces, and those who were far from him would say: "Blessed be his Name whose glorious kingdom is for ever and ever." Neither those who were near nor those who were far would move from their places until he had disappeared.

At first the High Priest would pronounce the Name in a loud voice. When the number of dissolute persons increased, he pronounced it in a low voice. Rabbi Tarfon said: I used to stand among my brother priests in line and bend my ear toward the High Priest, and I would hear him merge the Name in the sound of the singing of the priests. At first the Name could be communicated to every man. When the number of dissolute persons increased, it was communicated only to the worthy. [Yerushalmi, Yoma III. 7; see Babli, Yoma 39b]

THE PRAYER OF THE HIGH PRIEST

This was the prayer of the High Priest when he left the Sanctuary in peace on Yom Kippur: "May it be your will, O Lord our God and God of our fathers, that no exile shall come upon us, neither on this day nor in this year. And if exile is to come upon us on this day or in this year, may we be exiled to a place of Torah. May it be your will, O Lord our God and God of our fathers, that no dearth come upon us, neither on this day nor in this year. And if dearth come upon us, on this day or in this year, let it be as the result of our fulfilment of your commandments. May it be your will, O Lord our God and God of our fathers, that this year be a year when prices are low, a year of plenty, a year of commerce, a year of rain and warm weather and dew, and that your people Israel may not need one another's help. Do not heed the prayers of wayfarers. . . . And [I pray] for your people Israel, that they do not rise to rule over one another."

For the people of the Valley of Sharon he would pray: "May it be your will, O Lord our God and God of our fathers, that their houses may not become their graves." [Yerushalmi Yoma V. 3]

SIMEON BEN YOHANAN, THE HIGH PRIEST

It was Simeon the High Priest, the son of Onias,
Who in his life repaired the house again,
And in his days fortified the Temple:
And by him was built from the foundation the double height,
The high fortress of the wall about the Temple:
In his days the cistern to receive water, being in compass as the
    sea,

Was covered with plates of brass:
He took care of the Temple that it should not fall,
And fortified the city against besieging:
How was he honored in the midst of the people
In his coming out of the Sanctuary!
He was as the morning star in the midst of a cloud,
And as the moon at the full:
As the sun shining upon the temple of the Most High,
And as the rainbow giving light in the bright clouds:
And as the flower of roses in the spring of the year,
As lilies by the rivers of waters,
And as the branches of the frankincense tree in the time of
   summer:
As fire and incense in the censer,
And as a vessel of beaten gold
Set with all manner of precious stones:
And as a fair olive tree budding forth fruit
And as a cypress tree which groweth up to the clouds.
When he put on the robe of honor,
And was clothed with the perfection of glory,
When he went up to the holy altar,
He made the garment of holiness honorable.
When he took the portions out of the priests' hands,
He himself stood by the hearth of the altar,
Compassed with his brethren round about,
He was as a young cedar in Lebanon;
And as palm trees compassed they him round about
And all the sons of Aaron in their glory,
And the oblations of the Lord in their hands, before all the
   congregation of Israel.
And finishing the service at the altar,
That he might adorn the offering of the Most High Almighty,
He stretched out his hand to the cup,
And poured of the blood of the grape,
He poured out at the foot of the altar

A sweet-smelling savor unto the Most High King of all.
Then shouted the sons of Aaron,
And sounded the silver trumpets,
And made a great noise to be heard,
For a remembrance before the Most High.
The singers also sang praises with their voices,
With great variety of sounds was there made sweet melody.
And the people besought the Lord, the Most High,
By prayer before Him that is merciful,
Till the solemnity of the Lord was ended,
And they had finished His service.
Then he went down, and lifted up his hands
Over the whole congregation of the children of Israel,
To give the blessing of the Lord with his lips,
And to rejoice in His Name.
And they bowed themselves down to worship the second time,
That they might receive a blessing from the Most High.
Now therefore bless ye the God of all,
Which only doeth wondrous things everywhere,
Which exalteth our days from the womb,
And dealeth with us according to His mercy.
He granteth us joyfulness of heart,
And that peace may be in our days in Israel for ever:
That He would confirm His mercy with us,
And deliver us at His time!
[Ben Sira L]

THE ENTRANCE OF THE HIGH PRIEST INTO THE SANC-
TUARY, AND HIS DEPARTURE FROM IT

(An eyewitness account by Marcus, Roman consul and Justice of the Jews, who held office in Jerusalem during the days of the Second Temple.)

Seven days before the special day called Yom Kippur and the most important of their holidays, they would prepare a space and chairs to sit on, in the house of the High Priest, for the head of the Court, the patriarch, the High Priest, the prefect of the priests, and the King, besides seventy chairs of silver for the seventy members of the Sanhedrin. Then the eldest of the priests would stand up and address the High Priest with these words of admonition and exhortation:

"Look before whom you are about to enter, and know that if you fail to concentrate on what you are about to do, not only will you at once fall dead but the atonement of Israel will be lost as well. Lo, the eyes of all Israel are hanging upon you, so search your ways; perhaps you have committed a transgression, however slight, for one transgression may balance off many good deeds, and the scale is in the hands of the God of knowledge. Also search the ways of your brother priests and purify them; remember always that you are about to come before the King over all kings, who sits on a throne of justice and scatters all evil before him with his eyes. Then how shall you come before Him, the enemy being with you?"

Then the High Priest would say to them that he had already searched his deeds and repented for every transgression that was apparent to him, and that he had also called his brother priests together into the Court of the Temple and had adjured them by Him who rested his Name there, that each of them was to reveal the evil which he was aware of in his fellow, and the evil which he was aware of in himself, in order that the High Priest might give them the correct penance for each transgression.

The King too would speak warmly to the High Priest, and assure him that he would honor him when he came out of the Sanctuary in peace. After this, they would announce that the High Priest was going out to his chamber in the

Sanctuary, and then all the people would go out to accompany him, and go before him in perfect order. And this I have seen with my very eyes: first to go before him would be all those who were of the seed of the kings of Israel (for the more important a man, the nearer he stands to the High Priest), after them went all those who were descended from the kings of the house of David, all in their proper order, one following another. A herald would go before them, crying, "Give honor to the house of David!" After them came the house of Levi, and a herald crying, "Give honor to the house of Levi!" There were thirty and six thousand of them, and all the prefects wore clothing of blue silk, and the priests, of whom there were twenty-four thousand, clothing of white silk. After them came the singers, and after them those who played upon instruments, and after them the trumpeters, and after them the guards of the gate, and after them the incense-makers, and after them the curtain-makers, and after them the watchmen, and after them the treasurers, and after them a class called *kartofilos,* the chair-bearers, and after them all the workingmen who worked in the Sanctuary, and after them the seventy of the Sanhedrin, and after them a hundred priests with silver rods in their hands to clear the way, and after them the High Priest, and after him all the elders of the priesthood, two by two. And the heads of the academies stood at vantage points and cried, "Lord High Priest, may you come in peace! Pray to our Maker to grant us long life that we may engage in his Torah."

When the procession reached the foot of the mountain of the Sanctuary, they would there pray for the continuance of the kingship of the House of David, and after that for the priests and for the Sanctuary, and the noise was so great because of the great number of the people crying Amen, that the birds flying overhead fell to the earth. Then the High Priest would bow to all the people and turn aside in tears and awe. And the two prefects of the priesthood would lead him to his chamber, and there he would separate from all his brother priests. So much for his entrance.

But when he came out the honor was doubled, for all the people that were in Jerusalem passed before him, most of them carrying torches of white wax, and all of them dressed in white clothing; and all the windows were garlanded with embroideries, and lit with candles. Priests have told me that often the High Priest could not reach his home before midnight, because of the press of the people passing before him, and because of the great numbers, for although all the people were fasting, they did not go home until they had seen whether they could not reach the hand of the High Priest and kiss it. The day afterward he would make a great feast and invite his friends and relatives, and declare a holiday because he had come out of the Sanctuary in peace.

Afterward the High Priest would order a smith to make a gold tablet, and engrave upon it these words: "I [so and so] the High Priest, son of so and so, the High Priest, have served in the high priesthood in the grand and holy house in the service of Him who rested his Name there, and it was such and such a year after the Creation. May He who found me worthy for this service find my son after me worthy to serve before the Lord." [Shevet Yehudah]

FORMERLY IN ISRAEL

Rabban Simeon ben Gamaliel said: There were never any holidays in Israel like the Fifteenth of Av and Yom Kippur, for on those days the daughters of Jerusalem would go forth in borrowed white dresses, in order not to shame those who

had no rich dresses. . . . And the daughters of Jerusalem
would go forth and sing and dance in the vineyards. What
they sang was: Young man, lift your eyes and see what you
are choosing; do not set your eyes on beauty, set your eyes
on family. "Grace is deceitful, and beauty is vain; but a
woman that feareth the Lord, she shall be praised" (Prov.
31:30). And it is said: "Give her of the fruit of her hands;
and let her works praise her in the gates" (Prov. 31:31).
And it is also said: "Go forth, O ye daughters of Zion, and
gaze upon King Solomon, even upon the crown wherewith
his mother hath crowned him in the day of his espousals,
and in the day of the gladness of his heart" (Cant. 3:11). "In
the day of his espousals"—this is the revelation of the Torah,
and "in the day of the gladness of his heart"—this is the
building of the Temple, may it be rebuilt speedily in our
days, Amen. [Mishnah Taanit IV. 8]

Our masters have taught: The King's daughter borrows
a dress from the daughter of the High Priest, the daughter
of the High Priest from the daughter of the Deputy High
Priest, and the daughter of the Deputy from the daughter
of the [priest] Anointed for Battle, and the daughter of the
Anointed for Battle from the daughter of an ordinary priest,
and all the Israelites borrow dresses from one another, in
order not to shame those who have no richer dresses.

It has been taught: On Yom Kippur he who has no wife
goes to the vineyards. The sages taught: Those who were
beautiful used to sing, "Set your eyes on beauty, for woman
is made for beauty alone!" Those who came of good family
used to sing, "Set your eyes on family, for woman is made
to rear a family." Those who were ugly would sing, "Take
your purchase away for the sake of heaven, if only you adorn
us with jewels of gold."

Ulla Biraa said in the name of Rabbi Eleazar: The Holy
One, blessed be he, is destined to form a chorus for the righteous, and He will sit in their midst in the Garden of Eden,
and each and every one of them will point with his finger at
Him, for it is said (Isa. 25:9): "And it shall be said in that
day: Lo, this is our God, for whom we waited, that He might
save us; this is the Lord for whom we waited, we will be
glad and rejoice in His salvation!" [Taanit 31a]

THESE I DO REMEMBER

The liturgical poem beginning, "These I do remember,"
which is recited after the description of the Temple service,
is in memory of the ten who were martyred by Rome,
who were killed for the sake of the unification of the Name
of God. For when the Temple still stood and the altar stood
in its habitation, sacrifices were offered upon the altar every
day. But now what is offered are the souls of the righteous.

It is cited in the Midrash: Why were the ten martyrs, the
sages of Israel, given over to be slaughtered at the hands of
the wicked kingdom of Rome? Because his brothers sold
Joseph into slavery. For the quality of divine justice brings
charges every day before the throne of glory, and says, "Is
there any superfluous letter in your Torah? You have said,
'And he that stealeth a man, and selleth him, or if he be
found in his hand, he shall surely be put to death' (Exod.
21:16). The ten brothers sold Joseph, and yet You have not
punished them or their seed" [Ele Ezkerah]. Therefore the
decree against the ten sages of Israel was passed, in punishment for the sake of Joseph.

We have also found it stated in apocryphal books that the
sale of Joseph was on Yom Kippur, and the Book of Jubilees
says the same.

VIII. The Afternoon Prayer

THE BINDING OF ISAAC

The Afternoon Prayer is of greater importance on Yom Kippur than it is on all the other days of the year, for the Afternoon Prayer was established by Isaac, and Isaac was bound on the altar on the afternoon of Yom Kippur [see Zohar on Gen. 28:11]. Therefore it is fitting to read the portion about the Binding of Isaac during the Afternoon Prayer, although it was already read in the Morning Prayer, in order to recall the aiding merit of Isaac. That is what our rabbis, of blessed memory, said (Gen. Rabbah LVI): "Abraham said to the Holy One, blessed be he: May it be your will, that when the children of Israel come to commit transgressions and evil deeds, that then the Binding of Isaac may be remembered for their benefit, and you may be filled with compassion for them."

THE AFTERNOON PRAYER

In keeping with the order of prayer on all the other days of the year, it would be fitting to begin the Afternoon Prayer with the Psalm 145 and then to recite the prayer beginning, "And a redeemer shall come to Zion," but these prayers are set aside to be recited after the Afternoon Prayer in order to make a break between the Afternoon and the Closing Prayers. However, it is the Sephardic custom to recite them at this point. The Afternoon Prayer is opened with the taking out of the Torah Scroll.

THE READING OF THE TORAH

The Ark is opened and the Torah Scroll is taken out, and three men read the section about incest in the third book of

Moses (Lev. 18). Then the third man also reads the prophetic portion.

The reason why the section about incest is read during the Afternoon Prayer on Yom Kippur is because there is no atoning for sins on Yom Kippur until one has turned in Teshuvah. Hence, we read the section about incest so that if, God forbid, one of the children of Israel shall have broken the prohibition against incest, he will remember his transgression as soon as the prohibition is read before him, and will turn in Teshuvah, that he may be forgiven. [Otzar ha-Geonim, Megillah]

THE READING OF THE BOOK OF JONAH

For the prophetic portion, the Book of Jonah is read from beginning to end, in order to teach us that no man can fly away from God, as David, peace be upon him, said (Ps. 139:7–10): "Whither shall I go from Thy spirit? Or whither shall I fly from Thy presence? If I ascend up into heaven, Thou art there; if I make my bed in the netherworld, behold, Thou art there. If I take the wings of the morning, and dwell in the uttermost parts of the sea; even there would Thy hand lead me, and Thy right hand would hold me." [Avudraham; Hayye Avraham]

Another reason why we read the Book of Jonah is because it informs us that God pardons and forgives those who turn in Teshuvah, as we are told in the case of Nineveh. [Ibbur Shanim]

Another reason for reading the Book of Jonah is because the prophecy of Jonah purposes to teach us that the compassions of God extend over all that He has made, even idol-

ators—then how much more do they extend over Israel!
Therefore we make the Book of Jonah the prophetic reading
during the Afternoon Prayer, which is an hour of God's
grace, as our sages, of blessed memory, have said (Berakhot
6b): "Let a man always be careful of his Afternoon Prayer,
for lo, Elijah was only answered during the Afternoon
Prayer." [Joshua ibn Shoeb, Derashot al ha-Torah]

Israel said to the Holy One, blessed be he: Master of the
worlds, if we do Teshuvah, will you accept us?

He said to them: I have accepted the Teshuvah of the
people of Nineveh, and shall I not accept your Teshuvah?
[Pesikta de-Rav Kahana]

There are some who add another reading after the reading
from Jonah and say the verses beginning: "Who is a God
like unto Thee, that pardoneth the iniquity," which is at the
end of Micah. The reader of the prophetic portion recites the
benedictions the same as on public fast days through "Blessed
art thou, O Lord our God, the shield of David."

A PUZZLING CUSTOM

It is an ancient custom in the city of Candia when the portion
from the Book of Jonah is being read on Yom Kippur to
read only the first three verses in the holy tongue, and to
translate the rest of the book from the beginning to end into
the secular Greek; afterward they skip to the Book of Micah,
where they read three verses, and translate in the same way.
Rabbi Elijah Capsali [16th cent.] thought to abrogate this
custom, because it is not according to the law. But Rabbi
Meir [ben Isaac Katzenellenbogen, 15th–16th cent.], the
head of the academy at Padua, heard about it, and wrote to
Rabbi Elijah, to turn him from his purpose. In truth this is
a puzzling custom, but it is not right to rest entirely upon

our intelligence, and abrogate an ancient custom. It is necessary to find an explanation for it. That is what all our early sages did, whenever they came across a puzzling custom. [Likkutim Shonim mi-Sefer debe Eliyahu; see Responsa of Maharam of Padua, No. 78]

CONTINUATION OF THE AFTERNOON PRAYER

The Reader takes the Scroll and returns it to the Ark, reciting the customary prayers and Psalms. The congregation reads the Silent Prayer of Benedictions and the Confession. Then the Reader repeats the Prayer of Benedictions with the addition of several liturgical poems and penitential prayers.

One must be especially careful to recite this prayer with powerful concentration, for at the time of the Afternoon Prayer a hard judgment hangs over the world, and Isaac established this prayer to appease the Lord called "the Fear of Isaac" [cf. Gen. 31:42]; besides, the Binding of Isaac took place on Yom Kippur during the time of the Afternoon Prayer.

THE GATES

When the Afternoon Prayer is finished, the Closing Prayer is prayed. This is a prayer which was added to the other prayers on the holy day in order to awaken God's compassion during the time of the closing of the gates. What the closing of the gates means is explained in the Palestinian Talmud: "Rab says: It means the closing of the gates of heaven. And Rabbi Yohanan says: The closing of the gates of the Temple" (Berakhot IV. 1). And now that our Temple is in ruins, and the habitation of our glory is taken, we direct our hearts to heaven, praying that before the gates of the heavenly Temple are closed, prayers may enter in on high and be accepted with compassion and favor.

ix. Neilah: The Closing of the Gates

The time for the Closing Prayer is when the sun is over the tree tops. One must be careful to finish it with the coming out of the stars. One must be brief with penitential prayers and insertions in the middle of the prayer, and the Reader does not prolong every word the way he prolongs all the other prayers during the day, in order that he may finish before the coming out of the stars, because this prayer on the day of the fast of Yom Kippur corresponds to the closing of the gates of the Temple, which took place during the day, after the kindling of the twilight lamps. [Shulhan Arukh shel ha-Rav]

There are some who say that the Closing Prayer can be prolonged even past nightfall, despite the fact that that is after the closing of the gates of the Temple. For they think that "the closing of the gates" is the same as "the closing of the gates of heaven," and they interpret it to mean after the setting of the sun, which is nightfall. Rabbi Joel Sirkes [16th–17th cent.] wrote to the same effect [Hilkhot Yom ha-Kippurim, No. 623], despite the fact that Rabbi Moses ben Maimon [12th cent.] and Rabbenu Nisim ben Reuben Gerondi [14th cent.] and many other great men who are in the majority are of the opinion that the Closing Prayer ought to be ended while it is still daylight, while the sun is over the tree tops, that is, near the time of the setting of the sun. Nevertheless, it is the custom in all Israel to follow Rab's interpretation and to finish the prayer after nightfall, and Rabbi Isaac Alfasi [11th cent.] and Rabbi Asher ben Yehiel [13th–14th cent.], who believe the same as Rab, are worthy of being relied on and reason enough not to abrogate an ancient custom.

It is also the custom in most of the Diaspora of Israel for the rabbi of the city or the elder of the community to be the Reader of the Closing Prayer, and for two of the elders of the community to stand at his side, one at his right hand and one at his left. They recite Psalm 145, and after that the prayer beginning, "And a redeemer shall come to Zion." There are some whose custom it is to recite afterward the song of praise by Rabbi Judah ha-Levi [11th–12th cent.] beginning, "Give praise, O my soul, emanation from the Holy Spirit!" For at that time the soul is pure and clean and takes pleasure in giving praise and thanksgiving to its Maker. There are also some whose custom it is to recite afterward the prayer beginning, "May the Compassionate One remember."

Rabbi Judah bar Barzilai, the Barcelonian [11th–12th cent.] wrote in his Commentary on the Book of Creation: "Rav Saadia Gaon [9th cent.] said that it is the custom in Sura to take a Torah Scroll out of the Ark during the Closing Prayer on Yom Kippur, and to read the first portion of the Book of Genesis. But the Geonim who came after him did not agree with this custom, and said that it is not a part of the formula of the Closing Prayer."

It is the custom for the rabbi of the city or the elder of the community to speak strong words to the people, not in the way of scriptural exposition, but as exhortation. He does not prolong his speech, but rouses the people in a few words to prepare their hearts for awesome prayer during the hour when the judgment is being sealed, that they may wholeheartedly turn to God.

After the sage has concluded his speech, the Reader chants the Kaddish in a traditional melody sanctified by the early cantors who dedicated their voices to the Omnipresent and composed the melodies established for the prayers of Israel. Then the silent Prayer of Benedictions is recited, similar to that of the Afternoon Prayer, except that "seal us" is said for "inscribe us," and "sealed" for "inscribed." If it is on the Sabbath, the Sabbath is mentioned in this prayer, in the same way as it is mentioned in the other prayers of the day, for it is still the Sabbath day; even those who prolong this prayer past nightfall must mention the Sabbath, since they began it while it was still daylight.

THE REPETITION OF THE PRAYER OF BENEDICTIONS

The Ark is opened for the repetition by the Reader of the Prayer of Benedictions, and left open throughout the prayer. Hymns and liturgical poems are inserted in the prayer, and are to be found in our festival prayer books. It is the custom in Jerusalem and some other communities for the priests to bless Israel during the Closing Prayer as well.

x. 'Hear O Israel' and the Final Blast

HEAR, O ISRAEL

Then the Reader chants "Hear, O Israel" once, and the congregation respond once in a loud voice; every one must know in his heart that he must be prepared to offer himself up for the sanctification of the Name of God. Then the Reader says: "Blessed be his Name whose glorious kingdom is for ever and ever" three times, and each time the congregation answers after him. He says it three times [Mateh Moshe] because of the passage: "The Lord reigneth, the Lord hath reigned, the Lord shall reign for ever and ever," which means that the Lord reigned before the world was created, the Lord is reigning in this world, and the Lord will reign in the world to come.

Then the Reader says: "The Lord, He is God" seven times, and the congregation repeats the phrase after him each time. The seven times correspond to the seven firmaments which the Holy One, blessed be he, tore apart for Israel during the revelation of the Torah, to show them that there is none beside him. Another reason is [Mateh Moshe] that it is a symbol of the departure of the Divine Presence which rested in our midst from evening to evening. Now we are accompanying it through the seven firmaments.

Another reason for saying "The Lord, He is God" seven times is [Tosafot, Berakhot 34a] that it corresponds to the seven firmaments which praise the Creator, who dwells above the seven firmaments.

Then the Reader chants the full Kaddish in a joyful melody, because we are confident of God's compassion, and that our prayer has been accepted by him. In Jerusalem I have seen pious and devout men surround and dance around the Reader when he chants the full Kaddish during the Closing Prayer. He too dances and sings in a joyful melody: "May the prayers and supplications of all Israel be accepted before their Father in heaven."

THE FLUTE

A certain villager used to pray on the Days of Awe in the House of Prayer of the Baal Shem Tov [18th cent.]. He had a boy whose wit was dull and who could not even read the letters in the prayer book, much less recite a holy word. His father never brought him along to the city, because the boy was completely ignorant. But when the boy became Bar Mitzvah, his father took him with him to the city on Yom Kippur, so as to be able to watch him and keep him from eating from simple ignorance on the holy fast day.

Now the boy had a little flute on which he used to play all the time when he sat in the field tending his flock. He took the flute with him from home and put it in his coat, and his father did not know about it. The boy sat in the House of Prayer all Yom Kippur without praying, because he did not know how. During the Additional Prayer he said to his father: "Father, I want to play my flute." His father became terrified, and spoke sharply to the boy. The boy had to restrain himself.

During the Afternoon Prayer the boy repeated again: "Father, let me play on my flute." Again the father spoke sharply to his son, and warned him not to dare do any such thing. But he could not take the flute away from his son, because of the prohibition against unnecessary handling on Yom Kippur.

After the Afternoon Prayer, the boy said again: "Please let me play on my flute." Seeing that the boy wanted badly to play on his flute, his father said to him: "Where is the flute?" The child pointed to the pocket of his coat. The father took the child's pocket and held it in his hand, to keep the boy from taking out the flute and playing on it. Holding the pocket with the flute in this way, the man stood and prayed the Closing Prayer. In the middle of the prayer, the boy forced the flute out of his pocket and blew a blast so loud that all who heard it were taken aback. When the Baal Shem Tov (who was the Reader) heard the sound, he shortened his prayer.

After the prayer the Baal Shem Tov said: "With the sound

of his flute this child lifted up all the prayers and eased my
burden. For this child does not know anything, but, by dint
of his seeing and hearing the prayer of Israel all of this holy
day, the prayer's holy spark kindled an actual fire in him,
and the flame of his longing burned higher and higher until
his soul nearly expired. Because of the strength of his longing he played the note of his heart truly, without any dis-
traction, for the sole sake of the Name of God. Now, the
clean breath of his lips was very acceptable to Him, and by
this means all the prayers were lifted up. [Kehal Hasidim
he-Hadash]

ONE BLAST

After the full Kaddish, one blast is blown on the ram's-
horn; but there are places where the Tekiah, Shevarim,
Tekiah blasts are all blown. It is cited in the Mahzor Vitri:
"I have heard that they blow the Tekiah, Shevarim Teruah,
Tekiah blasts at the end of the prayer at the close of Yom
Kippur in the Land of Israel as they leave the House of
Prayer." But in the Diaspora the custom is to blow only one
blast, as a memorial of the Jubilee; except for the city of
Cologne, where the custom is to blow the Tekiah, Shevarim
Teruah, Tekiah blasts too.

RAM'S-HORN OF FREEDOM

Rav Hai [10th–11th cent.] wrote: It is the custom in all Israel
to blow the ram's-horn at the close of Yom Kippur; we have
found no reason to believe that it is an obligation, but it
seems to be a memorial of the Jubilee, as it is said: "Then
shalt thou make proclamation with the blast of the horn on
the tenth day of the seventh month; in the day of atonement
shall ye make proclamation with the horn throughout all
your land" (Lev. 25:9). Since the reckoning of the Jubilee

year is not certain, the custom was established of blowing the ram's-horn every year as a memorial of the Jubilee. This is the sense of the saying: "In the Jubilee year . . . on Yom Kippur, the Court blew the ram's-horn. Slaves were sent home and fields returned to their original owners" (Rosh ha-Shanah 8b). This is the memorial of the Jubilee which they kept during the time when the Temple still stood. [Avudraham]

IN REMEMBRANCE OF REVELATION

Another reason why the ram's-horn is blown at the close of Yom Kippur is because we find in Pirke Rabbi Eliezer that when our master Moses, peace be upon him, went up to Mount Sinai to receive the second set of tablets, he went up at the New Moon of Elul and came down on the tenth of Tishri, and ordered the ram's-horn to be blown both when he went up and when he went down. Therefore, later generations established the custom of blowing the ram's-horn on the nights of the New Moon of Elul and the close of Yom Kippur, as a memorial of those blasts with which Israel joyfully accepted the second set of tablets. [Shibbole ha-Leket]

Another reason is that the ram's-horn is blown in the hope that God may remember to our benefit the sounds of the blasts at the Revelation, and will remember that Israel received the Torah with a whole heart and willing soul. [Mateh Moshe]

THE DEPARTURE OF THE DIVINE PRESENCE

Another reason for blowing the ram's-horn is because it is an allusion to the departure of the Divine Presence, as it is said: "God is gone up amidst . . . the sound of the horn" (Ps. 47:6). [Bayyit Hadash]

NEXT YEAR IN JERUSALEM

After the blowing of the ram's-horn, we say: "Next year in Jerusalem!" There are some whose custom it is to say it three times; once for our exile in Egypt, the second time for our exile in Babylonia, and the third time for our exile in Edom [Rome]; may the Holy One, blessed be he, speedily redeem us in his compassion and return us to Jerusalem [Kol Dodi]. But in the Land of Israel it is the custom to say: "Next year in Jerusalem rebuilt!"

Twice during the year we say, "Next year in Jerusalem!"— once during the Seder on Passover eve and once at the Closing Prayer of Yom Kippur. For there is a difference of opinion in the Talmud between Rabbi Eliezer and Rabbi Joshua. The first says that Israel were first redeemed in Nisan and are destined to be redeemed in Nisan, and the second says they were redeemed in Nisan and are destined to be redeemed in Tishri (Rosh ha-Shanah 11a). Therefore, both in Nisan and in Tishri we say, "Next year in Jerusalem!" [Otzar Dinim u-Minhagim]

xi. The Close of Yom Kippur

THE EVENING PRAYER

After the blowing of the ram's-horn, the cantor opens with the prayer beginning, "And He, being merciful, forgives iniquity"; and the weekday Evening Prayer is prayed.

A PARABLE

Why do we say the prayer beginning, "Forgive us," during the Evening Prayer at the close of Yom Kippur; lo, Yom

Kippur has already made atonement for all sins? This may be compared to a parable about a king who was passing through a field. A countryman saw him and kicked him. The king's men wanted to kill the man. But the king said: "Let him be, for he does not know who I am. If he knew me, he would not have done what he did; put him in a school, and let him get understanding and manners." They put the man in a school, and he became a man of understanding. When he saw the respect the king was held in, and remembered what he had done to the king, he grew faint with shame and began to cry, "Forgive me!" For all the time he had been a coarse man he had not known how great his sin was, and it had not been clear to him in what way he had sinned.

So it is with us. So long as we are filthy with transgressions, we do not know either the depth of our sin or the greatness of the King who is King over all kings, the Holy One, blessed be he, against whom we have sinned. Now that we have cleansed ourselves, and our transgressions have been forgiven, we are ashamed over our past and beg: "Forgive us, our Father, for we have sinned; pardon us, our King, for we have transgressed. [Gedulat ha-Zaddikim II. 21, quoting Yitzhak of Vorki]

THE BLESSING OF THE NEW MOON

It is the custom to bless the New Moon immediately after leaving the House of Prayer, in order to begin the new year by fulfilling a religious duty. It is the custom to bless it while one is still wrapped in the prayer shawl and kittel, and with a happy heart. There are some who are careful not to bless the New Moon at once; but first they recite the Havdalah and eat a little in order to ease their hunger, so as not to bless

the New Moon with a weak heart. But this is not a sufficient
reason to set oneself apart from the rest of society. However,
if a person feels that because of his hunger he cannot concentrate as he should, let him first eat and then bless the New
Moon. If the moon is lightly clouded over, he may wait until
the next day. But if the nights are all cloudy and there is no
reason to suspect that it will be possible to bless the New
Moon later, he must bless it at once. [Mateh Efrayim]

THE HOLY DANCE

Once at the close of Yom Kippur the moon was nowhere to
be seen. By means of his holy spirit, the Baal Shem Tov saw
that if Israel were to fail this duty on the close of Yom Kippur, they would lose by it, God forbid. He became very sad
at this thought, and tried by exercise of his powers of concentration to make the moon come out, and asked many
times whether the moon had come out yet. But the sky was
clouded over and there was no hope that the moon would
come out that night. However, the hasidim of the Baal Shem
Tov, may their merit shield us, did not know what was going
on. Because it was their custom to have a holiday at the close
of Yom Kippur, having left the House of Prayer in peace at
the end of the service (for the service of their master, the
Baal Shem Tov, was actually like the service of the High
Priest)—it so happened that the hasidim were very happy
that night as well, and danced with a holy enthusiasm. At
first they danced by themselves, at last in the greatness of
their holy enthusiasm they pressed into the room of the Baal
Shem Tov and danced and rejoiced before him. When their
enthusiasm became overpowering, they dared to beg the Baal
Shem Tov to dance with them. So they took him into the
middle, and he too danced with them. They were still danc-

ing when suddenly someone called: "The moon is out!" At once they ran out to bless the New Moon.

The Baal Shem Tov said: "What I could not do by the exercise of my powers of concentration, the hasidim did with their joy."

BLESSINGS

After the blessing of the New Moon, every man greets his neighbor and wishes him the blessing of a good year, joyfully and with a good heart, as on a holiday. Then they all go home in gladness and joy, and everyone blesses all the children of his house; and seeing that he is pure and forgiven, his blessing bears fruit all that year. [Hemdat Yamim]

Another reason for this comradely blessing is because Yom Kippur only makes atonement for the transgressions that men commit in their relationship with the Omnipresent; now, after having appeased the Holy One, blessed be he, men appease one another, that they may be clean before God and man. [Seder ha-Yom]

HAVDALAH: BENEDICTION OF SEPARATION

Havdalah is recited over a cup of wine, but no benediction is recited over spices. But if Yom Kippur falls on a Sabbath, before Havdalah the prayer beginning, "Lo, God is my salvation," and the benediction over spices are recited, as on every other close of the Sabbath. Now the reason why the benediction over spices is recited at the close of the Sabbath is because the soul is in pain at the close of the Sabbath, and is therefore rejoiced and comforted with a goodly odor [Maimonides, Hilkhot Shabbat XXIX]. But on Yom Kippur, when the soul is not in pain at the end of the day, for Yom Kippur makes atonement at nightfall and the soul is at ease, there is then no need for spices, even if Yom Kippur falls on the Sabbath [see Orah Hayyim, No. 624]. But most of the Codifiers decreed that when Yom Kippur falls on the Sabbath the benediction over spices is recited, for it is the opinion of Rabbenu Gershom, "the Light of the Exile" [Mordekhai, Yoma], that the benediction is to be recited at the close of every Yom Kippur, even when it does not fall on the Sabbath.

Then the benediction over the light, ending, "the Creator of the lights of the fire" is said. The benediction is recited only over a light that has burned all day, which is a light that was burning but was not kindled the same day, or one that was legitimately kindled on the same day, as in order to save a life.

FROM STRENGTH TO STRENGTH

After Havdalah, one takes a bite to eat and goes out to prepare a spot for a booth to celebrate the Feast of Booths in, in order to begin the new year by fulfilling a religious duty.

Rabbi Jacob ben Moses ha-Levi [14th–15th cent.] expounded: Let every man begin making his booth immediately after Yom Kippur; the days of Teshuvah being completed and this being the first day when one is liable to sin, God forbid, everyone ought to spend the day in fulfilling a religious duty, in order to realize the verse (Ps. 84:8): "They go from strength to strength." [Maharil]

THE FEAST AT THE CLOSE OF YOM KIPPUR

Let every man set his table and eat joyfully and with a good heart, as on a night when a holiday is hallowed, for on this day all his transgressions are forgiven, the mercy of the Lord being with him. The same is written in the Midrash: "At the close of Yom Kippur a voice issues from heaven and says: 'Go thy way, eat thy bread with joy, and drink thy wine with a merry heart; for God hath already accepted thy works' (Eccles. 9:7); and your prayer has been heard" (Eccles. Rabbah III). The masters of the Tosafot (Shabbat 114), also, wrote that the close of Yom Kippur is a kind of holiday.

One ought to eat well at the feast, but not to turn one's thought away from the Master. But one ought rather to sit at the table with discretion, and pause between the courses, and eat in moderation.

BLESSING AND PEACE

He who has not managed to greet his fellow when going out of the House of Prayer ought to pay him a visit to greet him after the feast. In this way let every man appease his fellow and ask his forgiveness, though he had already done so before Yom Kippur, that it might not be said that it was because of the awe of Yom Kippur that he had forgiven his fellow, and now that the Day of Judgment was past his hatred had returned. But those who never bore hatred to any man, and are pure of all sin—their blessing bears fruit. [Hemdat Ya-mim]

It is the Sephardic custom in Jerusalem for men to visit the homes of their parents and their wives' parents to wish them well; the sages go to visit the Chief Rabbi. This practice of theirs is based on the early custom, during the time when the House still stood on its mound, of accompanying the High Priest to his home where he would make a banquet that night for all his friends. [Yerushalayim I]

A SECOND DAY OF YOM KIPPUR

It is the custom of the pious and saintly men of Germany to make Yom Kippur last two days and to pray in a quorum of

ten, repeating the whole prayer of Yom Kippur on the second
day. Rabbi Asher ben Yehiel [13th–14th cent.] tried to stop
them. There are some who say that the person who once
made Yom Kippur last two days can never change his practice without incurring extirpation. But Rabbi Asher ben
Yehiel used to allow those who wished to stop this practice
to ask about it; that is to say, to ask a sage to free them of it.
Rabbi Asher believed that since, according to the law, the
man was not bound to fast a second day, but took it upon
himself of his own free will, it is like an oath which can be
annulled.

We learn about the custom of fasting for two days from
the Talmud (Rosh ha-Shanah 21a): "Rabbah used to fast
for two days." Because of this many great men used to make
Yom Kippur last two days. [Hagahot Maimoniot, Shevitat
Asor]

Those who make Yom Kippur last two days must follow
all the laws of Yom Kippur, including the ban on work and
other deprivations on Yom Kippur. But in any event they
must pray the same as on a weekday, whether they be ten or
a hundred, and must put on phylacteries. They may chant
liturgical poems and penitential prayers if they wish, as well
as recite the Thirteen Qualities, but without prolonging
them, rather reading as a man reads the Torah Scroll. For
they may not recite these prayers among the other prayers,
but only afterward, and may not read in the Torah at all,
even the scriptural portion read on the fast-day, which begins: "And Moses besought the Lord his God" (Exod.
32:11). [Mateh Efrayim]

THE DAY AFTER YOM KIPPUR

I have heard it told of the Seraph of Strelisk [Rabbi Uri,

18th–19th cent.] that he used to say after the holy day: "Who will bring yesterday back to me! I would take more pleasure in it than in the honey of the comb!" [Hillula de Rabbi]

The Codifiers wrote that supplications are not to be said during the four days between Yom Kippur and the Feast of Booths, and one ought not to fast, even if these days include the day when one's father or mother died. If a Sabbath should happen to fall among them, the prayer beginning, "Your righteousness is an everlasting righteousness," is not recited. For those days are days of joy, because the Holy One, blessed be he, does not count the sins committed between Yom Kippur and the Feast of Booths. On these days, the First Temple was dedicated in the time of Solomon, and our sages, of blessed memory, said (Mishnah Taanit IV. 8): " 'In the days of the gladness of his heart' (Cant. 3:11)—that is the building of the Temple." May it be rebuilt speedily in our days. Amen.

ENDED IS THE THIRD BOOK OF THE DAYS OF AWE WHICH IS THE BOOK OF YOM KIPPUR AND THE ENTIRE WORK IS COMPLETED.

Bibliography

AGGADAT ELIYAHU (commentary on the Aggadot of the Palestinian Talmud) by Eliyahu ben Abraham Solomon ha-Kohen. Smyrna 1755; Salonika 1825.

AGRA de-KHALLAH (on the Pentateuch) by Zevi Elimelekh Shapira of Dynov. Przemysl 1879.

ALIM li-TERUFAH (hasidic teachings) by Nathan Sternhartz. Berditchev 1896.

ALUMAT YOSEF by Joseph Elijah Fried. Jerusalem 1909.

ARBA TURIM: see TUR

ASARAH MAAMAROT (kabbalistic treatises) by Menahem Azaria di Fano (16th–17th cent.). Venice 1597.

ASPEKLARIAH ha-MEIRAH (commentary on the Zohar) by Zevi Hirsh Horwitz. Fuerth 1776.

ATERET ZEKENIM (on the Shulhan Arukh) by Menahem Mendel ben Meshullam Zalman Auerbach. Printed with the text of Shulhan Arukh, Orah Hayyim, Lwow 1876.

AVODAT YISRAEL (homiletics) by Israel ben Shabbetai of Koznitz. Lwow 1850.

AVOT de RABBI NATAN (ethical tractate of the Talmud; two versions). Ed. Solomon Schechter, Vienna 1887.

AVUDRAHAM (on liturgy) by David ben Joseph Avudraham (14th cent.). Lisbon 1489.

BAYIT HADASH (commentary on the Arba Turim) by Joel ben Samuel Sirkes (16th–17th cent.). Cracow 1631–1640.

BEN SIRA (or, The Wisdom of Jesus the Son of Sirach, or, Ecclesiasticus; a book of the Apocrypha). Ed. H. Strack, Leipzig 1903.

BENE YISAKHAR (homiletics) by Zevi Elimelekh Shapira of Dynov. Zolkiev 1846; 1850.

BET ADEN: see EVEN SAPPIR

BET ha-MIDRASH (collection of midrashic and aggadic sources;

six volumes). Ed. Adolph Jellinek (19th cent.), Leipzig 1853–1857; Vienna 1873–1877.

BET YAAKOV by Jacob Aaron ben Moses of Zaloshin. Pietrokov 1899.

BET YOSEF (commentary on the Arba Turim) by Joseph Caro of Safed (16th cent.). Venice 1550; 1564; Sabionetta 1553; 1559.

BIKKURE ha-ITTIM (Hebrew Annual). Vienna 1820–1831.

BINYAN SHELOMO (on the Sayings of the Fathers) by Meir Judah ben Solomon. Przemysl 1896.

BIRKE YOSEF (on laws and customs) by Hayyim Joseph David Azulai (18th cent.). Vienna 1860.

BIURE HAGRA (commentary on the Shulhan Arukh) by the Gaon Elijah of Vilna (18th cent.). Printed with the text of Shulhan Arukh, Warsaw 1862.

DARKHE ha-TOV veha-YASHAR (biography of Rabbi Zevi Hirsh of Liska) by Zev Wolf Josefow. Munkacs 1910.

DARKHE HAYYIM (sayings etc. of Rabbi Hayyim Halberstam of Zans) by Raphael ha-Levi Segal Zimmetbaum. Cracow 1923.

DERASHOT al ha-TORAH by Joshua ibn Shoeb (14th cent.). Cracow 1573.

DEREKH HASIDIM (Hasidica). Lwow 1872.

DERUSH NAEH by Judah Loev ben Bezalel (the Maharal of Prague, 16th cent.). Prague 1589.

DEVAR YOM be-YOMO by Hayyim Knoller. Przemysl 1907.

DEVARIM AREVIM. Munkacs 1903–1905.

DEVASH le-FI by Hayyim Joseph David Azulai (18th cent.). Livorno 1801.

DIVRE TORAH (collected teachings). Josefow 1852.

DIVRE YEHEZKEL by Ezekiel Shraga Halberstam. Podgorze 1901.

DOR DEAH by Jekutiel Kamelhar. 1933.

DUTIES of the HEART: see HOVOT HA-LEVAVOT

ELE EZKERAH (Midrash on the Ten Martyrs). In Bet ha-Midrash, ed. A. Jellinek, Vol. II, Vienna 1873.

ELEF ha-MAGEN (on the Mateh Efrayim) by Meshullam Finkelstein (19th cent.). Pietrokov 1908.

ELIYAHU ZUTTA (commentary on the Levush) by Elijah ben Benjamin Zev Wolf ha-Levi Spira of Tiktin (17th–18th cent.). Prague 1688.

ELIYAHU ZUTTA: see TANNA DEBE ELIYAHU

EMEK BERAKHAH (on liturgic benedictions) by Abraham ben Sabbatai Sheftel ha-Levi Horovitz of Prague (16th cent.). Cracow 1597.

EMEK ha-MELEKH (kabbalistic compendium) by Naphtali ben Jacob Elhanan Bacharach (16th cent.). Amsterdam 1648.

EMUNOT ve-DEOT (system of religious philosophy) by Rav Saadia Gaon (9th–10th cent.). Leipzig 1859.

EN YAAKOV (compendium of Aggadot from the Babylonian Talmud) by Jacob ibn Habib of Zamora (15th–16th cent.). Constantinople 1516; Venice 1546. Numerous editions.

ESER OROT (Hasidica) by Israel ben Isaac Simhah. Pietrokov 1907.

ETZ YOSEF (commentary on En Yaakov) by Enoch Zundel ben Joseph. Printed with the text of En Yaakov, Vilna 1830.

EVEN ha-EZER (talmudic treatises and responsa) by Eliezer ben Nathan of Mainz (12th cent.). Prague 1610.

EVEN ha-EZER (laws on marriage and divorce), one of the four parts of the Shulhan Arukh.

EVEN SAPPIR (travels in Egypt, Arabia, British India, China, Australia; the part Bet Aden: on Yemen) by Jacob Saphir ha-Levi. Lyck 1866; Mainz 1874.

"THE GATES of SANCTITY" (Shaare Kedushah; kabbalistic discussion of reward and punishment and of sanctity) by Hayyim Vital Calabrese of Safed (16th–17th cent.). Zolkiev 1810.

"THE GATES of TESHUVAH" (Shaare Teshuvah; on repentance) by Jonah Gerondi of Toledo (13th cent.). Fano 1505.

GEDULAT ha-ZADDIKIM (Hasidica) compiled by Gerson Im-
manuel ha-Levi Staschevsky. Warsaw 1934–1937.

GUIDE to the PERPLEXED: see MOREH NEVUKHIM

HAARETZ (Palestinian Hebrew Daily). Tel Aviv 1919–

HAGGAHOT MAIMUNIOT (glosses on the Mishneh Torah)
by Meir ha-Kohen of Toledo (13th cent.). Printed with the text
of Mishneh Torah, Constantinople 1509.

HAYYE ADAM (manual of religious life) by Abraham Danzig
of Vilna (18th–19th cent.). Vilna 1812.

HAYYE AVRAHAM (commentary on parts of the Shulhan
Arukh) by Abraham Kalfon. Livorno 1826.

HEKHAL ha-BERAKHAH (on the Pentateuch) by Isaac Judah
Yehiel. Printed with the text of the Pentateuch, Lwow 1864–
1874.

Ha-MANHIG (on laws, customs, liturgy) by Abraham ben Nathan ha-Yarhi of Lunel (12th–13th cent.). Constantinople 1519.

HEMDAT YAMIM (kabbalistic work on the Jewish ritual) by an
anonymous follower of moderate Sabbatianism (end of 17th
cent.). Zolkiev 1732.

HILKHOT YOM ha-KIPPURIM by Joel Sirkes: see BAYIT HADASH

HILLULA de-RABBI (hasidic book) by Yehiel Mikhal Huebner.
Lwow, s.a.

HOVOT ha-LEVAVOT ("Duties of the Heart"; system of Jewish
ethics) by Bahia ibn Pakuda of Saragossa (11th and possibly
12th cent.). Naples 1490.

IBBUR SHANIM (on the calendar) by Issachar ben Mordecai
Maaravi. Constantinople 1564.

IGGERET RAV SAADIA GAON (Epistle of Rav Saadia Gaon;
9th–10th cent.). In: *Devir*, Vol. I, Berlin 1923.

IKKARIM: ("Principles" of Jewish religious philosophy) by
Joseph Albo (14th–15th cent.). Soncino 1486.

IN THE HEART OF THE SEAS (Bilvav Yamim). Story of a journey to the Land of Israel by Shmuel Yosef Agnon. English trans. I. M. Lask, New York 1948.

IR VILNA ("The City of Vilna") by Hillel Noah Maggid Steinschneider. Vilna 1900.

KAD ha-KEMAH (dogmatic and ethical homilies) by Bahia ben Asher of Saragossa (13th–14th cent.). Constantinople 1515.

KAF ha-HAYYIM by Hayyim Palaggi. Salonika 1859.

KAF ha-HAYYIM, JERUSALEM by Jacob Hayyim ben Isaac Barukh. Jerusalem 1933.

KAV ha-YASHAR (on ethics) by Zevi Hirsh Kaidanover (17th–18th cent.). Frankfort on the Main 1705.

KEDUSHAT LEVI (on the Pentateuch) by Levi Isaac of Berditchev (18th cent.). Hrubishov 1818.

KEHAL HASIDIM he-HADASH (Hasidica). Lwow 1906.

KENESET ha-GEDOLAH (commentary on the Shulhan Arukh) by Hayyim ben Israel Benveniste of Smyrna (17th cent.). Livorno 1658.

KENESET YISRAEL (hasidic teachings of Rabbi Israel of Rizhyn, 18th–19th cent.). Ed. Reuben ben Zevi David, Warsaw 1906.

KEREM SHELOMO (Glosses to parts of the Shulhan Arukh) by Solomon Haas of Dresnitz. Pressburg 1843.

KETER SHEM TOV (hasidic teachings) compiled by Aaron ben Zevi Hirsh Kohen of Apt. Zolkiev 1784.

KEVUTZAT YAAKOV by Jacob Margaliot. Przemysl 1897.

KIPPUR TAMIM (Prayer Book for Yom Kippur, Bagdad ritual). Bagdad 1925.

KITZUR LIKKUTE MOHARAN (hasidic teachings) by Nahman of Bratzlav (18th–19th cent.). S.l., s.a.

KITZUR SHULHAN ARUKH (manual of Jewish laws and rituals) by Solomon Ganzfried. Ed. David Feldman, Leipzig 1924.

KOL BO (on ritual law, liturgy and customs) by an unknown author. Naples 1490.

KOL DODI (in ms., in possession of the author).

KUNTRES MINHAG TOV. Ed. Meir Zevi Weiss, in *Ha-Tzofeh le-Eretz Hagar*, 1909.

KUZARI ("Book of Argument and Demonstration in Aid of the Despised Faith") by Judah ha-Levi (11th–12th cent.). Fano 1506.

LAHME TODAH (homilies and talmudic discourses) by Zevi Hirsh ben Pinhas ha-Levi Horwitz (18th-19th cent.). Offenbach 1816.

LAWS OF TESHUVAH (Hilkhot Teshuvah), part of Mishneh Torah.

LEKET YOSHER (on laws and rituals) by Joseph ben Moses (15th cent.). Berlin 1903.

LEVUSH (or, Levushim; compendium, in ten sections, of traditional Judaism) by Mordecai Jaffe (16th–17th cent.). First section, Lublin 1590.

LIKKUTE ETZOT (selected teachings of Rabbi Nahman of Bratzlav (18th–19th cent.). *S.l.*, 1816.

LIKKUTE ETZOT HADASH (teachings of Rabbi Nahman of Bratzlav) compiled by Nathan of Nemirov. Lwow 1874.

LIKKUTE ha-PARDES (discussions and decisions in Jewish law) by Rashi (11th cent.). Venice 1519.

LIKKUTE MAHARIAH by Israel Hayyim Friedman of Rochov. Marmaros Sziget 1911 (?).

LIKKUTIM SHONIM mi-SEFER DEBE ELIYAHU (excerpts from historical writings) by Elijah Capsali (16th cent.). Padua 1869.

LIKKUTE YEKARIM (or, Likkutim Yekarim; anthology of hasidic Bible interpretation) by Samuel ben Judah Leib Segal. Lwow 1792.

MAGEN AVRAHAM (commentary on Orah Hayyim, a part of

the Shulhan Arukh) by Abraham Abele Gumbinner (17th cent.). Dyrhenfurt 1692.

MAGEN AVOT (commentary on the Sayings of the Fathers; theological discussions) by Simeon ben Zemah Duran (14th–15th cent.). Livorno 1762; 1785.

MAGGID TAALUMAH by Zevi Elimelekh Shapiro of Dynov. Przemysl 1886.

MAHARIL (or, Minhage Maharil, compendium of the Ashkenazic ritual and liturgical customs) by Jacob ben Moses ha-Levi Moelln of Mainz (14th–15th cent.). Sabionetta 1556.

MAHAZIK BERAKHAH (discussion of parts of Shulhan Arukh) by Hayyim Joseph David Azulai (18th cent.). Livorno 1785.

MAHZOR BENE ROMA (Festival Prayer Book according to the ritual of Rome). First edition, Soncino and Casalmaggiore 1485–1486. Ed. S. D. Luzzatto, Livorno 1856.

MAHZOR OHOLE YAAKOV (Festival Prayer Book), ed. Jacob Yitzhaki. Jerusalem 1908–1910.

MAHZOR VITRI (compendium of prayers and synagogal usages) by Simhah ben Samuel Vitry (12th cent.). Ed. S. Hurwitz, Berlin 1889–1893.

MAIMONIDES: see MISHNEH TORAH

MASAE YISRAEL (travels) by Israel ben Joseph Benjamin ("Benjamin the Second"; 19th cent.). Lyck 1859.

MATEH EFRAYIM (laws and customs of the Penitential season) by Ephraim Zalman Margaliot (18th–19th cent.). Zolkiev 1835.

MATEH MOSHE (liturgic compendium) by Moses ben Abraham Premsla (16th cent.). Cracow 1591.

MEIL SHMUEL (abridgement and index of Shene Luhot ha-Berit) by Samuel ben David Ottolengo of Venice (17th–18th cent.). Venice 1705.

MEKHILTA de-RABBI SHIMON BAR YOHAI (halakhic Midrash on Exodus). Ed. David Hoffmann, Berlin 1905.

MEKOR HAYYIM (homilies) by Hayyim of Zans. Ed. Abraham Simhah Bunam Michelson, Bilgoraj 1912.

MENAHEM ZION by Menahem Mendel of Rymanov. Czernowitz 1851.

MENORAT ha-MAOR (compendium of religious ethics) by Isaac Aboab (13th–14th cent.). Constantinople 1514.

MENORAT ha-MAOR (compendium of religious ethics) by Israel al-Nakawa of Toledo (14th cent.). Ed. H. G. Enelow, New York 1930–1932.

MEOR ENAYIM (homilies) by Menahem Nahum of Tchernobil (18th cent.). Lwow 1848.

MIDBAR KEDEMOT (on Aggadot) by Hayyim Joseph David Azulai (18th cent.). Livorno 1793.

MIDRASH MISHLE (Midrash on Proverbs). Ed. Solomon Buber, Vilna 1893.

MIDRASH PINHAS by Phineas of Koretz. Bilgoraj 1929.

MIDRASH RABBAH (Midrash on the Pentateuch and the Five Scrolls). Numerous editions.

MIDRASH TEHILLIM (Midrash on the Psalms). Ed. Solomon Buber, Vilna 1891.

MIDRESHE ha-TORAH (commentary on the Pentateuch) by Solomon Astruc Gatigno (14th cent.). Berlin 1899.

MIGDAL DAVID by David Solomon ben Samuel. Lwow 1873.

MIKHTEVE MASEOTAV (description of a journey to Palestine by Obadiah of Bertinoro, 15th–16th cent.). Ha-Meamer III, Jerusalem 1920.

MINHAGIM le-RABBI YUSPA SHAMMASH: see YOSIF OMETZ

MISHNAH. Numerous editions.

MISHNEH TORAH (code of Jewish law) by Moses ben Maimon (Maimonides; 12th cent.). Soncino 1490; Amsterdam 1702. In the present volume Mishneh Torah is quoted by sections (e.g., Hilkhot Teshuvah).

MOED lekhol HAI (on laws and customs) by Hayyim Palaggi. Salonika 1861.

MORDEKHAI (or, Sefer Mordekhai; commentary on the Sefer

ha-Halakhot of Isaac Alfasi) by Mordekhai ben Hillel (13th-14th cent.). Usually printed with the text of Sefer ha-Halakhot. Constantinople 1509.

MOREH NEVUKHIM ("Guide to the Perplexed"; philosophy of Judaism) by Moses ben Maimon (Maimonides, 12th cent.). Venice 1551. Numerous editions.

NAGID u-METZAVEH (on the mystical meaning of prayers) by Jacob ben Hayyim Zemah of Safed (17th cent.). Amsterdam 1712.

NAHLAT YOSEF by Samuel ben Joseph Yeshuah. Jerusalem 1907.

NEFESH HAYYAH by Reuben Margoliot. Lwow 1934.

NEHAR PEKOD (Shaar ha-Mifkad) by Raphael Aaron ibn Simeon. Alexandria 1905.

NEHMAD mi-ZAHAV by Ezekiel of Kazmir. Pietrokov 1909.

NEHORA ha-SHALEM (liturgic notes) printed with the text of the Prayer Book; several editions.

OBADIAH of BERTINORO: see MIKHTEVE MASEOTAV

OHEL ELIMELEKH (teachings of Rabbi Elimelekh of Lizhensk, 18th cent.), compiled by Abraham Hayyim Simhah Bunam Michelsohn. Przemysl 1910.

OR ha-MEIR (kabbalistic commentary on the Pentateuch) by Zev Wolf of Zhitomir (18th cent.). Koretz 1796.

OR ha-YASHAR (mystical treatise) based on Or Zaddikim by Meir Popers of Jerusalem (17th cent.). Hamburg 1690.

OR YESHARIM (Hasidica) by Moses Hayyim Kleinman. Pietrokov 1924.

ORAH HAYYIM (laws on prayer, synagogue, Sabbath and festivals), one of the four parts of the Shulhan Arukh.

ORAH la-HAYYIM (commentary on the Pentateuch) by Abraham Hayyim of Zlotchov. Zolkiev 1817.

ORHOT HAYYIM (or, Orhot Hayyim ha-Arukh, commentary on Orah Hayyim) by Aaron ha-Kohen of Lunel. Florence 1750.

ORHOT HAYYIM by Nahman Kahane. Sziget 1898.

OR ZARUA (on the Talmud) by Isaac ben Moses of Vienna (12th–13th cent.). Zhytomir 1862; Jerusalem 1887–1890.

OTZAR DINIM u-MINHAGIM (cyclopedia of laws and customs). Ed. Judah D. Eisenstein, New York 1917.

OTZAR ha-GEONIM (collected responsa of the Babylonian Geonim). Ed. Benjamin M. Levin. Tractate Rosh ha-Shanah, Jerusalem 1933; Tractate Yoma, Jerusalem 1934.

OTZROT HAYYIM (on the Pentateuch) by Hayyim ha-Kohen Rappaport of Ostraha. Zhytomir 1858.

PALESTINIAN TALMUD: see YERUSHALMI

PARASHAT DERAKHIM (aggadic homilies) by Judah Rosanes of Constantinople (17th–18th cent.). Constantinople 1729.

PEER HADOR (or, Teshuvot ha-Rambam; responsa by Maimonides, 12th cent.). Amsterdam 1765.

PESIKTA de-RAV KAHANA (Midrash for festivals and outstanding Sabbaths). Ed. Solomon Buber, Lyck 1868.

PESIKTA HADATA: see BET HA-MIDRASH

PESIKTA RABBATI (Midrash for festivals and outstanding Sabbaths). Ed. Meir Friedmann, Vienna 1880.

PHILO of ALEXANDRIA, THE SPECIAL LAWS (*de specialibus legibus*). Loeb Classical Library, VII. Cambridge, Mass. 1937.

PIRKE RABBI ELIEZER (aggadic work on the Pentateuch, attributed to Eliezer ben Hyrcanos, 1st cent.). Constantinople 1514.

RAIA MEHEMNA ("The Faithful Shepherd"; a kabbalistic interpretation of the laws of the Torah; part of the Zohar). See ZOHAR

RASHI (abbreviation for Rabbi Shelomo [ben] Isaac; of Troyes, 12th cent.). Author of classical commentaries on the Bible and the Babylonian Talmud, printed with the texts. Numerous editions.

REMA (abbreviation for Rabbi Moses Isserles of Cracow, 16th

cent.). Author of Haggahot (glosses) to the Shulhan Arukh, printed with the text. Venice 1578. Numerous editions.

RESHUMOT (Hebrew Annual). Ed. H. N. Bialik, A. Drujanow and J. H. Rawnitzky, Tel Aviv 1925–1930.

RESPONSA, BAR LEVAI by Meshullam Issachar ha-Levi Horowitz. Lwow 1861; 1872.

RESPONSA HATAM SOFER, ORAH HAYYIM by Moses Sofer of Pressburg (18th–19th cent.). Pressburg 1855.

RESPONSA of MAHARAM of PADUA. Meir Katzenellenbogen (15th–16th cent.). Venice 1553.

RESPONSA MELAMED le-HOIL by David Zevi Hoffmann (19th–20th cent.). Frankfort on the Main 1932.

ROSH ha-SHANAH (New Year's Day), tractate of the Talmud.

SAYINGS OF THE FATHERS (Pirke Abot, or, Avot), an ethical tractate of the Mishnah.

SEDE HEMED by Hayyim Hezekiah Medini. Warsaw 1924.

SEDER ELIYAHU RABBA (Midrash). Ed. Meir Friedmann, Vienna 1902.

SEDER ha-DOROT he-HADASH (Hasidica). Lwow 1865.

SEDER ha-YOM (mystical commentary on the Prayer Book) by Moses ibn Makhir of Safed (16th cent.). Venice 1599.

SEDER OLAM RABBA (Midrash). Mantua 1513. Ed. B. Ratner, Vilna 1894.

SEFER ha-HAYYIM (five treatises on ethics and ascetics) by Hayyim ben Bezalel of Friedberg (16th cent.). Prague 1611.

SEFER ha-HINUKH (exposition of the 613 commandments) attributed to Aaron ha-Levi of Barcelona (13th cent.). Venice 1523.

SEFER ha-ITTIM (laws on Sabbath and festivals) by Judah ben Barzilai al-Barcelloni (12th cent.). Berlin 1736.

SEFER ha-MATAMIM by Isaac ben Mordecai Lipiec of Siedlce. Warsaw 1885.

SEFER ha-MINHAGOT (on laws and customs) by Asher ben Saul of Lunel (14th cent.). Ed. Simhah Asaf in Sifran shel Rishonim, Jerusalem 1935.

SEFER ha-MUSAR (religious ethics) by Judah ben Solomon Kalaz (15th–16th cent.). Constantinople 1537.

SEFER HASIDIM (ethical, mystical and ascetic teachings) by Judah ben Samuel he-Hasid of Regensburg (12th–13th cent.). Bologna 1538. Ed. J. Wistinetzki, Berlin 1891.

SHAAR ha-MELEKH (on ethics and ascetics esp. for the penitential season) by Mordecai ben Samuel (18th cent.). Zolkiev 1774.

SHAARE EFRAYIM (laws on the reading from the Torah) by Ephraim Zalman Margaliot of Brody (18th–19th cent.). Dubno 1820.

SHAARE RAHAMIM (collection of writings by the Gaon of Vilna and Rabbi Hayyim of Volozhyn). Vilna 1871.

SHEILTOT (compendium of Jewish law) by Ahai of Shabha, Babylonia (7th–8th cent.). Venice 1546.

SHEM mi-SHMUEL by Samuel ben Abraham of Sochaczow. Pietrokov 1932.

SHEM TOV KATAN (prayers and meditations) by Benjamin ben Judah Loeb Kohen. Sulzbach 1706.

SHEMEN ha-TOV (teachings of Rabbi Shmelke of Nikolsburg, 18th cent.). Compiled by Abraham Simhah Bunam Michelsohn, Pietrokov 1905.

SHENE LUHOT ha-BERIT ("Two Tables of the Covenant," exposition of Jewish doctrine) by Isaiah ha-Levi Horowitz of Prague (16th–17th cent.). Amsterdam 1649.

SHEVET YEHUDAH (history of Jewish persecutions and religious disputations) by Solomon ibn Verga of Seville (15th–16th cent.). Adrianople 1554. Ed. M. Wiener, Hanover 1855.

SHIBBOLE ha-LEKET (on laws and customs; commentary on prayers) by Zedekiah ben Abraham de Pietosi of Rome (13th cent.). Venice 1546.

SHISHIM SHENOT HAYYIM (autobiography) by Israel Isser Kasovich (18th–19th cent.). Berlin 1923.

SHIVKHE ha-BESHT (tales and teachings of the Baal Shem Tov). Kopust 1815.

SHULHAN ARUKH (authoritative code of Jewish law, in four parts) by Joseph Caro of Safed (16th cent.). Venice 1565. Numerous editions.

SHULHAN ARUKH shel ha-RAV (laws and customs according to the hasidic ritual) by Shneur Zalman of Ladi (18th–19th cent.). Vilna 1905.

SIAH SARFE KODESH (hasidic teachings) collected by Yoetz Kaddish. Lodz 1927–1928.

SIDDUR AVODAT YISRAEL (Prayer Book with commentary). Ed. S. Baer, Roedelheim 1868.

SIDDUR DEREKH ha-HAYYIM (annotated Prayer Book) compiled by Jacob of Lissa (18th–19th cent.). Ed. Hayyim Polak, Altona 1831.

SIDDUR ha-MINHAGIM by Solomon Zevi Szyk. Munkacs 1884.

SIDDUR RABBI JACOB EMDEN; see SIDDUR RABBI YAABETZ

SIDDUR RABBI YAABETZ (Prayer Book with commentary) by Jacob ben Zevi Emden (18th cent.). Lwow 1863.

SIFRAN shel ZADDIKIM (hasidic sayings), ed. Eleazar Dov ben Aaron. Lublin 1928.

SIHOT ha-RAN: see SIHOT MOHARAN

SIHOT MOHARAN (or, Shivhe ha-Ran im Sihot ha-Ran; tales and teachings of Rabbi Nahman of Bratzlav, 18th–19th cent.). Lwow 1909.

SIPPURIM u-MAAMARIM YEKARIM, compiled by Isaiah Wolf Cykernik. Warsaw 1903.

SOFERIM ("Scribes"), a tractate of the Talmud.

TAAME ha-MINHAGIM (on customs) by A. J. Sperling. Lwow 1928.

TALMUD (or, Talmud Bavli, Babylonian Talmud). Numerous editions. (Quoted according to tractate, folio and page.)

TANHUMA (Midrash on the Pentateuch). Ed. Solomon Buber, Vilna 1885.

TANNA DEBE ELIYAHU RABBA and TANNA DEBE ELI-YAHU ZUTTA (or, Seder Eliyahu Rabba and Seder Eliyahu Zutta; ethical Midrashim). Ed. Meir Friedmann, Vienna 1902.

TANYA (or, Likkute Amarim, theological system of Habad hasidism) by Shneur Zalman of Ladi (18th–19th cent.). Zolkiev 1799; 1805.

TASHBATZ (or, Teshuvot Shimshon ben Tzadok, or, Minhagim; on laws and customs) by Samson ben Zadok (13th cent.). Cremona 1558.

TESHUVOT ha-GEONIM (responsa of the Geonim). Leipzig 1858.

TESHUVOT ha-RAMBAM: see PEER HADOR

TIFERET ARYE LEIB mi-SPOLA (Hasidica) by Judah Yudel Rosenberg. S.l., s.a.

TIFERET YISRAEL (sayings of Rabbi Israel of Tchortkov). Husiatyn 1904.

TIFERET UZIEL by Uziel Meisels. Warsaw 1863.

TIKKUN HATZOT by Nisim Harari. Jerusalem 1897.

TOLEDOT ADAM by Joshua of Ostrovo ben Solomon Judah Leib. Josefow 1874.

TOLAAT YAAKOV (mystical commentary on the prayers) by Meir ibn Gabbai (15th–16th cent.). Constantinople 1560.

TORAT ha-OLAH (on the Temple, sacrifices, etc.) by Moses Isserles of Cracow (16th cent.). Prague 1569.

TOSAFOT ("Additions," comments and discussions on the Talmud). Printed with the text of the Talmud.

TUR (or, Arba Turim; compendium of Jewish law, in four parts) by Jacob ben Asher (13th–14th cent.). Pieve di Sacco 1475. Numerous editions.

TURE ZAHAV (commentary on Yoreh Deah, a part of the Shul-han Arukh) by David ben Samuel ha-Levi (16th–17th cent.). Printed with the text of Shulhan Arukh, Lublin 1646.

YAFE la-LEV by Isaac Palaggi. Smyrna 1872–1876.

YALKUT (or, Yalkut Shimeoni, midrashic compendium) compiled by Simeon Kara ha-Darshan of Frankfort (13th cent.). Salonika 1521.

YAM shel SHELOMO (notes to seven tractates of the Talmud) by Solomon ben Yehiel Luria of Lublin (Maharshal, 16th cent.). On tractate Hullin, Cracow 1615.

YERUSHALMI (or, Talmud Yerushalmi, Palestinian Talmud). Numerous editions. (Quoted according to tractate, chapter and halakhah.)

YERUSHALAYIM (Annual), ed. A. M. Luncz. Vol. I, Vienna 1882.

YESH SAKHAR (laws mentioned in the Zohar) by Issachar Baer ben Petahiah. Prague 1609.

YESOD ha-TESHUVAH (on repentance) by Isaac ben Moses Elles. Munkacs 1897.

YESOD ve-SHORESH ha-AVODAH (liturgic rules) by Alexander Suesskind ben Moses of Grodno. Amsterdam 1754.

YISMAH MOSHE by Moses Teitelbaum. Lwow 1871.

YOMA ("Day" of Atonement), tractate of the Talmud.

YOREH DEAH (dietary laws, laws on purity, vows, honor due to parents and teachers), one of the four parts of the Shulhan Arukh.

YOSIF OMETZ (or, Minhagim le-Rabbi Yuspa Shammash; on laws, rituals and customs) by Joseph Yuspa Hahn of Frankfort (16th–17th cent.). Frankfort on the Main 1723.

ZIKHRON TOV (on Rabbi Isaac of Neskhizh). Pietrokov 1892.

ZIKHRON la-RISHONIM (hasidic tales and teachings) compiled by Moses Hayyim Kleinman. Pietrokov 1912.

ZOHAR (kabbalistic commentary on the Pentateuch) by Moses de Leon (13th cent.). Cremona 1560; Sulzbach 1684.

Publisher's Note

Days of Awe is an abridged version of S. Y. Agnon's Hebrew work, *Yamim Noraim*.* The wealth of illustrative material contained in the original has been condensed by the editor, Nahum N. Glatzer; in particular, many of the lengthy references to the order of prayers have been omitted.

The major portion of the book was originally translated by Rabbi Maurice T. Galpert, and the translation was revised, completed, and prepared for publication by Jacob Sloan under the supervision of the editor.

Hebrew names are spelled in accordance with English usage (e.g., Isaac for Yitzhak); however, the Sephardic transliteration has been retained where titles of books are quoted.

The Bibliography lists the major works from which the author culled his material. Individual passages of the text are separated by an extra space. The source quotation following at the end of a passage refers to the entire passage. Biblical, talmudic, and midrashic source references are enclosed in parentheses; later sources, indications of periods, and other explanatory matter are enclosed in square brackets. Passages for which no sources are given are by the author; they serve as an introduction or transition, and are most of the time summarizations of source material.

Grateful acknowledgment is made to Professor Abraham J. Heschel of the Jewish Theological Seminary and to Professor Simon Halkin of the Jewish Institute of Religion, who assisted in making the selection; to the Jewish Publication Society of America for permission to use passages from the Society's English translation of the Holy Scriptures; to Harvard University Press for permission to reprint an extract from their translation of Philo (*Philo*, Vol. VII, pp. 425–435, translated by F. H. Colson; Loeb Classical Library); to Messrs. E. P. Dutton of New York for a portion of the translation of Ecclesiasticus (*Ancient Hebrew Literature*, Vol. IV, pp. 212–214, Everyman's Library); and to Mr. Abraham Berger of the New York Public Library for his kind advice in the compilation of the Bibliography.

* Third edition, Schocken Books, New York, 1946.